Gaston Bachelard: A Philosophy of the Surreal

For Kristina

Nothing is absolutely dead. Every meaning will have its homecoming festival.
Mikhail Bakhtin

Gaston Bachelard: A Philosophy of the Surreal

Zbigniew Kotowicz

EDINBURGH
University Press

Edinburgh University Press is one of the leading university presses in the UK. We publish academic books and journals in our selected subject areas across the humanities and social sciences, combining cutting-edge scholarship with high editorial and production values to produce academic works of lasting importance. For more information visit our website: edinburghuniversitypress.com

© Zbigniew Kotowicz, 2016, 2018

Edinburgh University Press Ltd
The Tun – Holyrood Road
12(2f) Jackson's Entry
Edinburgh EH8 8PJ

First published in hardback by, Edinburgh University Press 2016

Typeset in 11/13 Adobe Sabon by
Servis Filmsetting Ltd, Stockport, Cheshire,
and printed and bound in Great Britain by
CPI Group (UK) Ltd, Croydon CR0 4YY

A CIP record for this book is available from the British Library

ISBN 978 1 4744 1721 1 (hardback)
ISBN 978 1 4744 3223 8 (paperback)

The right of Zbigniew Kotowicz to be identified as the author of this work has been asserted in accordance with the Copyright, Designs and Patents Act 1988, and the Copyright and Related Rights Regulations 2003 (SI No. 2498).

Contents

Acknowledgements	vii
Abbreviations	ix
Introduction	1
1. The New Scientific Mind	23
The Epistemological Rupture	23
The Epistemological Obstacle	29
The Ruses of Prejudice	31
Naïvety	34
Science and History	43
Rationalism	48
Truth, Dialectics, the Philosophy of No	51
Mathematics, *la phénoménotechnique*	52
Against Substance	59
Pythagorism (and further thoughts on *la phénoménotechnique*)	66
Some Concluding Remarks	71
Appendix to Chapter 1: 'Surrationalism' by Gaston Bachelard	77
2. The Imaginary	82
The Turn	82
The Imagining Faculty	86
Imagination and Violence	88
Narcissism	92
The Body, Hylozoism	95
A Psychoanalysis of a Philosophical Mind	98
The Four Elements	100
The Imaginary and Philosophy	103

vi Contents

	Overcoming Pain, Overcoming Death	105
	Topophilia	107
	Masculine Death, Feminine Death	115
3.	**The Poetics of Time**	119
	The Instant	119
	Duration	124
	The Void	126
	Rhythm and Vibration	129
	Against Bergson	131
	The Void and Nothingness	136
	Concluding Remarks	144
	Appendix: Bachelard and Atomism	157
	Some Preliminary Remarks on Democritus, Epicurus and Pierre Gassendi	157
	Democritus and Hylozoism	162
	The Atom in Contemporary Thought	164
	The Void	168
	Four Atomist systems	171
	Bachelard and Atomism (Epistemology)	172
	Bachelard and Atomism ('Metaphysics')	176
	On Philosophical Aspirations	178
	Notes	182
	Bibliography	198
	Index	206

Acknowledgements

This book was written while I was recipient of a research grant for a project entitled 'Gaston Bachelard: A Theory of the Subject and Epistemological Thought' from Fundação para a Ciência e a Tecnologia of Lisbon (grant no. SFRH/BPD/70880/2010) under the European Community financial programme FSE POPH. I have been carrying out this research since early 2011 based at the Centre for Philosophy of Science of the University of Lisbon. Olga Pombo, the director of the Centre, is a great admirer of Bachelard. For over a decade now, a research line, 'Bachelard: Science and Poetics', has been active with a number of publications on Bachelard coming from the Centre's imprint. Conferences, seminars and graduate teaching are regular activities of the group. The Centre might in fact be unique in its longstanding exploration of Bachelard's work.

This was not, however, my first engagement with Bachelard's thought. He was the subject of my doctoral dissertation in the Department of Philosophy of the University of Warwick well over 20 years ago. In the intervening years I was involved in other projects and the present study is effectively a new work reflecting the activities of the last years (although, of course, some insights from my doctoral thesis found their way into this new venture).

Finally, I want to express my gratitude to those who were directly involved with this book: to Carol Macdonald and everyone at Edinburgh University Press for steadfast support; to Tim Clark for the excellent copy-editing job he has done (this is something the reader never notices but for which the author is invariably grateful); and to Iain Bamforth, Silvia Di Marco, Aldous Eveleigh, Baudouin Jurdant, Anthony Rudolf, Isabel Serra and David Webb, all of whom read the whole or parts of the typescript and made valuable suggestions. None, needless to say, can be held responsible for the views expressed in this work or for any deficiencies in their presentation.

Permission to translate 'Le surrationalisme' from Gaston Bachelard, *L'engagement rationaliste*, copyright © 1972 by Presses Universitaires de France. Any third party use of this material, outside of this publication, is prohibited.

Excerpts from 'Collected Poems in English and French', copyright © 1977 by Samuel Beckett. Used by permission of Grove/Atlantic, Inc. and Faber and Faber. Any third party use of this material, outside of this publication, is prohibited.

Excerpts from 'Stories and Texts for Nothing', copyright © 1967 by Samuel Beckett. Used by permission of Grove/Atlantic, Inc. and Faber and Faber. Any third party use of this material, outside of this publication, is prohibited.

Abbreviations

For full details of these and a more complete list of Bachelard's publications see the Bibliography. Page references are to the French editions, followed by page references to the English translations which have been consulted. (The full list of translations into English can be found in the Bibliography.) In some instances, I may have first spotted a line or two in an English translation and have kept it, but on the whole, the translations are my own, so there are differences, but not significant, in the way Bachelard's prose is rendered in English (with the exception of Arthur Goldhammer's translations from *Le Nouvel esprit scientifique*, which I have used throughout as I found them to be regularly better than my own).

ARPC	*L'Activité rationaliste de la physique contemporaine*
AS	*L'Air et les songes*
DD	*La Dialectique de la durée*
E	*Études*
ECA	*Essai sur la connaissance approchée*
EEPC	*L'Expérience de l'espace dans la physique contemporaine*
EngR	*L'Engagement rationaliste*
ER	*L'Eau et les rêves*
FC	*La Flamme d'une chandelle*
FES	*La Formation de l'esprit scientifique*
FPF	*Fragments d'une poétique du feu*
IA	*Les Intuitions atomistiques*
II	*L'Intuition de l'instant*
L	*Lautréamont*
MR	*Le Matérialisme rationnel*
NES	*Le Nouvel esprit scientifique*
PCCM	*Le Pluralisme cohérent de la chimie moderne*
PE	*La Poétique de l'espace*

Abbreviations

PF	*La Psychanalyse du feu*
PN	*La Philosophie du non*
PR	*La Poétique de la rêverie*
RA	*Le Rationalisme appliqué*
TV	*La Terre et les rêveries de la volonté*
TR	*La Terre et les rêveries du repos*

Introduction

I

The work of Gaston Bachelard was introduced to me well over twenty years ago, in 1989, to be precise, by an artist friend of mine who told me about, and praised, *La Poétique de l'espace*, the book he was reading at the time. I bought the book, flicked through the pages and put it on the shelf; it became one of those volumes that sit around waiting to be picked up at an indeterminate free moment. Some months later, while preparing to teach a course on the philosophy of Marx, I was going through Hegel's *Phenomenology of Spirit*. One evening, fatigued by Hegel's text and needing a break, I pulled Bachelard's book from the shelf; I did not put it down until I had finished it, which was the following morning.

At the time, I was well into the second year of my doctoral research. The subject of my work focused on how our Western tradition constructed the concept of psychical interiority conceived as a separate interior space that is subject to its own laws, independent, autonomous and different from the laws of the external world; we are supposed to 'have' a psyche that defines who we are, locked away in our interior. This research had a historical dimension. The notion of a psychical interiority was largely absent from Greek thought[1] and the study was to begin with St Augustine, specifically with his reflections on memory and time in *Confessions*; it was meant to end with an analysis of the elaborate construct of the Freudian psyche. I then intended to subject this concept of the psyche to a critical examination from a phenomenological (Husserlian, Heideggerian) perspective. But, there I was, fascinated by a text which had absolutely nothing to do with my research. After some time I decided to abandon the early project in order to explore the world that Bachelard seemed to open up. Looking back, this was a very rash decision, to say the least; in fact, almost incomprehensible, since, after all, I knew nothing about Bachelard and had read one single book.

What was it that provoked such a strong reaction? Today the memory of that time is a little hazy, but I do remember thinking something like 'this is pagan' – nothing of the Greek tradition is present, none of the great philosophical figures appear in the text, there is not a whiff of the transcendent, immanence, *telos* – in fact, the book did not provoke any association with anything I knew about philosophy. By philosophical standards the text comes across as nothing more than haphazard wanderings, pleasant and insightful but somewhat inconsequential; but I sensed that there was more to it than that; it was clear to me that it was a philosophy book (and I also quite quickly dropped the adjective 'pagan').

The first intimation of something very different is contained in a short sentence: 'Being starts with well-being' (PE 103, 104). Coming to Bachelard from a background in psychoanalysis and phenomenology, I found this deceptively simple utterance difficult to understand. But, further still, this is not just an isolated utterance. *La Poétique de l'espace* is filled with an unrepentant search for well-being, with an unrestrained joy, with a kind of philosophical *joie de vivre* which did not agree with my intellectual habits. I had been developing a sophisticated (or so I thought) understanding of madness, fallenness, alienation, 'bad faith', the 'human condition', the 'end of man', etc., etc. (the list is long) – basically, about all that is wrong and tragic about human existence – while in Bachelard one finds a quest for the knowledge of sanity, creativity, happiness, notions which were, I realised, hidden from me. I was certainly ill-prepared to enter this territory.

Bachelard's *oeuvre* comes in twenty-seven volumes. He published in his lifetime twenty-three books. His last unfinished work was brought out posthumously; most of his articles are collected in three volumes. Of this output, thirteen books can be classified as 'philosophy of science', eleven deal with questions of the poetic image, and two, which are often referred to as Bachelard's 'metaphysical' texts, are reflections that one would put under the heading 'philosophy of time'. This is a considerable output (even if three or four of the volumes are quite slim) representing a wide palette. Although the writings cover seemingly unrelated subjects there is nothing eclectic about Bachelard's project; there is a consistency in it that could only come from a strong and coherent programme.

However, to begin with, I could only *sense* this consistency, yet it was not clear to me what was holding these writings together. The *joie de vivre* of La Poétique de l'espace is often present but this is hardly sufficient to give it philosophical consistency; and this I found elusive. To try to illustrate the difficulty I was facing, I would compare it to a reaction to hearing and immensely enjoying a piece of music written in an unfamiliar scale. But it is one thing to enjoy music; it is another to understand it. For this we have, first of all, to work out the scale in which the music is written. If the keyboard we use for this kind of task has all the notes that are used in the particular scale, the matter is not too difficult. But should we try to tackle a scale of an Indian raga, for example, the keyboard will not do; we discover that the pitch is wrong and that the intervals between the notes are different. Something analogous was happening here. The keyboard that I had been using to construct what I thought would be my doctoral thesis was not suitable for working out the scale on which Bachelard arranged his thought. In other words, I had to change my thinking habits. But old habits die hard; so it took time.

These were difficulties that were specific to me, but there are others which are of a more objective nature. First of all, there is no obvious point of entry into Bachelard's *oeuvre*; there is no key text that one can recommend to start the exploration (although one would perhaps advise the reader *not* to begin with the somewhat idiosyncratic La Formation de l'esprit scientifique). We enter Bachelard's work and we find ourselves dealing with a patchwork. In time, we will begin to read into this patchwork some pattern, but we have to do it by ourselves; Bachelard himself never overtly coordinated his ideas, he rarely made references to his own earlier writings, and he did not have the habit of alerting the reader to a change of mind. He is reported to have said in one of his lectures: 'I should like to develop a philosophy that would have no point of departure' (Gaudin 1987: xxxiv).

A further factor must be kept in mind. Bachelard held an *agrégation* in philosophy so he was more than familiar with the entire history of philosophy.[2] Yet he seemed to put together his project without inheriting any of the philosophical past, even though it is evident from his writings that he is always aware of it, as he borrows from it when it suits his needs, and, in general, he exudes an impressively deep erudition (which was another reason for not sticking with the term 'pagan').³ A friend who is familiar with Bachelard's work once described him as 'making it all up by himself'. Very much so, it seems. Bachelard will speak of phenomenology or psychoanalysis but there is little of Husserl or Freud in them; he will use philosophical terms such as dialectics or employ the phenomenon/noumenon distinction but he gives them his own specific meaning.

Finally, there is the question of Bachelard's style. His writings defy philosophical expectations: there is little philosophical terminology, many an imprecise formulation, and not much debate; and he is unsystematic. One commentator remarked that 'Bachelard's language is characterised by a strange lack of rigour, great versatility, and an overabundance of neologisms', but he then adds that 'Bachelard performs a miracle of an extremely lively writing' (Quillet 1964: 49). Indeed. Most of the time, Bachelard is a pleasure to read. There is nothing of the buttoned-up academic drone in his writing, never a convoluted sentence. There is a lightness and nimble tempo in his pen. Since it is necessary to get through a good number of his works to begin to see a pattern emerge, Bachelard's readability is not a negligible factor; it really helps.

2

An unusual man, with an unusual career and a still more unusual mind, Gaston Bachelard was so modest that probably few of his contemporaries will remember him as a young man, when he was slowly working his way from small jobs in public administration up to a chair of philosophy in the Sorbonne. The Bachelard they will remember is the last one, a debonair patriarch, with a marked provincial accent, dearly loved by his students to whom he was so generously devoted, but chiefly known to his neighbours as an old man fond of choosing his own cut of meat at the market or of buying his own fish.

I wish I could make clear how his provincial origins and his familiarity with things of the earth affected his intellectual life and influenced the course of his philosophical reflections. Owing to his courageous efforts, Bachelard finally succeeded in giving himself a university education, got all the university degrees one can get and ended as a university professor; yet, unlike most of us, at least in France, he never allowed himself to become molded by the traditional ways of thinking to which universities unavoidably begin by submitting their students.

His intellectual superiority was such that he could not fail to succeed in all his academic ventures. We all loved him, admired him and envied him a little, because we felt he was a free mind, unfettered by any conventions either in his choice of the problems he wanted to handle or in his way of handling them.

These are the opening two paragraphs of the Foreword to the English translation of *La Poétique de l'espace* penned by Étienne Gilson. Gilson was his generation's greatest scholar of mediaeval philosophy, Thomas Aquinas and Descartes, and spent all his life in prestigious institutions, from the Lycée Henri IV to the Collège de France and the Académie française; in brief, Gilson was everything that Bachelard was not, and being a Christian philosopher he did not share any of Bachelard's philosophical tastes. All of which makes his words of praise and admiration so much more remarkable. These few words from Gilson tell us a fair bit about some of the sources of Bachelard's unusual quality. Gilson traces them to his non-Parisian roots, to his earthliness and to the fact that he was not moulded by the State's prestigious institutions such as the École Normale Supérieure. These account for the remarkable sense of freedom which is evident in his work.

Here are a few more details about Bachelard: He was born in Bar-sur-Aube, a small town in Champagne. His father was a cobbler and his mother owned a tobacco/newsagent boutique; so his origins were not only provincial but also 'humble'. He lived in Bar-sur-Aube till he was 46. He then moved to Dijon, and began his university career. After ten years in Dijon he moved to Paris to take up his post at the Sorbonne. Bachelard was the most un-Parisian Sorbonnard. He spoke with a strong provincial accent, had a long beard and long hair. He apparently disliked the city, the cinema, sport, jazz, the car, the telephone. He lived near Place Maubert and he treated it as his village.

Perhaps the most notable detail is that there was no Parisian input into Bachelard's intellectual development. Such input would have come from philosophers who, in this telling description by one commentator, had received an 'education, at the École Normale, [which was] classical in nature, primarily based on Greek and Latin authors, and more or less Kantian as well [...] They had read the same traditional authors, most notably those of the seventeenth century; they thought in an orderly, methodical way, measuring their words. [...] All were born of bourgeois families and with Parisian souls' (Poirier 1974: 11). Bachelard had an extremely negative view of the intellectual habits of the philosophical milieu of his day: 'we can surely say that a head well made [*tête bien faite*] is unfortunately a closed head. It is a product of a school' (FES 15);[4] and he held this milieu responsible for what he considered France's sclerotic education system: 'The physics textbooks, patiently copied year after year for half a century now, furnish our children with a well socialised science, fully immobilised and, thanks to a very curious permanence of programmes for university entry examinations, this science passes for a *natural* one' (FES 24).[5]

Bachelard was modest, as Gilson remarked, but he could speak his mind. A good number of other disparaging remarks of this sort could be cited, and Bachelard took a real interest in questions of education; he himself was a science teacher for many years and he sometimes referred to these experiences in his writings. But it is not central to Bachelard's project (at least not from the point of view of this study), and we shall not concern ourselves with this matter further. It is mentioned because his views on the educational establishment add one more dimension to his eccentricity. He was certainly not in the typical mould of those who held a Chair at the Sorbonne, which was a rather conservative place.

3

It is now time to give some further details about Bachelard's professional trajectory. He was born in 1884 and spent his early years working in the post office. In 1912 he received his *licence* in mathematics. At first, Bachelard planned to train as an engineer and took the entry examination to obtain a training post; he came third but did not gain entry as there were only two places on offer (this is the nearest he came to a failure, if coming third in a nationwide competition can count as one).[6] He was mobilised during the First World War and spent thirty-eight months in the trenches. In 1920, he obtained a *licence* in philosophy; in 1922, he entered and obtained the *agrégation*; in 1927, he was awarded a doctorate, his principal thesis being *Essai sur la connaissance approchée* (directed by Abel Rey), followed by the complementary thesis *Étude sur l'évolution d'un problème de physique: la propagation thermique dans les solides* (directed by Léon Brunschvicg). Three years later he took the Chair of Philosophy at the *faculté des lettres* of the University of Dijon where he taught philosophy, psychology and French literature (!). Thereafter appeared a number of works on epistemology (*La Valuer inductive de la relativité*, *Le Pluralisme cohérent de la chimie moderne*, *Le Nouvel esprit scientifique*, *L'Expérience de l'espace dans la physique contemporaine*, among others). These writings are striking for the original way in which Bachelard understands the nature of scientific discovery and development. His analyses often draw on historical material and they present two key points which Bachelard held on to from the beginning to the end of his authorship: firstly, facts as dealt with by scientists are not hidden in nature to be discovered by the efforts of experimentation and rationality, and thereafter to be treated as objective givens; rather, facts are created, so that it would be more precise to speak of them as artefacts. Secondly, science does not develop through a continuous accumulation of objective knowledge but is characterised by breaks and intermittencies; these have become known as epistemological ruptures. New inventions change the material and epistemological terrain in which scientists operate. The structure of Bachelard's argument is based on the conviction that scientists move forward not through an accretion of knowledge but by ridding themselves of the past in order to open a free field for the new to emerge. Today, after the writings of Paul Feyerabend, Bruno Latour, Thomas Kuhn, Isabelle Stengers, Ian Hacking, Michel Serres, among others, these ideas may seem fairly obvious, but when Bachelard was developing them they were genuinely new. (And because his idea of the epistemological rupture was already so well known in France, when the French translation of Kuhn's *The Structure of Scientific Revolutions* appeared, it had little of the novelty it had brought to the English speaking milieu.) Bachelard's writings established his reputation as his generation's leading philosopher of science.

During this earlier period he also published two books on the philosophy of time, *L'Intuition de l'instant* and *La Dialectique de la durée*. In these two works Bachelard expounds an intriguing concept of time as consisting exclusively of isolated instants; the instant is the only reality that time offers us. The time we live is a perpetual renewal; we carve out new destinies while lodged in the instantaneity of what is given to us.

In 1940, Bachelard was appointed Chair of History and Philosophy of Science at the Sorbonne. His arrival at the Sorbonne brought about a change in direction. Instead of continuing with his work on the philosophy of science, as, presumably, he was expected to, he started bringing out books on the nature of the poetic imagination. This in fact he announced earlier with the 1938 publication of a work with an unusual title: *La Psychanalyse du feu*. He followed it with a quartet of beautiful monographs: *L'Eau et les rêves*, *L'Air et les songes*, *La Terre et les rêveries de la volonté* and *La Terre et les rêveries du repos*, which were all published between 1942 and 1948. This work on the poetic imaginary[7] is quite unlike that on the philosophy of science in mood, and reading it we enter another world. Bachelard seeks to root the imaginary in the Greek division of the four elements, fire, water, air and earth. Each imaginary life, he argues, is organised around a principal element.

After the writings on the imaginary and the four elements, Bachelard returned to philosophy of science, publishing three major works between 1949 and 1953: *Le Rationalisme appliqué*, *L'Activité rationaliste de la physique contemporaine* and *Le Matérialisme rationnel*.

In the final years of his life Bachelard was exclusively preoccupied with the question of the poetic imagination. From this late period of activity comes *La Poétique de l'espace*, by far his best known work in the English speaking constituency, as well as *La Poétique de la rêverie*, *La Flamme d'une chandelle* and his last unfinished, posthumously published *Fragments d'une poétique du feu*.

At the time Bachelard was active, something new was happening on the French philosophical scene, in terms of an opening towards and engagement with German philosophy. The year 1929 is perhaps the symbolic date. On February 23 and 25, Edmund Husserl gave two double-session lectures (in German) entitled 'Introduction to Transcendental Phenomenology'. They took place at the Sorbonne. An extended version of the lectures was published in a French translation in 1931 as *Méditations cartésiennes* (of which there are five). This was the arrival of phenomenology in France. Between 1933 and 1939, at the École des Hautes Études, Alexandre Kojève gave hugely influential lectures on Hegel's philosophy, principally *The Phenomenology of Spirit* (they were later prepared for publication by Raymond Queneau and came out in print in 1947 (Kojève 1947)). Hegel, Marx, Freud, Husserl and

Heidegger became principal references for leading figures of the Parisian intellectual scene such as Jean Hyppolite, Louis Althusser, Jacques Lacan, Maurice Merleau-Ponty, Jean-Paul Sartre, and a number of others. Bachelard does not belong anywhere near this movement, which was quite dominant at the time, but he did not go unnoticed. His contemporaries read him widely and his works reverberate in many of their writings. Those who wrote texts specifically devoted to Bachelard include such prominent figures as Maurice Blanchot (1959), Eugène Minkowski (1963), George Canguilhem (2002), Jean Hyppolite (1957), François Dagognet (1965), Michel Serres (1970), Jean Starobinski (1984) and Jean-François Lyotard (1970). There are some two dozen monographs on Bachelard, the first of which came out shortly after his death (Pierre Quillet 1964, François Dagognet 1965, Dominique Lecourt 1969); one of the most recent, a comprehensive presentation of Bachelard's work, comes from Vincent Bontems (2010). As for his wider influence it will be better to give some thought to this in the concluding part of this work.

In the Anglophone world Bachelard hardly registered. There are three books and a handful of articles.[8] The most recent book, *Gaston Bachelard: Critic of Science and the Imagination*, from 1996, is by Cristina Chimisso. Chimisso situates Bachelard in the social and cultural context of his day, and explores the relation between this and the idea we have of it and of his work. The focus of the book is altogether different than in the present study, since it is not strictly speaking a philosophical engagement with Bachelard's thought. The title of an earlier book, *Surrealism and the Literary Imagination: A Study of Breton and Bachelard*, by Mary-Ann Caws (1966), is self-explanatory. Although the subtitle of the present work has the word 'surreal' in it, it does not locate Bachelard in the context of the Surrealist movement. There is a case for undertaking such a study but it belongs in literary criticism rather than philosophy and Caws deals with the matter comprehensively as she is a leading expert on Surrealism. Finally, a 1984 book, *Bachelard: Science and Objectivity* by Mary Tiles, has been very helpful to me. Tiles concentrates exclusively on Bachelard's philosophy of science and pays particular attention to the role that he assigns to mathematics in scientific thinking. Tiles has a background in mathematics as well as philosophy and her analyses are incisive and elucidate a great deal. She also confronts Bachelard's views with those of the philosophers who emerged from the Vienna Circle. As she shows them to be incompatible, it comes as no surprise to find that Bachelard's thought has not affected Anglophone philosophy of science (with the notable exception of Ian Hacking).[9] Similarities (superficial, it must be said) have been noted between Kuhn's concept of scientific revolutions and Bachelard's concept of epistemological rupture, but this has not provoked much curiosity about Bachelard's views. After reading Tiles's detailed study one comes to the conclusion that comparing Bachelard with Vienna Circle-inspired epistemology is like trying to compare Surrealist productions with landscape painting. Such diversity is not troubling (to most) in art, but in philosophy of science it may seem disconcerting.

4

There are two principal entrances into Bachelard's philosophical universe: the first through his writings on the philosophy of science, the second through his meditations on the nature of the imaginary. Bachelard always insisted on a radical separation between the activities of scientific rationality and poetic imagination. Between a concept and an image there cannot be any filiation, he often repeated, as they are the products of different faculties; consequently, if a poem is laden with concepts, the image that gives the poem its poetic resonance will be weakened; conversely, images tend to obfuscate scientific concepts. Bachelard held this view throughout his writings. In his earlier work he referred to scientific activity as diurnal and the poetic as nocturnal; later he maintained that the concept belongs to the workings of the *animus* while the image comes from the *anima*. The result of this separation is that there are considerable differences between the writings on science and on poetry. *Le Nouvel esprit scientifique*, for example, reflects on the changes in scientific rationality brought on by the emergence of relativity theory and quantum physics. The analysis of the emergence of new rationalities is one of Bachelard's central preoccupations. It rests on the thesis that rationality, rather than being fixed by permanent rules, evolves and proliferates through ruptures with the past. To illustrate changes in the structures of rationalities Bachelard often draws on historical material, whereas his writings on the imaginary are strictly ahistorical. Further, Bachelard frequently stressed that a scientific effort is a collective effort, whereas the poetic image opens the world of solitude: 'The image is in fact less social than the concept, it is more likely to reveal a solitary being, a being at the centre of its will' (TV 176).

The two parts of Bachelard's work also differ immensely in their mood. Science is a hard and uncompromising enterprise with a long development which can be traced, analysed and judged by its results; poetry is elusive and fragile. These two distinct lines of investigation have also met with different fates: Bachelard's epistemological writings entered the academic syllabus, becoming part of the basic teaching in France; his writings on the poetic imagination have been to a large extent ignored by 'official' philosophy but have had a great success with the larger public, writers, poets, artists, and some philosophers as well, of course.

Anyone who wants to come to grips with Bachelard's work has to somehow deal with this radical duality, which, one should note, did not in the least inconvenience Bachelard himself – quite the opposite, in his last work he stated 'I only knew tranquil work after I had neatly cut my working life into two almost independent parts, one put under the sign of the concept, the other under the sign of the image' (FPF 33). Some view these two aspects as completely separate projects, Bruno Latour going so far as to say that Bachelard was 'schizophrenic, and was proud of it' (in Serres 1992: 51); whereas others see a continuity between them.

There is of course nothing schizophrenic about Bachelard's project. Although the differences between the world of poetic images and the world of scientific concepts have been just spelt out, there are a number of threads that hold Bachelard's work together. One of them is an aspiration that runs through the whole of his philosophy. All of Bachelard's thought is devoted to one singular question: how to understand, philosophically, a mind that is at work. This commitment is behind one of his often repeated charges against various philosophical ways of thinking: that they are lazy – a rather unusual epithet to be found in a philosophical discourse. They are lazy, either because they contemplate reality passively, as Bachelard holds is the case with phenomenology, or they deal with concepts that the mind cannot really get hold of, such as 'Being' or 'universe'; for example, 'the universe is the infinity of my inattention' (EngR 104). This has been noted by others: 'Bachelardism is not a philosophy of Being [. . .] but a philosophy of *work*, of work for itself and not as a mode of elucidation of Being, not as an enterprise of overcoming, in contemplation, in a Heideggerian fashion, but work as an absolute creation. The philosophy of Being is a laziness' (Quillet 1964: 10).

What does Bachelard mean by a mind at work? This is not a mind attempting to penetrate reality, to be a perfect eyewitness to what reality presents us with, but a mind engaged in creating new realities; this is when a mind is at its most exceptional. Science and poetry are the two domains of human activity that furnish Bachelard with material for his analyses: the scientific effort carves out newer and stranger realities and likewise the poetic imagination conjures up new worlds. Both scientists and poets are prime examples of a mind creating domains that surpass reality. Bachelard is a surrealist. He is a surrealist with a small 's' as he never belonged to the movement, and he did not agree with all of the Surrealists' theorising; for example, he did not share André Breton's fascination with the Freudian unconsciousness. But he was attracted to the Surrealist poets (some of whom were his friends, being particularly close to Paul Éluard, and he cited many of them in his writings). Like them he believed that the way to new realities is to be sought through language: 'Surrealism places itself, first of all, almost uniquely on the plane of language' (Breton 1985: 101); like them he endows the poetic image with the power to transform reality. He also wrote a commentary on Lautréamont's *Les Chants de Maldoror*, a work the Surrealists held in especially high esteem. Bachelard's affinity with them is not limited to his writings on the poetic imagination; his analyses of scientific developments are also conducted from a surrealist angle. Bachelard's unflinching commitment was to render philosophically intelligible ways of quitting, sidestepping, eluding, so to speak, reality as it is given and to show how new realities can be forged. Thus the aspiration that holds together the two distinct paths is clear: *philosophy is not in the business of contemplating reality but of surpassing it.*

5

Presenting the difference between Bachelard's philosophy of science and that inspired by the Vienna Circle as akin to comparing landscape painting to a Surrealist work is not an exaggeration, at least as far as Surrealism goes. Bachelard quite explicitly drew comparisons between Surrealist activities and the developments in new science. In 1936, Roger Caillois, an unclassifiable essayist, invited Bachelard to participate in a new review *Inquisitions*. Other contributors were similarly unclassifiable, including George Bataille, Jules Monnerot, Michel Leiris, the science-fiction writer Jacques Spitz and the Dada poet Tristan Tzara, who also edited the review. All of them at one point or another were linked with the Surrealist movement.[10] The subtitle of the issue (which turned out to be the only one) was *Du Surréalisme au Front Populaire*. Bachelard's six-page 'Le Surrationalisme' was the opening text and it reads like a manifesto (see the Appendix to Chapter 1 for a full translation). In the opening passages we read:

> We almost always confuse decisive acts of reason with a monotonous resort to the certitude of memory. What we know well, what we have experienced several times, what we repeat loyally, easily, warmly, gives the impression of an objective and rational coherence. So rationalism acquires a taste of school. It is easy and tiresome, cheerful as a prison gate, welcoming like a tradition.

It is clear that Bachelard had little patience for rationalism as it was taught in his time; the good old Cartesian method that aims to establish once and for all the first principles and rules of acquiring knowledge was to him an obsolete idea on which to found scientific rationality. This, in his view, will not do; developments in twentieth-century science demand an approach in a new spirit.

> When surrationalism eventually finds its doctrine it will be possible to put it in relation to surrealism as fluidity will be restored to sensibility and reason. The physical world will be experienced in new ways. We will understand differently and feel differently. We will establish an *experimental reason* which will surrationally organise the real in the way Tristan Tzara's *experimental dream* organises poetic freedom surrealistically. We can, therefore, foresee two orders of spiritual tasks which are already beginning to be visible, in their early stages, in scientific developments of our time: reason will divide itself through an internal dialectic – reason will be divided by experimental obstacles through an external dialectic. The conjunction of these two dialectics will determine in the third place the *surempiricisms* of a strange mobility and of a strange innovative force.

The invention of non-Euclidian geometries was a scientific event that Bachelard often singles out as one of the decisive moments;

he praises these inventions because they freed scientists from the confines of Euclidian space.

> In applying the spirit of finesse to the geometrical spirit, [the Russian mathematician] Lobachevsky created geometrical humour, *he promoted polemical reason to the rank of constituting reason*; in making supple the principle of contradiction, he founded the freedom of reason in relation to itself.
>
> Here you have in front of you a hardened rationalist spirit that repeats the eternal example given in every school philosophy book by philosophers who block rationalism with elementary scientific culture: the sum of the angles of a triangle equals two right angles. You will reply calmly: 'It depends'. In fact, it depends on the choice of axioms. With a smile, you will disconcert this elementary reason that gives itself the right of absolute ownership of the elements. You will give suppleness to this dogmatic reason by making it play with axioms. You will teach it to unlearn in order to understand better. What variety there is in this disorganisation of a sclerotic rationalism! And, reciprocally, what variations on surrational themes; what brusque mutations for the suddenly dialectised minds!
>
> Unfortunately, no positive, real, surrealist usage has been made of this liberty, which could have renewed all the notions by arriving at them dialectically; the logicians and formalists arrived. Instead of realising, surrealising the rational liberty which the spirit experienced in these precise and fragmentary dialectics, the logicians and formalists, quite to the contrary, de-realised, de-psychologised the new spiritual conquest.

Yet Bachelard is convinced that the tide can be turned:

> A psychic revolution has come about in this century; human reason has been un-anchored, the spiritual voyage has begun and knowledge has quit the shores of the immediately real.

For a philosopher with an analytical bent these kinds of utterances coming from someone described as a 'philosopher of science' must seem positively perplexing. But perhaps it will be a little less so if we are more precise about Bachelard's aims. To begin with, the label 'philosopher of science' is not quite accurate: none of the terms that we would expect to find in a philosophy of science work, such as 'verification' or 'refutation', are present in

Bachelard's writings. His aim is not to determine the logical structure of scientific theory or the correct conditions of justification. It would be more accurate to say that he explores the workings of scientific rationality. Rationalism is a term that looms particularly large in Bachelard's thinking, it appears in the titles of three of his last books that deal with questions of science (*Le Rationalisme appliqué*, *L'Activité rationaliste de la physique contemporaine*, *Le Matérialisme rationnel*) and a great part of his earlier opus is also devoted to various aspects of the problem. The key question that he seeks to answer was imposed upon philosophy, as Bachelard sees it, by Einstein's relativity theory and quantum physics: namely, what are the conditions for the emergence of new scientific realities, surrealities, as they are neither extensions of the 'natural' world, nor derived from it? Some of the features of the new science, Schrödinger's Cat, for example, are no less strange than André Breton and Philippe Soupault's *Champs magnétiques*, and yet they are products of purely rational efforts. To emphasise this surrealist quality of new scientific developments Bachelard points out that they can be just as disquieting and unsettling as the productions of Surrealist artists that perturb our everyday view of the world: 'Contemporary physics gives us an unknown world. Its messages are delivered in "hieroglyphs" to use the expression of Walter Ritz. In trying to decipher them, we realise that these unknown signs sit uneasily with our psychological habits' (E 12).

Another way of describing the difference is that for an adherent of the Vienna School rationality is logical whereas for Bachelard it is mathematical – and mathematicians invent new things, some of them very strange indeed. Articulated in this way, Bachelard's surrationalism may seem a little less puzzling, although his evident disdain for traditional rationalists, logicians and formalists will remain hard to swallow for an analytical philosopher.

6

Well-being and surrealism are the two notes on Bachelard's scale that have been identified so far. More will come, but these two are enough to begin with. This is how the present work will proceed:

The first chapter, 'The New Scientific Spirit', will be devoted to Bachelard's epistemological thought. His publications on the philosophy of science span a quarter of a century. The first part of his doctoral thesis, *Essai sur la connaissance approchée*, was published in 1927; the last significant work was *Le Matérialisme rationnel*, published in 1953.

Bachelard's writings on the subject evolve along two axes: the first concentrates on the historical developments of science, the second analyses the future to which contemporary science points. Out of these two evolve somewhat independent and not always connected themes, concepts and problems.

The historical dimension is characterised by Bachelard's argument that scientific developments are discontinuous in nature rather than a steady accumulation of knowledge and technique. This is not an unfamiliar view; Kuhn came to a similar conclusion. But Bachelard's way of arguing this point is quite different: for him, it is the very structure of rationalist thought that produces discontinuities, whereas for Kuhn the breakdowns of scientific paradigms are due to the accumulation of anomalies within science. Moreover, where Bachelard finds discontinuities, Kuhn speaks of incommensurabilities, which is quite a different concept, although the two are not incompatible. Here we have a first sighting of Bachelard's notion of an epistemological rupture, a notion that had a considerable influence on French philosophical thought and that went beyond the philosophy of science. This will be accompanied by an analysis of his concept of an epistemological obstacle, which in his view is a hindrance to scientific progress. These obstacles need to be eradicated from scientific thinking through a procedure Bachelard called the psychoanalysis of the scientific mind.

According to Bachelard, such a psychoanalysis is necessary in order to open the mind to the challenges set by new scientific developments. In the process, he dismisses what he calls 'naïve' experience of the world as being an obstacle to scientific thought; he goes as far as to contend that rationality presents interests that are different from those presented by life and that attract the naïve spirit. This aspect of Bachelard's thought met with severe criticism from the next generation of Francophone philosophers of science, Michel Serres, Isabelle Stengers and Bruno Latour in particular. These criticisms will be analysed and evaluated. Since most of them will be found to be fair (at least up to a point), their importance in the bigger picture presented by Bachelardian epistemology will need to be assessed.

The other dimension of Bachelard's writings on science is his analysis of the new rationality of contemporary science, principally in physics and chemistry. Since we will find that his much criticised concepts of the epistemological obstacle and psychoanalysis of the scientific mind have little bearing on lessons to be drawn from his analyses of theory of relativity and quantum physics, the value of these lessons is not affected. Amongst the several themes elaborated in these we can identify:

1. Bachelard's concept of rationality.
2. The role of mathematics (non-Euclidian geometries, tensor calculus, Paul Dirac's work) in scientific thinking.
3. Bachelard's contention that new science 'quits nature and enters the factory of phenomena'; that is, while in the traditional view science was understood to be a practice of observing and analysing natural phenomena, the new science, in Bachelard's rendering, produces new phenomena, phenomena that are not encountered in 'nature'. In this context the original and influential concept of the *phénoménotechnique* will be explored.
4. Bachelard's rejection of the classical concept of substance/matter and his redefinition of it in terms of resonance, frequency and vibration together with the mathematisation of chemistry.
5. Bachelard's highly unusual understanding of how we should view the historical dimension of science.

The chapter will end with an analysis of Bachelard's argument that rather than imposing rules of practice on science, as some philosophers have proposed, philosophy should learn from the new surrational scientific mind. Recognition of this shift is not specific to Bachelard alone. One could say it is another version of the end of transcendental philosophy, and perhaps more specifically of neo-Kantianism. But Bachelard's programme is remarkably radical as he seeks to reverse a number of trends in philosophical and scientific thinking; he advocates a non-Aristotelian logic, non-Baconian science, non-Cartesian epistemology, non-Lavoisian chemistry and non-Euclidian geometries.

The other aspect of Bachelard's work is devoted to the study of the poetic imagination. This will be the subject of Chapter 2, 'The Imaginary'. It differs from the previous one in both its subject matter and in its style of presentation. While Bachelard's writings on scientific thought take the form of an argument that requires a careful and rigorous analysis, his reflections on the poetic image are, to use his own words, a fruit of the observations of a 'botanist out on a walk who through haphazard readings collected "poetic flowers"' (FPF 28). However, there is nothing haphazard in the way Bachelard presented his thinking on the imaginary, and this chapter will follow the flow of his exposition. It explores the evolution of Bachelard's thought about the imaginary from the violent early *Lautréamont*, to the writings on the four elements, fire, water, air and earth, to *La Poétique de l'espace*, which is quite rightly considered one of Bachelard's *chefs d'oeuvre*, and his final unfinished *Fragments d'une poétique du feu*. Although these writings have a poetic tinge, the philosophical interest of this part of Bachelard's opus is far from negligible. Most intriguingly, in the early phase of his work on imagination, he turns to Presocratic thought and presents poetic imagination as organised around the four elements; also in a Presocratic manner, we find ourselves immersed in a hylozoic world, that is, the world of the Ionian Greeks in which all matter is intrinsically alive, in which all material substance has the capacity to initiate changes to which it is subject, and where there is no external design or *telos*, independent of nature, which gives these changes shape or direction. In the second phase of his writings on the imaginary, which constitute Bachelard's last writings, he develops a phenomenology of the image and of the soul. In this period, his closeness to Surrealist thinking again becomes very apparent.

During this period, Bachelard sheds his prejudice towards what he referred to as the 'naïve' in his epistemological writings and now welcomes it: 'Through this reverberation, by going *immediately* beyond all psychology or psychoanalysis, we feel a poetic power rise naïvely within us' (PE 7, xix). This change of value that he now attaches to the term 'naïve' changes the tone of his scale.

Like many philosophers, Bachelard, too, meditated on death. This comes in the last work that he published *La Flamme d'une chandelle* and in the posthumous *Fragments d'une poétique du feu*. A discussion of this will close the chapter.

'The meditation on time is the preliminary task of all metaphysics' (II 13). This comes in two early books, *L'Intuition de l'instant* (1932) and *La Dialectique de la durée* (1936); the analysis of these will be the subject of Chapter 3, 'The Poetics of Time'. Bachelard seemed to put considerable effort into these texts and there are good reasons to consider them central to his overall project, yet they are relatively little commented on and some presentations of Bachelard make no mention of them at all. One commentator says that these essays 'use in parallel psychological and epistemological arguments, they associate analyses of poetry with scientific works. [. . .] They are the most arduous and most thankless [*ingrats*] as the reader never knows on which foot to dance or where the argument is situated' (Bontems 2010: 167).[11] What is the cause of this difficulty? On the one hand, these two texts are quite deceptive as they are easy to read; on the other hand, it is true that Bachelard drew his arguments from very disparate domains: Pierre Janet's psychology, Gaston Roupnel's *Siloë* (which is a quite mystical text), quantum physics, as well as poets and theoreticians of music. But most of all, we are faced with an unfamiliar territory; this is clearly a philosophy of time but of a kind that seems without precedent in our philosophical heritage. A great deal of reflection is needed to grasp the implications of Bachelard's conception of time as a series of disconnected instants. The discontinuous conception of time is at the heart of Bachelard's understanding of the structure of consciousness, and also plays a key role in his understanding of progress in science (reason itself produces discontinuities); finally, it is the root of the poetic image.

This chapter comes in three parts. The first is an exposition of Bachelard's conception of the instant, of how in his view duration is created, and of how, despite the fact that the instant is our only temporal reality, we can create habits and launch and sustain projects. The second deals with Bachelard's critique of the philosophy of Henri Bergson and principally with Bergson's main thesis that time is a flowing duration of the *élan vital*. There is quite an extensive literature (in French) on the Bachelard versus Bergson debate.[12] Some of the arguments in that debate will be presented here, but there is one question that seems not to have been addressed, namely, the *reason* Bachelard engages in his dispute with Bergson's philosophy, a reason which, at first sight, is not quite clear. First of all, Bachelard does not need this confrontation in order to clarify his own views; second, it is out of character with the rest of his writings, as Bachelard never engaged in sustained disputes with other philosophers (although there were some that he clearly disliked; he was apparently allergic to Jean-Paul Sartre); and, third, he is remarkably uncompromising and trenchant in his criticisms, referring to Bergsonians as his 'adversaries'. Bachelard clearly sees Bergson's duration of the *élan vital* as a trap; he also refers to it as a philosophy of laziness. An isolated passage seems to spell out yet another reason for this hostility: if the time we live were a continuous duration, as Bergson holds, we could re-live the past, which we cannot, and it would also bring into our lived experience the fear of death: 'To relive the time which has disappeared, is [. . .] to learn the anxiety of our death' (DD 33, 51).

The chapter ends with a presentation of a dispute that took place in Indian philosophy between Buddhists and Brahmins and is principally based on a work by Lilian Silburn: *Instant et cause: Le discontinu dans la pensée philosophique de l'Inde* (Silburn 1989). The Brahmins were partisans of duration, while discontinuity was central in the thought of the Buddhists, and their disagreements are much the same as the disagreements voiced by Bachelard in relation to Bergson. Reading Silburn's work, especially the chapter on the logicians of the School of Dignāga, one is struck by the similarities between Bachelard's thinking and what we find to be the Buddhist views; it is thus difficult to resist presenting them, even if in a very abbreviated fashion. This is not meant to be an exercise in comparative philosophy, a kind of East meets West, which is a dubious practice (although in many respects Bachelard does indeed think like a Buddhist). But Bachelard can sometimes be overly laconic, and reading Silburn's work helped me better understand his texts. Silburn's work has the depth typical of a *thèse de doctorat d'État* of that period: it is rich in detail, her analyses are very precise and extended, and what at times may seem obscure in Bachelard's text (the different types of duration, for example) becomes clearer after reading Silburn.

The Concluding Remarks will be followed by an Appendix, 'Bachelard and Atomism'. Some key notes of Bachelard's scale have been identified, but atomism is another thread that can be seen in Bachelard's thought. In fact, thinking of Bachelard as an atomist helps to clarify a great deal of his thought and reveals a coherence and consistency that runs throughout his writings; it is one of the key notes on his scale, and it is a recognisably philosophical note. But this obviously needs fleshing out in more detail. In order to do so it will be necessary first to have a closer look at the atomist systems of Democritus and Epicurus, then the seventeenth-century atomism of Pierre Gassendi, and finally at some of the developments in atomist thinking in contemporary science. It will be then possible to locate Bachelard in this universe.

Talk of atomism in relation to Bachelard may provoke puzzlement, as the term conjures up the image of billiard balls bouncing haphazardly off each other, which is clearly alien to Bachelard's world. But this image is misleading, and already in the earlier Greek versions of atomism we find that the thinking is far more subtle and complex. Furthermore, with developments in contemporary physics, atomism has evolved and new questions of an ontological nature have arisen.

A few caveats must be voiced. The first of which is that this is not an attempt to fit Bachelard's thought into a Procrustean bed of atomism. In fact, in preparing this work, the opposite happened: it was reading Bachelard that led me to look closely at atomism. Another point must be emphasised. We are not dealing with atomism as a 'natural' philosophy, as an ontological hypothesis that tries to describe the hidden reality behind the world as it presents itself, as a way of explaining why the world is the way it is. This is not the kind of question that would be of much interest to a surrealist; Bachelard welcomes the atomism of contemporary science because it is within this world that the surrationalist programme can be acted out. Further, we are dealing with what atomist *thinking* entails, with how it proceeds, how it determines its philosophical choices, which options are rejected and which adopted. And, finally, a matter of considerable importance: the atomist doctrine opens up the question of *aspirations* in philosophy. Aspirations determine the shape that the thought takes and what it attempts to promote.

This Appendix, which is the length of a chapter, is not included in the main body of the text for a number of reasons. First, epistemology, poetics and time are clearly recognisable themes in Bachelard's work, and in a sense the main text is a presentation of these themes and an attempt to see how these seemingly different facets interrelate, or resonate one with another; here I stay close to Bachelard's writings throughout. In the Appendix we will stray from the texts to first lay out some of the problematic related to atomism. Also, the three chapters that make up the main text are in a sense finished presentations, while the Appendix is more of an interpretative essay that puts Bachelard in a wider philosophical context and has a somewhat different feel. It could be extended and elaborated, but the discussion here will be restricted to those features of atomism that are pertinent to our thinking about Bachelard's project.

For now, all that can be done is to name the few notes that

have already been identified as belonging to Bachelard's scale; here they are, listed alphabetically, like keywords at the end of an abstract of an article: *atomism, Buddhism (?), naïvety, surrealism, well-being* . . .

I

The New Scientific Mind

The Epistemological Rupture

Henri Poincaré, Émile Meyerson, Pierre Duhem, Léon Brunschvicg are but a few names that have ensured the prominence of philosophy of science in the French milieu. One of the features that these thinkers have in common is the conviction that to understand science one has to understand its history: 'to give a history of a physical principle is at the same time to make a logical analysis of it' (Duhem 1962: 269). A sizeable part of Bachelard's writings deal with questions related to the history of science, however, he introduces an original feature into his analyses. George Canguilhem, Bachelard's successor at Sorbonne's Chair of History and Philosophy of Science, who excelled in his writings on the philosophy and history of medicine and biology, described Bachelard's work as a 'new art of writing the history of sciences. This history cannot any longer be a collection of biographies or a table of doctrines, in the fashion of natural history. This must be a history of conceptual filiations.' Then, in the following sentence, Canguilhem states that 'This filiation has a status of discontinuity, much like in Mendelian heredity' (Canguilhem 2002: 184). This point must be underlined: what marked out Bachelard's views on the history of science, and has had a considerable influence on the thinking of subsequent generations of Francophone philosophers of science, is his argument that the scientific *episteme* does not develop through a continuous accretion of knowledge, a refinement of techniques, an accumulation of discoveries and a more and more coherent theory; rather, the *episteme* develops through a series of ruptures and discontinuities.

There are discontinuities of different types and Bachelard will accord varying degrees of importance to them. The first type of discontinuity, and the one that would appear to be the most obvious, occurs when a particular theory is shown to be erroneous because it followed the wrong line of reasoning. A good example would be the case of the seventeenth-century phlogiston theory of combustion. This theory stated that when bodies burn they release a substance called phlogiston, which was meant to account for their loss of mass when they burn. In time, the theory ran into difficulties as it was discovered that some metals, such as magnesium, gain rather than lose mass when they burn, but most of all the existence of the mysterious phlogiston was never made in any way apparent. The theory was finally refuted when a century later the French chemist Antoine Lavoisier demonstrated that the process of burning does not release anything like phlogiston from the burnt body but quite the opposite – it takes from air a substance which he called oxygen. This is a clear rupture. The new theory refuted the old one so completely that nothing of it remained.

But this was just one specific theory with a limited impact on the larger scientific scale and so this kind of discontinuity was not of great interest to Bachelard; and there is not much to be learnt from it either. Looking at it closely, one can glean something about the old scientific mind-set. The concept of phlogiston was rooted in the old idea that substance, mass and size are somehow equivalent, hence if a body diminishes in size it has to release the missing substance in some other form. Some old ways of reasoning can be elucidated from this example but this will not tell us much about today's scientific mentality.

Something similar can be said of the prevailing world-view of what Bachelard refers to as pre-scientific thought. The guiding conception in the early speculations, from the Greeks until the emergence of modern chemistry, was the scheme of the four elements: water, air, earth and fire. Bachelard comments on the various efforts that were made to match the four elements with four different temperaments, on how body organs were grouped according to similar structures, or on some of the attempts to link different planets to different elements (MR 44–8). Speculations of this kind lasted until the eighteenth century. The decisive blow to this world-view was the discovery (also by Lavoisier) that water and air were not simple elements but compound bodies. Oxygen was isolated and then within a few decades it was found that it mixes with nitrogen (then called azote) in air, combines with hydrogen in water, and that it also mixes with metals. The world that was emerging had little to do with the ancient constructs. In Bachelard's estimation, what was most important in these developments was not an accretion of knowledge nor a better understanding of nature's laws; it was that these discoveries led to a new realisation: nature does not present our immediate experience with pure elements; a pure substance is not a given fact but is the result of conscious human endeavour, it has to be extracted from nature. 'Such discoveries rupture history. They mark a *complete defeat of the immediate*' (MR 74).

But the discontinuities that are of principal interest to Bachelard are those that occur inside verified science, as he sees it – that is, science that has a consistent theoretical and experimental body, that has put into place an ongoing, mathematically founded research programme. An example of such a discontinuity that Bachelard returned to on a number of occasions was the development from Newtonian mechanics to relativity theory. This is the bare outline of his argument: the first breach in the order of the Newtonian scheme began with the creation of non-Euclidian geometries (by János Bolyai, Nicolai Lobachevsky and Bernhard Riemann). These constructions remained in the realm of pure mathematics until the advent of relativity theory, as non-Euclidian concepts were indispensable for the formulation of the new theory. Within two decades science underwent a profound transformation.

This transformation is a rupture rather than a smooth transition and the extent of the rupture can be gauged by its consequences. In this case, one of the consequences was a change in our understanding of space. Euclidian geometry is a system which designs a space in which all objects of the world can be located and their relations calculated, or, to put it in Bachelard's own caustic words:

> The indefinite character of Euclidian space, its isotropy, its uniformity, its indifference to whether it is inhabited or not [*au peuplement*], the possibility of displacing objects in it without the occurrence of any deformation, all this contributed to legitimise a monotonous use of the same frame; one space, one experience, one reason. (EEPC 139)

Spaces in the non-Euclidian world are of a different order. Bachelard will say 'One does not find space; it always has to be constructed', and he then quotes from the physicist Jean-Louis Destouches.

As it transpires from the works of Poincaré, neither experience nor the senses can completely fix space, not even its topology ... To fix a physical space it is necessary, also, and first of all, to have a theoretical idea: it is this that determines the choice of space that our senses or experience can only accept or reject. (EEPC 124)

The move from Euclidian geometry to the non-Euclidian realm led to a proliferation of new geometrical methods that cannot be conceived in the old system. But in moving out of the world of Euclid the new geometries do not refute it, instead they incorporate its results and the world of geometry expands. This means that while the results of the new geometries cannot be comprehended from within the Euclidian system the problems posed in the old system can be tackled by the new ones. To leave the world of Euclid it was necessary to break away from some old assumptions, but it is, nevertheless, possible to move back: 'when we go from non-Newtonian physics to Newtonian physics, we do not encounter contradiction but we do experience contraction' (NES 62, 60). Euclidian geometry was not refuted by the new developments, only its limits became apparent.

This is an example of a profound change in science. One should point out that these are not ruptures in one line, interrupted here and there, along which the scientific discourse develops; instead the ruptures lead to a multiplication of *episteme*. For example, we observe discontinuities when we change scale. The spaces of microphysics, of the human scale and of an astrophysicist are not arranged on a single scale *from* the infinitely small *to* the infinitely big. There is no continuity between these different spaces, there is no *passage* from one to the other, and neither do they negate each other; they co-exist in different epistemological realms. That they are different is quite clear. Notions such as 'weight', 'distance' and 'speed' mean one thing on the sub-atomic level, another on the metric scale and yet another in the world of an astrophysicist; and their 'measurements' are obtained with the use of very different instruments/technical set-ups. As a consequence we are dealing with a proliferation. Discontinuities that produce shifts happen at all levels of scientific activity: they are the nature of inventiveness; a sewing machine could only be invented, remarks Bachelard, after attempts to imitate the action of hand sewing were abandoned (RA 134). This is an interesting example as it is not drawn from mathematical physics or chemistry, Bachelard's usual terrains, but from quite a common observation, and so his argument is very accessible. Indeed, anyone who has sewn by hand and later tries to fathom how a sewing machine works will be at first puzzled, as the one has nothing to do with the other.

The example of the invention of the sewing machine is interesting but also somewhat paradoxical in being derived from a common observation, since the rupture between common knowledge and scientific thinking is the one that Bachelard seems to consider the most fundamental. He identifies the year in which this break or rupture becomes most pronounced, namely 1905, which is when Einstein proposed the first theory of relativity (FES 7). The reason this date is decisive is that Einstein's theory, and the later developments of quantum physics, simply cannot be comprehended within the parameters of common knowledge. They represent a total break with our 'natural' understanding of the world.

This rupture is marked by the move from visual representation to mathematical thinking. Bachelard points out that although terms that suggest visual images are sometimes used, they should not be taken in a literal 'naïve' sense. The following extended quote shows what Bachelard has in mind.

> The epistemological problem of the electron spin goes beyond the bounds of intuition for two related reasons:
> 1. The mathematical idea of rotation is the pretext that justifies the use of the spin metaphor. The best proof of this is that rotation is very easily quantized. If physicists were actually imagining the rotation of real particles, with all the extra baggage that such an image would entail, quantization would be much more difficult and complex. Furthermore, spin is justified when spin-states are composed. With an isolated electron spin makes no sense. Thus spin is *conceptualized*, not imagined.
> 2. The rotation of the electron, indeed the electron itself, makes no sense to the ordinary imagination. Bear in mind that *we imagine with our retinas* and not with some mysterious and all-powerful faculty. [...] The imagination takes us no further than sensation. Merely attaching numbers to images is not enough to give an idea of how small the object is. The path of least resistance for the imagination is not the same as for mathematics. We can no longer think in any way but mathematically. Precisely because our sensory imagination fails us, we must move onto the plane of pure thought, where objects have no

reality except in relations. Hence there are limits to what we humans can imagine reality to be; or to put it another way, there are limits to the image-defined *determination* [*la détermination imagée*] of the real. (NES 135–6, 131–2)

This, one should point out, is in keeping with the early theoreticians of quantum physics who quite specifically stated that quantum physics can be apprehended but is not something to be visualised. An object apprehended in pure thought is not a phenomenon but, as Bachelard argues throughout, a *noumenal* object.

The phenomenon/noumenon distinction is old; it was introduced by Plato to distinguish between the ideal forms that can only be apprehended by reason and things displaying themselves to the senses. Kant also employed the distinction but he did not ascribe to Plato's ideal forms. To him the noumenon is 'unavoidably bound up with the limitation of our sensibility'; Kantian categories have limits and, therefore, 'a place remains open for other and different objects' (Kant 1950: A287/ B343). A different object, other than an object of our sensibility, is known as a 'thing-in-itself'. One would not expect Bachelard to even contemplate Plato's scheme and, indeed, he makes no comment on it, but he also rejects Kant's concept of the noumenon quite explicitly:

[a noumenal object is] conceived in reaction to the usual notion of reality, as a polemic against the immediate; it consists of realized reason, reason subject to experimentation. The 'reality' to which this realism corresponds is not transferred into the realm of the unknowable thing-in-itself. It has a noumenal richness of quite another order. *The thing-in-itself* is a noumenon by exclusion of phenomena, whereas scientific reality, I would argue, consists in a noumenal context suitable for defining axes of experimentation. Scientific experiment is thus reason confirmed. (NES 9, 5–6)

In a later text Bachelard adds:

An object perceived and an object thought belong to two different philosophical instances. Therefore, one can describe an object twice: once as we perceive it, once as we think it. The object is a phenomenon and a noumenon. And as a noumenon it is open to being perfected to which the object of common knowledge is not. A scientific noumenon is not a simple essence; it is the *progress* of thought. In its first traits it denotes a progress of thought, and it calls for further progress. To fully characterise an object that realises a scientific conquest, one should therefore speak of a nougonal noumenon, of the essence of thought that engenders thought. (RA 110)

The term 'nougonal' adds a further dimension to the concept of a noumenon. It is certainly obscure (and that is how it is spelt in French); it is one of Bachelard's neologisms, only it is not clear what he derived it from as it does not have an obviously identifiable root; but one can work out easily what Bachelard has in mind. His noumenon is certainly not a 'place' in which objects are thought to 'reside'; it is not a passive 'thing-in-itself'; it is the dynamic principle that engenders thought, it is like an engine behind concepts, a machine that makes concepts evolve. These concepts are mathematical in nature. (Perhaps Bachelard derived 'nougonal' from the Greek *nous*, as it is used by the Presocratic Anaxagoras, where *nous* puts the ultimate seeds into motion, engendering movement.)

Scientific thought is noumenal. And Bachelard argues that visual images do not and cannot aid noumenal thought; further, not only can they not aid, they are an obstacle.

The Epistemological Obstacle

That rationality is progressing is for Bachelard beyond doubt. In *La Philosophie du non* he distinguishes five prevalent philosophies which pertain to scientific thought – naïve realism, clear and positivist empiricism, Newtonian or Kantian rationalism, complete rationalism, and dialectical rationalism (PN 42, 36); the last, which is another name for surrationalism, is the epistemology of the new scientific mind.

Bachelard further argues that progress in scientific thinking demands an ability to discard old epistemological assumptions. However, as the scientific thought develops, ushering in new epistemologies, the old ones remain, appealing to the archaic, naïve sentiments. In effect, the process of progress in scientific conceptualisations has to contend with several epistemological layers which more often than not contradict each other. These differences pertain to different stages in the development of scientific thought. But Bachelard's analyses are driven most of all by the sharp distinction he makes between common experience and scientific rationality. It is not just a question of them being different, since rationality works *against* the ordinary experience. In other words, rather than feed, for example, on the images of the world that we might have, the scientific spirit must, according to Bachelard, abolish them from its discourse; the first experiences are not only of little use for scientific discourse – they hinder it, and therefore must be eliminated.

The need to eradicate these obstacles led Bachelard to one of his better known concepts – the psychoanalysis of the scientific mind. The first experience, meaning the sensory experience, leaves traces which operate in the psyche like an archetype, infecting rationalist thought. They are 'infections' because they infuse knowledge with subjective opinions and values and therefore knowledge gets confused with needs and wishes. The first naïve experience nourishes values such as animism, substantialism, the myth of interiority – traits so frequently found in old scientific texts. The four element theories, for example, excited an immense amount of imagination because they appealed to various anachronistic needs that have nothing to do with scientific rationality. All these need to be weeded out from scientific thought, somewhat in the way a psychoanalyst helps to eradicate negative feelings deposited in the unconscious mind.

It is interesting to note that the idea that scientific developments necessitate profound changes in the psychological make-up goes back at least as far as the programme put forward by Francis Bacon at the beginning of the seventeenth century. Much as Bachelard would later, Bacon argued for the necessity of moving away from the Aristotelian world-view due to the unreliability of the senses. Paul Feyerabend makes these observations about Bacon:

> Bacon realized that scientific change involves a reformation not only of a few ideas, but of an entire world-view and, perhaps, of the very nature of humans. 'For the senses are weak and erring', he writes in *Novum Organum*, Aphorism 50. 'For man's sense is falsely asserted to be the standard of things; on the contrary, all the perceptions, both of the senses and of the mind resemble those uneven mirrors which impart their own properties to different objects from which rays are emitted and distort and disfigure them' (Aphorism 41). Bacon repeatedly comments on the 'dullness, incompetence and errors of the senses' (50) and permits them only to 'judge . . . the experiment' while it is the experiment that functions as a judge 'of nature and the thing itself'

(50). Thus when Bacon speaks of 'unprejudiced senses' he does not mean sense-data, or immediate impressions, but reactions of a sense organ *that has been rebuilt* in order to mirror nature in the right way. Research demands *that the entire human being be rebuilt*. (Feyerabend 1993: 112)

However, despite the fact that the need for the psychological revolution advocated by Bacon looks similar to what Bachelard was proposing later, it should be emphasised that Bachelard was against the Baconian programme of experimental science (although, as we shall see later, experiment in Bachelard's vision of scientific rationality's progress is essential, but it plays a different role).

The Ruses of Prejudice

Several commentators on Bachelard's epistemological writings have pointed out that his tone is rife with an attacking rhetoric.[1] And indeed, the poor 'unpurified' scientist is chastised in a hectoring and moralising tone. Bachelard is merciless towards the old scientific thinking; as far as he is concerned, it is no more than a history of human folly; and since it has not disappeared from the scientific idiom no effort should be spared to fully stamp it out.

And, again, a similar line of thinking is present in Bacon. To return to Feyerabend, he notes that Bacon's language is in this respect unequivocal:

> [It is] a 'demolishing branch' (115), an 'expiatory process', a 'purification of the mind' (69) must precede the accumulation of knowledge. 'Our only hope of salvation is to begin the whole labour of the mind again' (Preface) but only 'after having cleansed, polished, and levelled its surface' (115). Preconceived notions (36), opinions (42ff), even the most common words (59, 121) 'must be abjured and renounced with firm and solemn resolution' (68). (Feyerabend 1993: 112)

Feyerabend also points out that 'this idea of a physical and mental reform of humanity has religious features'. The same has been said of Bachelard. As one commentator tellingly put it: 'In the language of an inquisitor one could say that the "Augustinism" of Bachelard breaks severely with the "semi-Pelagianism" of the current epistemology' (Quillet 1964: 22–3).

This harsh and unforgiving attitude, which guides a great deal of Bachelard's historical analyses, operates in his system with a force of prejudice. Everything that comes under the term 'common knowledge', or 'everyday experience', or the 'naïve' view of the world (Bachelard uses these terms interchangeably) is subjected to harsh rejection. If we were to put together from Bachelard's various pronouncements a photo-fit of this common-sensical individual we would find it to be a rather simple creature. In constructing its world it relies on the senses and has constructed a geometrical and logical system to support this world-view. It has an unhealthy appetite for images. Furthermore, it is a creature that confuses knowledge with its bodily needs. In *La Formation de l'esprit scientifique* Bachelard goes through the whole gamut of possible needs that confuse the scientific mind. He combs texts from the seventeenth and eighteenth centuries to demonstrate that pre-scientific thought is a 'museum of horrors' (FES 21). These texts are full of 'infantile regressions' (FES 36), reveal the 'sclerotic state' of Baconian methods (FES 60), show the 'detestable solidarity of erudition and science, of opinion and experiment' (FES 63), and display a 'primitive consideration of the privileged object which is our body' (FES 149); the pre-scientific mind constitutes a 'veritable fetishism of life' (FES 149).

Bachelard's thesis is that in order to progress science has to detach itself from the values that life presents and serve the liberated mind. In the

> veritable destiny of human thought [. . .] we see that the interests that life presents are supplanted by the interests that the mind presents [. . .], the brain is no longer an absolutely adequate instrument of scientific thought, one might as well say that the brain is an *obstacle* for scientific thought. It is an obstacle in the sense that it coordinates gestures and appetites. It is necessary to think *against* the brain. (FES 251)

Such a radical rejection of everyday experience, or common sense, or the naïve view of the world is only possible when it is left vague as to what exactly this view of the world really means. As was mentioned in the Introduction, Bachelard's prejudice against common knowledge has drawn severe criticism from the next generation of Francophone philosophers of science, Michel Serres, Isabelle Stengers and Bruno Latour being the most prominent among them.

Serres wrote an essay devoted to Bachelard, 'La réforme et les sept péchés' (Serres 1970), in which he analyses the cleansing procedure advocated by Bachelard that is meant to purify the mind. Serres views it from an unexpected angle: it is an exercise in eradicating the cardinal sins from our psychological make-up: greed, sloth, pride, lust and gluttony are the insidious epistemological obstacles. But these are not all the sins; there remain anger and envy. These last two, by contrast, are necessary for the new scientific spirit to acquire the aggressiveness necessary to overcome the obstacles and destroy the old concepts. Bachelard compared the idle mind of the phenomenologist with the *penetrating* mind of the scientist, but we have here, in fact, more than just a penetrating mind: it is a mind which thrives on obstacles, a mind which is most alert when it is contradicted, a mind which wants a 'philosophy of no'. It is an aggressive mind and it feeds on its hostility to the naïve experience.

> [I]ntelligence must be *cutting*. It attacks a problem [...] it aggresses and transforms [...] sooner or later it must wound. Intelligence is always a factor of surprise, of a stratagem. It is a hypocritical force. When it resolutely attacks, it is after a thousand ruses. Intelligence is a claw that breaks while scratching. (L 146, 85)

Serres goes on to say that an archaeology of our scientific thought is necessary but that it has to go deeper. He cannot share Bachelard's enthusiasm for the feats of contemporary science because he sees science to be conducted under a malevolent sign. The malevolent sign is Mars, who turns science into a martial art. Knowledge is a hunt, science is poisoned; it is linked to power. To build scientific knowledge on such hostility to everyday experience must lead to an inhuman disembodied knowledge. A rationality which takes leave of the senses and aims to create its own new reality without any reference, conciliation or cohabitation with the immediate must grow into a monster. And it often does. Serres argues for another science, a science born under the sign of Venus. Here science would be conducted under a different contract with nature, and in this context he sees Bachelard's writings on the four elements as 'more' scientific (Serres 1978).

Latour stated his disagreement in *Nous n'avons jamais été modernes* (1997). He takes issue with the Bachelardian epistemologists' obsession with 'decontaminating' science (Latour

34 Gaston Bachelard

1997: 126), although, otherwise, he in fact rarely pronounces on the matter. One notes that Latour owes a number of concepts to Bachelard, but that is not the point. Latour casts a wider net, and he is certainly not trying to capture the essence of a rationalist activity. It is not the fine scientific minds that draw his attention but the ways in which science works. The title of one of his earlier books, *Science in Action* (1987), tells us about the focus of some of his thinking. Within his perspective science includes artisans as well as scientists, those working in agriculture as well as countless others who partake in scientific activities. Latour's work is as much anthropology of science as sociology or philosophy. There is also a political dimension in his work. Bachelard's judgements about 'common' knowledge or distinctions between the interests that life presents and those of the mind are completely irrelevant in Latour's world.

Stengers is another critic of Bachelard. Her comments are brief, they usually come in one-off sentences, and they are invariably hostile. She objects to Bachelard's distinction between the interests that life presents and those presented by reason, to the fact that he seems to conceive them as being in conflict and that science should chose between the two. This Stengers simply sees as wrong-headed because, if taken to the extreme, it would mean that science could not be put at the service of life (Stengers 1994: 34). The whole drift of Bachelard's thought is to her unacceptable. Stengers' view, which is quite close to Serres', is that science needs to forge a new contract with nature, and she has expressed her thought particularly incisively in *La Nouvelle alliance*, written with the eminent physicist Ilya Prigogine (Prigogine and Stengers 1978).

These criticisms are severe and quite understandable, but since they tend to be brief the matter needs to be looked at in more detail.

Naïvety

One of Bachelard's arguments is that sensations are not only limited but also that if we follow them we foreclose the possibility of some crucial aspects of scientific knowledge. He illustrates this point with his comments on the light spectrum that we see as it comes through the prism. The two extreme ends of the spectrum, violet and red, look so similar that it is common to join them and present the spectrum as a circle. This can lead to an interesting observation: if we spin the circle fast enough we will note that the prism becomes white; we realise that black is absent; it is in a sense a non-colour. These observations are real enough but their scientific import is minimal. Furthermore, from the point of view of physics there is no rationale for joining the spectrum into a circle as violet has the shortest wavelength and red the longest. But more importantly, joining the two extreme ends of the visible spectrum prevents the discovery of infrared and ultraviolet waves, which although not detectable by the human eye can be seen by some species: bees, for example, as well as many other insects and some birds can detect ultraviolet light.

But Bachelard's thesis goes further. He argues that sensory experience not only limits the scope of scientific activity, something which is quite obvious, but is, in fact, an obstacle to this activity. It is an obstacle because Bachelard seems to be arguing that thinking that takes its clue from sensory data is the source of our conception of matter as a unitary substance. A number of Bachelard's arguments are constructed in order to combat this concept of substance which must be rejected in current scientific thought. Since this concept derives, in Bachelard's view, from our first sensory experience of the world it follows that scientific rationality must work against this first experience. This is the thesis: our sensations are the source of our conception of matter as a unitary substance. Bachelard never quite *demonstrates* this, the nearest he comes to it being in his commentary on the early Greek doctrine in which the concept of the atom was formulated for the first time, the doctrine of Leucippus and Democritus. The title of the chapter in question, 'The Metaphysics of Dust' (in *Les Intuitions atomistiques*), already suggests the line of reading that he will take. Legend had it that the idea of atoms came to Leucippus when he saw motes of dust dancing in a shaft of sunlight coming through the window's closed shutters, a common sight in the Mediterranean. The picture was quite precise – the tiny specks of dust, dancing hither and thither, are the image from which the atomists' system grew. But it was the very preciseness of the initial image, argues Bachelard, which led them into a cul-de-sac of a naïve materialism. Following their intimate and immediate experience of dust, they believed that there is an immutable substance. This engenders the idea that the world is made of three-dimensional objects suspended in a three-dimensional space. Such materialism operates with the conviction that there is a finite constant amount of matter and that each individual bit of matter has a definable constant existence and its location can be determined. These tiny specks of matter as well as the objects they constitute will then, as science developed, be made to interact following some determinable and immutable laws.

This is how Bachelard presents his reading. It is telling that he draws attention to the image of dust as the founding image of the doctrine (although he makes no explicit reference to the legend about Leucippus) but omits the view, already expressed in antiquity, that the way the actual properties of the atom were conceived (as impenetrable, unchanging, indivisible, imperishable) was to reconcile this thinking with Parmenides' doctrine of the One. Bachelard, however, argues that 'dust [...] is easily posited as indestructible' (IA 29). Maybe; but it can be argued with equal conviction that dust is the image of the ultimate destructibility of all things: from dust to dust. At any rate, it is certain that the idea of an indestructible unity, material or ideal, was already formulated by the time of Leucippus; and it is just as certain that this idea does not come from the world of the senses, as Bachelard would have it, but belongs to the speculative tradition. The tradition that seeks indestructible unity, beginning with Parmenides, rejects the evidence of the senses as too varied and uncertain to be trusted. Truth, which is One, is hidden from the senses. In fact, it is not quite correct to state that Bachelard was unaware of the role played by speculative thought; he often accuses philosophy of introducing the idea of unity into scientific discourse and on various occasions Aristotle, Descartes, Hegel or Kant are mentioned in this context. But these tend to be loose comments rather than part of a sustained argument. It is the 'naïve' worldview that is the principal target of Bachelard's attacks. It is the senses that constrain rationality. Dust is too close to life; the fact that Einstein's relativity theory and quantum physics abuse the naïve understanding of the world, which indeed they do, was to Bachelard sign of progress.

What is strikingly at odds with the general thrust of Bachelard's thinking is that he takes 'naïvety' to be a state of mind which is not subject to historical (or geographical) variations. 'Naïve' always means the same. At least in one respect this leads to a contradiction. If it were true that the first experience does, let alone must, lead to the conception of primary, unitary substance, which bedevils all science, it would mean that there is some immutable structure of sensory experience. This in turn would run counter to Bachelard's own contention that the ego changes with the changing sensations, as he argued in his comments on Descartes' 'wax meditation', which we find in *Le Nouvel esprit scientifique* (NES 171–4, 165–8). There, Bachelard contests that there is no such thing as some stable entity called the 'rational mind' which would be engaged in processing data from the world. He made a point of rejecting Descartes' idea of a thinking substance engaged in discovering the truth. His comments on the origin of the immutable *cogito* make this sufficiently plain. This came to Descartes, it will be remembered, when he pondered in *Meditations* the changeable and unstable nature of things that surround us through the example of the changing properties of wax ('Meditation II' in Descartes 1968). At first it is hard and smells of flowers and honey, but when put near the fire it melts, loses its scent and seems to become an altogether different substance. This observation prompts Descartes into a long meditation which leads him to conclude that we cannot but doubt all our sensations and that the only certainty that we can have, the only thing which is immutable, is our mind – that which we have come to know as the Cartesian *cogito*. To this Bachelard gives the following reply:

> If the wax changes: I change; I change with my sensation, which is the moment I conceive it, the entire content of my thought; for to feel is to think in the broad sense that Descartes attaches to the *cogito*. But Descartes has a secret confidence in the reality of the soul as substance. Dazzled by the sudden light of the *cogito*, he never doubts the permanence of the *I* that is the subject of *I think*. Why is it the same being who feels hard wax and soft wax, when it is not the same wax that is felt on two occasions? If the *cogito* were recast in the passive voice as *cogitatur ergo est*, would the active subject vanish along with the inconsistency and vagueness of its impressions? (NES 172, 167)

It would seem that the term 'naïve knowledge' could only be posited as stable and unchanging when it is seen as some imprecise approximation denoting unschooled knowledge. The term 'naïve' is strange and vague, and it is almost always used in a pejorative sense, in order to dismiss. It can mean crude, simplistic, commonsensical, uncritical, uncouth, or simply stupid. The phrase 'this is naïve thinking' is not uncommon, but curiously one never really finds out what naïve thinking really is. What we usually learn is that this is what philosophy is not, that philosophy stands in opposition to naïve thinking. But although the real meaning of naïvety is vague it is somehow considered as self-evident; if we want to degrade a thought, an opinion, a concept, it is enough to say 'this is naïve'. Sometimes a clearer intimation of its meaning does however emerge; we find an example of this in Husserl:

> If the Ego, as naturally immersed in the world, experiencingly or otherwise, is called '*interested in the world*', then the phenomenologically altered – and so altered, continually maintained – attitude consists in a *splitting of the Ego*: in that the phenomenological Ego establishes himself as '*disinterested onlooker*' above the naïvely interested ego. (Husserl 1982: 35)

So, naïvety is some sort of 'immersion' in the world, a being 'interested' in it. Husserl has a clear notion of naïvety and he makes just as clear that a genuine philosophical project has to reject it.

The origin of the term 'naïve' gives a clue how it has acquired such a negative resonance. It derives from the now obsolete *neif* which meant serf. A serf is a peasant, a pagan, of whom real thought cannot be expected.

But occasionally, we come across an odd admiring reference to naïvety. Nietzsche commented on the personalities of the Old Testament that they had the 'incomparable naïvety of the strong heart' (Nietzsche 1968: 580). Marx had this to say about the Greeks of the Hellenistic period, particularly Epicurus: 'The Greeks will forever remain our teachers by virtue of this magnificent objective naïvety, which makes everything shine, as it were, naked, in the pure light of its own nature, however dim that light may be' (Marx 1975: 500). We also find an occasional appeal to the naïve in contemporary philosophy; one example is Giles Deleuze. Once, when asked what he thought Foucault had in mind when he said 'one day, perhaps, the century will be Deleuzian', Deleuze answered:

> I was the most naïve among the philosophers of our generation. One finds with us the themes like multiplicity, difference, repetition, but I put forward concepts almost raw while the others worked with more mediation. I was never touched by the overcoming of metaphysics, the death of philosophy [...] It is perhaps this that Foucault wanted to say: I was not the best, but the most naïve, a kind of brute art, so to

speak, not more profound but the most innocent (the most devoid of the guilt of 'doing philosophy'). (Deleuze 1990: 122)

However, Bachelard's diatribes against 'naïve knowledge', as presented here, are a little bit of a caricature, but one for which he himself is largely responsible. In his earlier writings odd disparaging remarks about old scientific thinking can be found, but it is in the 1939 *La Formation de l'esprit scientifique* that his prejudice spills out. Dominique Lecourt, who prepared a volume of *Textes choisis* of Bachelard's epistemological opus, wrote in the brief *Avertissement*:

> But, most of all, one did not want to feed the image – very widespread – of a debonair Bachelardism, which on a single reading of this ambiguous work *La Formation de l'esprit scientifique* is reduced to an inorganic juxtaposition of some general methodological principles, to some judicial pedagogical advice and some fine psychological observations unified under the likable banner of a watered down psychoanalysis. (Lecourt 1971: 5)

La Formation de l'esprit scientifique also happens to be one of Bachelard's most widely read books on epistemology, at least so it seems; it was on the syllabus at the lycée level (prejudice is easy to teach). And, as it happens, we find that in their criticisms of Bachelard, Serres, Stengers and Latour go, practically exclusively, for this text. (This is particularly telling in the case of Serres who wrote an article criticising Bachelard's epistemology commenting on this text alone).

When Bachelard returns to epistemological problems after his writings on the poetic imagination and the four elements, the tone is different. He does not change his views; for example, he still holds that the image and the concept are not reconcilable, but he seems less intransigent about the negative role of images in scientific thought. He does find some images 'manifestly absurd': 'In what way will a keen spirit that wants to learn be helped by a page where Whitehead tells us that a classical electron is a horse galloping freely on the prairie while the electron of Bohr is a bus guided by a trolley?' (ARPC 95). Nevertheless, there is some place for images in scientific thought: 'Images, like the languages that Aesop concocted, are, at the same time, good and bad, indispensable and prejudicial; it is necessary to use them with measure while they are good and get rid of them immediately when they become prejudicial' (ARPC 94). This seems to be recognition of the quite obvious fact that however potent noumenal thinking might be scientists cannot do without images. A good example would be the image of a miniature solar system as used by Rutherford and Bohr, when they were working out the internal structure of the atom. The image is obviously not the right one but it seemed to be necessary; yet it was no more than a crutch to get the thinking going, and once the thinking got going the image needed to be discarded. However, still today, in popular accounts, the size of the electron in relation to the atom is said to be comparable to putting a grain of sand in the dome of St Paul's cathedral, or even more precisely we will read that if the nucleus of the atom were a centimetre across, then the electron cloud that surrounds the nucleus would be a kilometre away. This is misleading; nuclear physics cannot be conceived within the parameters of Euclidian geometry. Also, to evoke the image of a cathedral's dome to help us understand something that is *unimaginably small* does not seem right.

Bachelard himself commented on Bohr and Rutherford's image of the atom. The image was wrong for a number of reasons. There is no such thing as an orbit in the sense we think of one because the ordinary conception of space is not valid in the interior of the atom, the 'jumps' or 'leaps' of the electron are not what we would imagine, and the electron cannot be localised in the way the image suggests. Bachelard quotes Arthur Eddington who said: 'In short, the physicist draws up an elaborate plan of the atom and then his critical mind will lead him to erase one detail after another.' Bachelard then adds: 'the atom is exactly *the sum of the criticisms* to which the first image of it was subjected. [...] The diagram of the atom that Bohr proposed a quarter of a century ago has acted as a good image: nothing of it remains' (PN 139–40, 118–19).

Yet this is not an annihilating procedure, even if Bachelard quite often speaks of the need to 'destroy' images (although some, like the galloping horse and the trolley guided bus, clearly need to be thrown out, if not destroyed). However, if the image of the atom as a miniature solar system disappears, this does not mean that the orbit, the electron and its 'jump' lose their existence; rather, instead of being objects of the Euclidian world, they become *noumenal* objects and acquire a dynamism that an image cannot have.

Bachelard also continues to distinguish between common

knowledge and scientific knowledge. He still holds that there is a radical discontinuity between the two but his arguments are measured and do not display any of the negative judgements about common knowledge. For example, in *Le Matérialisme rationnel*, published almost fifteen years after *La Formation de l'esprit scientifique*, Bachelard comments on the changes in meaning of certain notions. One instance would be the notion of temperature. We have a common understanding of what this means, but temperature with an arbitrary zero measured with the expansion or contraction of mercury is only relevant on a human scale: when a physicist speaks of the temperature of the atom's nucleus, the notion of temperature is altogether different; and certainly, scientists do not think of manufacturing a thermometer to measure it. In these instances, the common terms are often put in inverted commas, and Bachelard compares this to the *epoché* of the phenomenologists; when a concept such as temperature is applied to a new context, it is put in inverted commas so the common understanding has to be bracketed out. This is not just a matter of pointing out that terms or concepts acquire different meanings in different contexts, a rather banal observation; Bachelard makes a more precise point:

> As soon as an old word is thus put by scientific thought in inverted commas, it is the sign of a change in the method of knowledge touching a new experimental domain. We could say that from the epistemological point of view, it is a sign of a rupture, of a discontinuity of sense, of a reform of knowledge. (MR 216–17)

Bachelard is simply demonstrating an example of a discontinuity when there is a change of scale from the human scale to microphysics. The argument is clear and it does not bear any trace of animosity towards common knowledge. We see the same when we read his analysis of the first experiments on colour photography in relation to the linear and circular representation of the light spectrum. The circular scheme he refers to as our common or everyday view of colours. Its basic discovery is that there are three elementary colours, red, yellow and blue, and that by mixing them all other colours in the spectrum can be obtained, as green is a mixture of yellow and blue, for example. This might be of great use to manufacturers of paint, but a physicist would find no reason for isolating elementary colours because it is wavelengths not colours that have meaning for a scientist; there is also no scientific reason for joining red and violet. Furthermore, as we have seen, keeping the linear arrangement made possible the discovery of infrared and ultraviolet frequencies. But Bachelard does not diminish common knowledge. In fact, he points out that early photographic developments followed both the circular and linear schemes. He gives the example of Charles Cros, a mid-nineteenth-century French experimentalist, who based his work on the circular scheme of the three elementary colours. This involved photographing the same scene three times using red, blue and yellow filters so that when superimposed these images would recreate (at first rather roughly, to put it kindly) the original colour scheme. Some decades later, Gabriel Lippmann developed a technique whereby all wavelengths of the spectrum, without any selection or separation, were imprinted directly on the photographic plate. Bachelard comments: 'it is philosophically remarkable that two very different photographic techniques solved the problem of colour photography, one playing in a way with the circular arrangement of colours, the other with the linear one'. And he adds: 'The second technique [...] gives more pleasure to a scientific mind, even though it is clear that it cannot be developed on an industrial scale' (RA 117). And, indeed, Lippmann may have received the Nobel Prize for his invention (in 1908), but it was too complex; it required very special conditions, the exposure had to be very long, and duplicates of images, on paper or otherwise, could not be obtained. In time the technique was dropped and photography developed along trichromatic lines.

Again, the tone is much different from what we find in the earlier period. To begin with Bachelard may refer to the circular arrangement of the spectrum as common knowledge, but he also gives it the proper name 'psychological/biological knowledge', as it is a function of our psychology of colour that depends on the structure of our retinas that gives us trichromatic colour vision. And he accords it value: it is superior to the more 'scientific' method when questions about scaling it up industrially are asked. One gets the feeling that he could not bring himself to such an admission at the time of writing *La Formation de l'esprit scientifique*.

(It is also interesting to note that Bachelard reminds us what the principal nature of his interest in science is – not the technological prowess of science, in this case, but rationalist satisfaction, *tout court*. He ends this account of the beginnings of colour photography by recounting an occasion when he assisted in a projection of plates of the Fontainebleau forest taken by Lippmann. He speaks of a 'strange mixture of the joy of the eyes and the joy of the mind' (RA 118).)

In general, Bachelard's position is far more nuanced than the text of *La Formation de l'esprit scientifique* read alone would have us believe. But as it is, Bachelard is often reduced to a philosopher of the epistemological rupture and obstacle; his idea of psychoanalysing the scientific mind also gets a frequent airing. These are his easiest concepts, particularly because tinged with prejudice. The demonstration of ruptures in scientific developments has had an appreciable impact on thinking about science in the Francophone zone. As for the obstacle, Bachelard did not seem to attach a great deal of importance to this concept in the second phase of his epistemological work.

Science and History

Bachelard's writings on science evolve around two axes, the one his scrutiny of the past where he analyses the various forms taken by scientific rationality and how it progressed by breaking with previous forms of reasoning, the other his reflections on the challenges set by the science of the twentieth century for philosophical thought. Ordinarily, we take it as obvious that studying the past will help us better understand the present, as suggested by Duhem's dictum that 'to give a history of a physical principle is at the same time to make a logical analysis of it', which implies that there is a link between history and reason. However, we find something different in Bachelard's expositions. Two books with titles evoking one another illustrate this. *La Formation de l'esprit scientifique* was published five years after *Le Nouvel esprit scientifique*. From just looking at the titles one could reasonably expect that the second work would in some ways deepen the themes of the first, perhaps further elucidating certain points so that one way or another the stakes of the new science would become clearer. But nothing of the sort happens. In the first work we read about the changes brought about by the introduction of non-Euclidian geometries into physics, about the challenges to our everyday view of reality that Heisenberg's uncertainty principle sets, about the new freedom offered by the introduction of the tensor calculus into scientific thinking. Although the text was written eighty years ago it still comes across as remarkably fresh – we are reading an intellectual adventure of immense quality. When we turn to *La Formation de l'esprit scientifique*, we learn about the putative obstacles that bedevilled seventeenth-century pseudoscience, and a sort of psychoanalysis is proposed in order to weed out these obstacles from scientific thought. But none of this helps to provide a more acute understanding of the make-up of the contemporary scientific mind. This, at first, comes across as surprising but on reflection we realise that although Bachelard offers a great number of historical insights, he is throughout attempting to demonstrate how in its development science detaches itself from the past. Already in *La Formation* we read that 'the intellectual past [...] should be taken for what it is, the past' (FES 251). Elsewhere, commenting on developments in chemistry, he states that it 'is the science of the future because it is more and more a science that *deserts its past*' (MR 6): there is no resemblance, he will argue, between the kind of problems tackled by an alchemist and those that a contemporary chemist is dealing with.

What are we to make of these comments? One could go as far as to say that Bachelard is a historian who dislikes the past. He is scornful of historians who try to trace back concepts to their origins, who 'like to sojourn in the zone where science is elementary' (MR 210). But then, what is the point of doing a history of past scientific activities which are manifestly erroneous, if they do not elucidate anything about the present? *But this seems to be precisely what Bachelard is at pains to demonstrate.* He does not state this explicitly but re-viewing his various utterances on this question one can formulate the following thesis: While analysing the activities of science's past, Bachelard's other (and perhaps principal) aim is to argue against a conception of history that is deeply ingrained in our culture, a conception which is in the shadow of St Augustine's *City of God*, and which runs through our tradition via Hegel and Marx to contemporary pronouncements about the 'end of history'. History is a metaphysical entity that marches on purposefully; it has meaning, it has a *telos* and a finality; events come about because they are historically necessary; we are 'in' history, we can never escape it. This view of history seems to have percolated down into the common consciousness (how many times have we heard the utterly meaningless phrase 'history is against us' coming from sports commentators before a football game?). All these views can be summed up by the term *historicity*. On giving the matter further thought, it would seem that if one wanted to argue against our common understanding of history then to demonstrate that there is a radical discontinuity in scientific developments would be a particularly effective way of going about it, far more so than any 'metaphysical engagement' with the concept of history (such 'engagements' often give a lease of life to the concept that is meant to be dismantled). After all, it would appear obvious that Lavoisier's 1789 *Elements of Chemistry* laid the foundation for Mendeleyev's periodic table or that today's field theories evolved inevitably out of the insights of Michael Faraday (it was he who introduced the concept of the 'field'). Science is a collective pursuit, something that Bachelard himself stressed on a number of occasions; knowledge is transmitted, scientific societies are set up to improve the transmission of knowledge and this would seem to make the historical continuity of science even more obvious. And even when we realise that most of the old scientific theories are wrong, a view often advanced is that we learn from past mistakes, and this constitutes a form of continuity. Not so, Bachelard will argue: 'there is a total discontinuity between the difficulties of the past and the difficulties of today' (MR 215). In brief, to demonstrate, as he does, that science's developments do not constitute an uninterrupted line strikes a deep chord that goes against the orthodox view. Yet it is abundantly clear that Bachelard's entire thought is pitched against the idea of historical continuity, hence the choice of the term 'rupture', rather than, say, 'shift', 'transformation', 'realignment' or any number of others that could account for changes in scientific thought while preserving its essential continuity. It cannot be by chance that in one of his clearest remarks on the matter Bachelard refers specifically to historicity when he says that rationality can achieve a level at which

> it declares itself free with regard to all culture's historicity. The history of scientific thought ceases to be a necessary avenue; it is no more than an exercise of a beginner who has to give us examples of emergence of intellectual events. (RA 80)

And, 'In many respects, because of its revolutionary discoveries, contemporary science can be considered as a *liquidation of a past*' (EngR 137). However, this does not mean that scientific concepts drift in some timeless zone; they are anchored in the future: 'Paradoxically, it is the new that is fundamental' (MR 7). To put it differently, Bachelard is eliminating all forms of the *a priori* from his thought.

Bachelard is driven by the need to break the shackles of history. He was not alone in this: Roland Barthes, Elias Canetti, James Joyce expressed a similar sentiment.[2] But clearly the past cannot be liquidated just like that, by fiat. The above quotes come from different works; they are not wrenched out of context but, nevertheless, are not part of a sustained argument; they come more in the form of throwaway statements and, strung together as they have been here, come across as an unjustified rejection of any value in studying science's past, without truly arguing the case. However, we find a more nuanced discussion of the question of history in *L'Activité rationaliste de la physique contemporaine*. First, Bachelard points out that some scientific concepts and theories are based on ways of reasoning so blatantly erroneous that they simply fall away, such as the phlogiston theory. They are irrelevant, nestling like Descartes' physics, another example of a misbegotten theory, in a 'historical solitude' (ARPC 50). An epistemologist cannot be interested in this kind of episode without a tinge of bad faith since it is akin to doing palaeontology; the mind-set of a scientist who subscribed to the phlogiston theory is now extinct – it is a fossil (ARPC 37). In this scheme of things Bachelard's earlier 'psychoanalysis of the scientific mind' is a palaeontological activity.

There are also developments which are interesting in that, although of no real interest to a scientist today, they are nevertheless of importance as they formed barriers against scientific irrationality. Bachelard gives the example of the publication of *L'Éncyclopédie*, but one can perhaps see more clearly how Lavoisier's chemistry performed the role of a barrier. For example, Newton was one of the greatest minds in our scientific culture but he was also intensely drawn to alchemy, 650,000 words on the subject (unpublished) came from his pen, and he often had an alchemist's furnace on the go as well. This was no secret; he corresponded on alchemy with some of the most prominent men of his time, John Locke and Robert Hooke amongst them, and a number of his Cambridge colleagues knew about and shared his interests. After Lavoisier, a group of top scientists and philosophers indulging in alchemy at an institution like Cambridge is unthinkable.

Phlogiston is a case of erroneous thinking, a confusion of substance, mass and volume; Lavoisier's chemistry lost its pertinence because it was qualitative. The concept of the epistemological obstacle in *La Formation de l'esprit scientifique* is linked with these developments as it reveals outdated modes of scientific reasoning. But in the later *L'Activité rationaliste de la physique contemporaine* Bachelard introduces the concept of an *epistemological act*, which, he says, 'corresponds to these bursts of scientific genius that bring unexpected impulsion in the course of scientific development'. These scientific events form a 'positive heritage of the past constituting a sort of *actual past* and its action in present scientific thought is manifest' (ARPC 36); such events form a '*recurring history*'. Bachelard gives no example but Mendeleyev's periodic table can clearly be considered one such act.

One needs to ask: Why is it that Lavoisier's chemistry is only a 'barrier' against the irrationality of alchemy but has no pertinence to a contemporary chemist, while events like Mendeleyev's table constitute a sort of *actual past*? Bachelard does not state it clearly, but the answer is not difficult to formulate: it is scientific thought that sets an experimental programme based on sound mathematics that ushers in *epistemological acts*.[3] Today's periodic table has evolved immensely from the first scheme of 1871 (it is almost twice as big), but the kernel of it, Mendeleyev's insight about the law of periodicity that led to the systematisation of the elements, remains true. Mathematics, Bachelard points out in an earlier text, is a remarkable discipline in that once a result surmounts the hurdle of proof and check it never gets refuted later; it is 'a wonder of regularity. It knows periods of stagnation, but not of error' (FES 22). Scientific experiment based on sound mathematics is not refuted; further work might reveal its limits and there may be some refinements, but the mathematical nucleus around which it evolves remains intact.

Still, this is merely trimming from science's past what is of legitimate, so to speak, interest to an epistemologist; it hardly dents the sense of history: now we have an *actual past* of a *recurring history*; it has been detached from palaeontology, but that is all. But Bachelard goes further still. He borrows from an English text the distinction between *story* and *history* (and he gives it in English as French does not have a similarly neat pairing). He quotes from a 1934 book, *Introduction to Modern Science*, in which F. K. Richtmayer traces a short history of physics and states that the works of Maxwell should be studied 'as an integral part of a fascinating *story* of modern physics rather than part of the *history of physics*'. Bachelard comments:

> The doubling of *story* and *history* presents itself here as an opposition in all its vigour. The *story* of science, the history lacking the finality of reason, the finality of truth, the finality of technical accomplishment, that is what 'fascinates' the scholar. The *story* presents a greater interest than the *history*. The *story* has a notable pedagogical value which goes further than simple values of erudition. (ARPC 39)

Here Bachelard targets the idea of finality, mentioning it three times; finality is one of the stings of historicity. Science does not have a *history*. The developments of scientific rationality present themselves as a good many fossils of barren scientific mentalities that did not produce anything (phlogiston theory, for example), barriers that prevent irrationality from creeping back into the scientific discourse (Lavoisier), instructive stories (Mendeleyev), and surrationalist actions that carve out new realities (artificial isotopes, for example). In an earlier text, Bachelard makes this succinct remark: '*Elsewhere* acts no more on *here* than *times past* [*jadis*] act on *now*' (II 60).

The corollary to this is that if one wants to absorb Bachelard's lessons about changes in the structure of rationality that have come about due to developments in contemporary science, one can legitimately ignore what he tells us about seventeenth-century scientific musings. In fact, Bachelard himself effectively advises us to ignore them.

Rationalism

In his conception of rationalism Bachelard is at odds with the entire philosophical tradition that he inherited. He knew this tradition well, and was more than familiar with developments coming from the Vienna Circle, having reviewed Popper's first German edition of *The Logic of Scientific Discovery* and a few other works coming from these philosophers.[4] However, he never engaged in any sustained critique of this tradition, but simply went ahead with his own conception of what constitutes rationalist activity and in the process re-structured the relationship between philosophy and science.

It does not seem an oversimplification to say that throughout the history of philosophy rationalism has been understood as an effort to describe the nature of reality through the power of reason. What exactly the nature of this reality is and how much of it can be known with certitude may be subject to debate, but all agree, seemingly taking it for granted, that reality is a definite and determinate unity governed by immutable laws. Rational activity is a perfecting of knowledge of reality (its laws, truths, etc.) by honing the correct procedures for acquiring this knowledge, procedures that are mostly of a logical nature. Rationality proceeds by establishing first principles; and they always remain first principles.

This concept of rationality operates with an assumption that there is a symmetry between the mind which apprehends, calculates, speculates, and so on, and the world (or the facts, laws and truths that make up this world). To what extent, if at all, the mind or the world can be known might be disputed, but it is agreed by most parties, albeit tacitly, that both the world and the mind are deep down, so to speak, stable entities. This is a view which is found, it seems, right across the analytical spectrum. It holds for Gottlob Frege, Bertrand Russell and Karl Popper. It also holds for Émile Meyerson, an eminent French philosopher of science from an earlier generation, who was sometimes the butt of Bachelard's criticisms. Popper, to give an example, argues that objective and absolute truth exists, but he does not claim that we may know or recognise it. Instead, he claims that we can establish criteria of progress towards truth. These criteria hold true for ever, and in all circumstances all knowledge gained with the use of these criteria is valid. Facts are facts and so factual knowledge is considered as objective as anything can be and naturally must be governed by immutable rules.

> Although I shall confine my discussion to the growth of knowledge in science, my remarks are applicable without much change, I believe, to the growth of pre-scientific knowledge also – that is to say, to the general way in which men, and even animals, acquire new factual knowledge about the world. (Popper 1972: 216)

This is an extreme ahistorical position as it leads to the conclusion that since the criteria validating the truth of statements are applicable to such a wide range there cannot be any essential philosophical difference between Aristotle's qualitative science, Bacon's inductive method or the Copenhagen interpretation of quantum physics (and how birds go about building their nests).[5]

The difference between the logical rationality of the Vienna Circle and Bachelard's mathematical rationality has already been signalled in the Introduction. Mary Tiles makes two very important and precise observations about Frege's logic, which forms the basis for the analytical thinkers but contrasts with the position that Bachelard took. She remarks that 'the whole direction of his [Frege's] thought rests on acceptance of the idea that subjective passivity is a necessary condition of objectivity' (Tiles 1984: 74). This Bachelard would obviously oppose; he reproaches Meyerson for that very reason, for holding a '*static conception* of the psychology of the scientific mind' (RA 9). Second, within the Fregean scheme concepts need to be clarified and have stable meanings as they relate to statements of truth; Tiles writes: '[Bachelard's] concepts are, like Frege's, defined via their role in judgment, but not in judgment as to what is or is not actually the case, but in judgment about what is possible or impossible' (Tiles 1984: 153), Bachelard also states: '*It is when a concept changes its meaning that it is at its most meaningful*. For it is then that it becomes, in all truth, an event, a conceptualization' (NES 56, 54).

Two further points must be made. Since logic establishes timeless rules and criteria it cannot found a science that points to the future, which Bachelard insists science does. 'How do we provoke an event of reason? Such a question makes no sense for those who reduce the *rational* to *logic*' (RA 44). And one more, perhaps not negligible point: Bachelard speaks of the joy of reason when seeing Lippmann's photographic plates; elsewhere, he will speak of the 'aesthetics of scientific thought' (ARPC 35). This is not a rare sentiment among scientists who frequently refer to the aesthetic quality of some theories but is meaningless within Frege's logic. Nevertheless, mathematical rationality is creative; in some of its aspects mathematics is an art. All creativity, music, painting, writing has its specific aesthetic tonality, and so does the creative side of scientific activity. And this is why Bachelard had no compunction about introducing the psychological factor into the scientific mind; in fact, from this point of view it is perfectly reasonable (not to say logical).

Bachelardian rationality is not seeking knowledge that would be constant and universal. Bachelard notes that: 'No doubt there are some kinds of knowledge that seem to be immutable. So it is believed that the stability of the contents is due to the stability of the container, that is, that the forms of rationality are permanent and no new method of rational thought is possible' (NES 56, 54). However, these seemingly immutable kinds of knowledge refer to everyday, non-reflected knowledge but do not represent true scientific activity in which knowledge is ceaselessly rectified. This rectification is not, in Bachelard's account, an ever more precise penetration of nature but, in fact, the opposite: it breaks free from the common experience of the natural world.

These views lead to an entirely different concept of rationalism. To see it as merely engaged in exploring reality is to deny it the fundamental drive that propels it – rationalism does not explore reality but constructs it. Bachelard means this in a literal sense: knowledge is a construction, and it is the activity of a scientific mind that reveals this facet of rationalism – the scientific mind is not satisfied with mere knowledge of the objective world but has an insatiable need to create new realities. A scientific rationality, he never ceases to argue, is a mind at work. His comment on the phenomenological concept of intentionality is interesting in this context:

> when intentionality is directed towards a natural object it leaves us with an occasional objectivity. It is an intentionality without great subjective depth and without any real objective import. Such an intentionality will give us in addition the revelation of an idle consciousness, of a consciousness free because it has not found a real interest in objective knowledge, a veritable engagement. (MR 208)

By contrast the intentionality of the scientific mind is of a *penetrating* kind: the scientific rationality is not content to contemplate natural objects; modern chemistry, Bachelard tells us, 'cannot and should not leave anything at its natural state, [. . .] it must purify everything, rectify everything, recompose everything' (MR 209). Rationalism is a capacity to transcend reality as it presents itself; it is an open-ended quest that creates new realities. Scientific thinking is rationalism at work.

Truth, Dialectics, the Philosophy of No

Rationality is not a quest for truths, 'Innate truths naturally have no place in science' (NES 176, 171). To put rationalism to work is to enter into a dialectics, or as Bachelard says 'We should mistrust a concept that we have not managed to dialectise' (PN 134, 114). In the last chapter of *La Philosophie du non* Bachelard spells out in some detail how he understands this. First of all, his 'philosophy of no' is 'not a will for negation' (PN 135, 115). Bachelard is quick to point out that he is not thinking of a Hegelian dialectics which proceeds with an *a priori* scheme and operates solely through contradiction. The 'negative ontology' of his contemporary Jean Wahl, who states that 'negations speak a plenitude of reality which is situated above all negations', Bachelard finds 'overconfident' (PN 137, 117). So although Bachelard is promoting a 'philosophy of no' he has little taste for outright negation and contradiction. Concepts are juxtaposed, opposed, but also welded together, like the wave and particle electron, for example; or older concepts are incorporated in new developments. He also does not think of rationality as incessantly dialectising scientific concepts like a shredder, which was the view of Stéphane Lupasco, another of his contemporaries. Bachelard in fact praises Lupasco's work but does not agree that the dualising activity of the mind is of an 'incessant' nature (PN 136, 116). In his 'philosophy of no' rationalism proceeds carefully, one dialectised axiom can lead to a new scientific kaleidoscope.

One further point needs to be made. Bachelard's insistence on the dialectical nature of scientific thinking is one of the reasons why he rejects objects of sensation since he assumes that they are not subject to a dialectical process. This needs pointing out as it is not just prejudice that led Bachelard to the rejection of the experience of the world as a valid component in rationalist activities.

Mathematics, *la phénoménotechnique*

Rationalism is mathematical thinking, thinking which by going through the rigours of proof and check becomes irrefutable. Mathematical thought is as old in European scientific thinking as are the speculations around the four elements, and as was his custom, Bachelard did offer some thought on the state of the discipline in the past. The Pythagoreans were the first; they claimed that the design of the universe was mathematical and that number was the ultimate essence of reality ('everything that can be known has a Number; for it is impossible to grasp anything with the mind or to recognize it without this [*Number*]' – Philolaus fr. 4).[6] Apart from a few sporadic remarks praising the spirit of these early thinkers Bachelard does not comment on them. He does, however, offer a more extended commentary on Plato's geometrical theory of the four elements that we find in *Timaeus* (54c–57c).

Plato ascribes geometrical forms to the four elements. Fire is made of tetrahedrons which have four triangles (a familiar shape, like a pyramid), air of octahedrons made of eight triangles, water of icosahedrons which are structures of twenty triangles. The fact that fire, air and water are built from the same basic triangles accounts for the transformations between them – the transformation of one element into another is a rearrangement of the same triangles but in different numbers and forms. (Earth, which is made of cubes, cannot transform into another element.)[7] Plato's formula has been subjected to various analyses; it has been found to have some sort of coherence and can even be given an algebraic form (by Duhem in *Le Système du monde* and Thomas Heath in *Greek Mathematics*), which Bachelard comments on (MR 52).

However, Bachelard argues that it is another set of values that dominates Plato's speculation. The progression that Plato proposes – from fire via air and water to earth – is not, goes Bachelard's argument, a result of a mathematical insight but is derived from values that have their origin in the immediate experience of the elements. Fire being the lightest is assigned the smallest form and the progression through air and water to earth is based on the properties (weight, mobility) of the elements. These experiences therefore led Plato to *imagine* forms that would account for how the elements appear to us (also, for example, the sensation of being hurt by fire is due to the piercing quality of the imaginary pyramids which make up fire). These various experiences trigger values that are the opposite of the intelligibility of geometric forms and have nothing to do with rationalist procedures: it is for this reason that Plato's geometrical construct cannot, in Bachelard's view, be considered a truly mathematical construct, even if scholars were later able to give it an algebraic form. Plato was not ready for the Pythagorean teaching because he was not able to emancipate himself from sensory experience, and could therefore only produce a 'premature' form of mathematical rationality (MR 51–4).

That mathematics cannot rely on sensory experience seems rather obvious and one would expect Bachelard to point this out, but it is perhaps a little more surprising to read that 'in the arithmetic of nature [. . .] *one does not begin by counting*' (MR 102). The statement is clearer if we understand that Bachelard does not mean the arithmetic of a five-year-old who is learning to count; the preceding sentence makes it clear that he has in mind nature on the microphysical level. Here, indeed, counting has no role; the numbers of neutrons, protons, etc., in the atom are not counted, they are inferred. It is not only that counting deals with objects/phenomena on the human scale, while inference takes place at the noumenal level. There is another difference of an epistemological nature that needs to be underlined: in counting (or measuring) on the human scale it is necessary to isolate the object/phenomenon that is to be counted or measured; in noumenal inference this act of isolating does not take place; 'speeds', 'weights' 'distances' in the microphysical world are inferred in relational terms, never in isolation. A particle is never isolated, and indeed cannot be isolated.

Mathematical thought has always taken place in tandem with scientific activity and the forms it adopts are numerous: all these have been well analysed and are well known. Looking at various texts one gets the impression that everything about the role of mathematics in science has been subjected to detailed scrutiny,[8] yet Bachelard states that 'what leads some to believe that despite the most profound changes the scientific mind is fundamentally the same is that the true value of mathematics in scientific thought has not been appreciated' (NES 57, 55). Bachelard draws our attention to two features of mathematics which in his view are the most pertinent for our understanding of contemporary science. The first is its ability to predict as yet unknown realities. One example would be Mendeleyev's mathematical grid in which he arranged elements but also predicted the existence of some that were still unknown; James Clerk Maxwell's work on electric, light and magnetic phenomena that led him to predict the existence of radio waves (later confirmed by Heinrich Hertz) would be another. The second feature of mathematics, and this one Bachelard considers the most important, is its 'power [...] to create reality' (*la valeur réalisante de l'idée mathématique*) (NES 43, 41), or as Tiles puts it so aptly: Bachelard recognises that the mathematician 'has a tendency to ontologise, to give reality to his creations' (Tiles 1984: 88). In other words, the mathematical constructs do not remain in the realm of pure mathematics; mathematics is a noumenal activity which gives rationality its ontologising power, its constructs become realised as physical phenomena, the new realities that scientists invent begin in mathematical theorems.

The mathematical concept itself is not a physical phenomenon; it only announces its possibility; this phenomenon must be constructed. For this instruments are necessary; Bachelard already signalled the 'primordial role of instruments' in contemporary physics in his first work *Essai sur la connaissance approchée* (ECA 61). In that work we also find a chapter on 'Knowledge and technique'. In a 1932 article, 'Noumène et microphysique', Bachelard introduced a term *phénoménotechnique*. However, this term is not a development of earlier thought but announces a somewhat new dimension. The chapter on 'Knowledge and technique' deals with the interface between science and technology and there is also a sense that in that work there is some notion of a scientist probing reality. La *phénoménotechnique* is a set-up necessary for the production of new scientific phenomena.[9]

> We could say that mathematical physics corresponds to a noumenology quite different from the phenomenography [*phénoménographie*] to which scientific empiricism condemns itself. This noumenology implies a *phénoménotechnique* by which new phenomena are not simply found, but invented, constructed piece by piece. (E 18)

It is often stated that Bachelard formulated the notion of *phénoménotechnique* in opposition to phenomenology. However, this first time that Bachelard uses the term it is to contrast it with what he described by coining the term 'phenomenography', that is, a description of physical phenomena, which is quite different to the Husserlian phenomenological programme. It is true that Bachelard often used the term 'phenomenology', but this is an instance of his previously noted 'strange lack of rigour' since when he uses the term to contrast it with the *phénoménotechnique* it should be understood as 'phenomenography', or a mere description of phenomena. To assume that Bachelard could be so confused to oppose phenomenology, which is a rich idealist philosophical doctrine dealing principally with the structure of consciousness, with a concept that pertains to scientific activity is a little absurd. Although there are a number of borrowings from Husserl in his work, such as the notion of the *epoché* for example, there does not seem to be any real engagement with Husserl's philosophy.[10] In fact, while the term phenomenology appears frequently in Bachelard's writings, Husserl's name is hardly ever evoked, being mentioned only two or three times. At times Bachelard refers to 'phenomenologists', usually in order to criticise the passivity of their concept of intentionality, and not only in the context of science. In *L'Eau et les rêves* he makes the following comment:

> All the objects in the world receive their true *coefficient of adversity*. These activist nuances do not seem to us to be sufficiently expressed by 'phenomenological intentionality'. The examples the phenomenologists give do not make satisfactorily clear the degrees of tension in intentionality; they remain too 'formal', too intellectual. A doctrine of objectivisation that objectifies forms but not forces lacks principles of intensive material evaluation. There must be at once a formal intention, a dynamic intention, and a material intention so that an object can be understood in its force, resistance and matter – that is, completely. (ER 180–1, 159)

This comment is one of a number in which Bachelard reproached phenomenology for what he perceived to be its essential idleness. The phenomenology of a poetic image and of the soul that Bachelard announced in *La Poétique de l'espace* has little to do with Husserl, although the term phenomenology seems to be accurate to describe his aims. In any significant engagement with Husserl we would expect some pronouncements on the eidetic reduction, the transcendental ego, or something about Husserl's work on mathematics; yet none of these are found in Bachelard's writings. (We can see more clearly the relative insignificance of Bachelard's relation to phenomenology when we contrast this with the work of his contemporary Jean Cavaillès, who was deeply engaged with Husserl's thought, particularly his conception of mathematics.)[11]

'[N]ew phenomena are not simply found, but invented, constructed piece by piece' (E 18); they are constructed in a factory. 'Modern science is becoming more and more a science of *effects*. The effects are named after their inventors. We speak of the effect of Zeeman, Stark, Compton, Raman' (IA 139). The creation of these new phenomena requires experimental set-ups, sometimes relatively simple as in Zeeman's effect (splitting a spectral line into several components in the presence of a static magnetic field), which can be obtained by holding a flame between strong magnetic poles, but at times the support of massive technology is necessary, such as the gigantic Large Hadron Collider at CERN, for example. And these technical set-ups are constructed following very precise mathematical rules; they are 'reified theorems' (RA 103). 'Following contemporary science we quit nature to enter a *factory of phenomena*' (ARPC 17).

Reflecting on this formula one wonders whether it is only relevant to contemporary science; in a way, it would seem this is how we begin to learn science. The very first chemistry lessons in school are just that: exercises in producing phenomena. Children are not asked to go into a garden, scoop up some soil and start analysing it as a way of 'exploring nature'; instead, they are ushered into a laboratory, given some well-prepared substances, plus receptacles in which they can be heated or mixed, and various effects are obtained; the more spectacular, the more enjoyable these lessons are, and the more memorable for that. And if children go into nature, into a forest, for example, they will never see the things they have seen in a chemical laboratory. But perhaps it is not just limited to these early lessons; quitting nature may well be the very first condition for doing science at all – a view that has been voiced by others.[12]

Bachelard might agree with these last comments, but this is not quite what he is arguing in this instance. When he asserts that science quits nature in order to enter a factory of phenomena, it is not just as a mere change of terrain, a question of walking into a laboratory to refine the exploration of nature. He points out that new kinds of objects, concepts, and new forms of judgement that mathematics devises are not abstracted from the experience of the natural world; these constructs have nothing to do with a description of reality, as, for example, there is nothing in nature that would correspond to non-Euclidian geometries; rather, they start their lives as pure mathematical speculations. Bachelard notes that most mathematical tools were invented before any use for them was conceived (EEPC 122). This was certainly the case with non-Euclidian geometries and with the tensor calculus ('contemporary physical science has been created by this mathematical concept, much as microbiology was created by the microscope' (NES 58, 56)). And yet, although these mathematical constructions were not derived, in however a complex way, from natural phenomena, they were necessary for the fabrication of a *phénoménotechnique* that could produce transuranian elements, that is elements that are not found in nature, and a vast number of artificial isotopes. At the time Bachelard was writing the book (MR 1953) the number of elements had reached 100, but he thought that further ones would be created as there was no theoretical reason denying this possibility. (And indeed, over half a century later the number of elements stands at 120.)

> It is the question of nothing less than the primacy of reflection over apperception, of the noumenal preparation of technically constituted phenomena. The trajectories that allow the separation of isotopes in a mass spectroscope do *not exist* in nature, they have to be produced through a technique; they are reified theorems. We will show that what man *makes* in a scientific technique does not exist in nature and is not even a *natural* development of *natural* phenomena. (RA 103)

This is of course far away from a chemical laboratory in an elementary school where children have their first chemistry lessons and in which natural phenomena are manipulated to obtain effects. The *phénoménotechnique* produces effects that Mother Nature, as we know her, could not produce, even with a human helping hand.

A further point argued for by Bachelard is that new mathematical reality changes the structure of reasoning. This is an important point. Although he speaks of mathematical tools, the usage of these tools affects rationality itself:

> [T]he mathematical tool affects the craftsman who uses it. [. . .] Tensor calculus, for example, is a marvellously flexible tool, and with it the mind acquires a new capacity for generalization. Prior to the mathematical age, during the age of the solid, it was essential that reality offer the physicist an abundance of examples pinpointing the idea to be generalized: An idea was then a summary of experiments already carried out. In the new relativistic science, a single mathematical symbol rich with significance indicates the thousand traits of a hidden reality: An idea is now a program of experiments still to be carried out. (NES 59, 57)

This is perhaps one of Bachelard's more compelling arguments against the concept of a fixed nature of rationality and for the view that rationality evolves in adapting to new scientific (mathematical) concepts. Compelling, but for a non-mathematician it is perhaps a little difficult to appreciate how the tensor calculus might modify one's way of thinking. Although this specific way in which reasoning is affected may be difficult to understand, the idea that ways of reasoning change need not be too hard to grasp; it is sufficient to shift to any domain that one is familiar with and think in terms of a change in mind-set. This is of course reasoning understood in a wider sense than Bachelard's mathematical rationality but the principle would seem the same. Mind-sets can be very different, one incommensurable with another (for example, behaviourism and introspection are two psychologies that follow very different lines of reasoning), and therefore there is a discontinuity. In France historians now speak of *histoire des mentalités*, possibly influenced (via Marc Bloch) by Bachelard.[13]

Against Substance

While Bachelard explores the various challenges that the new science sets to our conception of rationality there is also a philosophical import of a different order: the analyses of the activities of contemporary scientists lead us to question the concept of 'substance'.

The term 'substance' corresponds to the Greek *ousia*. The Latin rendering *substantia* means 'something that stands under or grounds things'. Therefore, substance is the fundamental or foundational layer of reality; if there were no substance, there would be no objects, no things; it is the essence of substantial kinds. Substance ensures identity over time; it is what gives permanence. Properties, a colour for instance, must belong to something, to substance, in other words, they cannot subsist without something to support them. A substance is an ultimate subject, an indivisible unity; a substance is the cause of itself.

The list that would recount all variations on the concept of substance would be long. What is noteworthy is that it seems a concept of a purely philosophical origin. It is difficult to see how it can be derived from sense data (this has already been noted); it does not relate to common experience of any kind, even if it has found its way into everyday parlance in such expressions as 'substantial' or 'man of substance'; it is not of divine origin like Parmenides' One. Moreover, the concept of substance does not bear any traits of what will later be named 'ideology': no value can be attached to it, it cannot be 'superior', 'good', 'more' or 'less' in any meaningful way; in this sense it is neuter, no more than a building block in a philosophical system.

If we take the Ionian thinkers' water, air and fire as first intimations of the concept of substance, then it has been present from the very beginnings of philosophy. The first full formal treatment of the subject was undertaken by Aristotle in his *Categories* and *Metaphysics*, and from then on the concept of substance, in one guise or another, seems to have been omnipresent throughout philosophy; until David Hume, who was the first to cast doubt on the concept. Hume's treatment of substance is much the same as his treatment of causation, in that he sees both as a projection onto the natural world of a tendency of our minds either to pass from one thing to another or to associate them in some way: 'the same habit, which makes us infer a connexion betwixt cause and effect, makes us here infer a dependence of every quality on the unknown substance' (Hume 1978: 222). This prefigures Kant's decision to put the concept of substance in the *a priori* structure. Nietzsche rejected the concept: although 'indispensable to logic, [. . .] in the strictest sense nothing real corresponds to it' (Nietzsche 1974: 171).

Every aspect of substantialism is rejected by Bachelard explicitly; it is a necessary condition for his philosophical project. Bachelard's anti-substantialism is evident in his reflections on the world of the new physics. It is in this context that one has to place his insistence that the realm of objects and things is the world of common knowledge, but science, more specifically microphysics, deals with phenomena, not objects: 'An object is merely an arrested phenomenon' (PN 109, 94).

Most of the direct arguments against the traditional conception of substance are formulated in texts that deal with developments in chemistry since this is where the notion of substance is most entrenched, manifesting itself as physical matter. Bachelard approaches the question from different directions. He analyses the relation between matter, light, radiation and energy,[14] presents it as a structure of temporality, and shows how through a progressive mathematisation chemistry loses its seemingly obvious substantial character. It might be best to begin with his observations on the nature of colour, something that had often been assumed to be a property of physical matter; it gives a good glimpse into the way Bachelard tended to organise his thinking.

> A *substance*, studied in detail, reveals itself to be an *ex-tance*. The properties of the substance are in solidarity with the experiment that conditions it *externally*. [. . .] It has been known for some centuries that gold has the colour that it refuses. If we illuminate it with white

colour, it absorbs all the other colours but sends back the yellow. If we illuminate it with a light without a yellow in it, it will no longer be yellow. The colour is not therefore a veritable *attribute* of substance. It is an activity – or better, a reactivity – which manifests itself in determined conditions; this activity is, in a fashion, extantial and not substantial. (MR 199)

In demonstrating that gold's colour is an extantial property Bachelard argues again that a substance, or object, cannot be seized in isolation: 'The unique has no properties' (MR 197); modern science deals with relations. This Bachelard underlined on a number of occasions. In this next passage he also introduces a temporal dimension to his analysis:

Lavoisian substance posits itself as a permanent existence, described within space; radiation, which is a non-Lavoisian entity, posits itself as an essentially temporal existence, like a frequency, like a structure of time. One can even ask oneself if this structured energy, vibrant, a function of a *number of times*, would not be enough in itself to define the existence of a substance. In this view, substance would be no more than a multi-resonant system, a group of resonances, a sort of collection of rhythms capable of absorbing and emitting certain gamuts of rays. One can foresee, in this sense, a completely temporal study of substances which would be the complement of the structural study. (PN 69, 58–9)

The mathematisation of chemistry is a longer tale.[15] Glancing at chemistry's past we quickly realise how much it lagged behind physics. In 1669, phosphorus was discovered by the German chemist Henning Brand. It was the first element discovered since the Middle Ages and, moreover, it was the first discovered element that could not be simply found, stumbled upon, so to speak, as it does not exist in nature in an isolated state; in other words, it had to be isolated in a chemical process. (This was the state of affairs at the time of Brand, since then, traces of isolated phosphorus have been found.) Here is how Brand arrived at this breakthrough achievement (on coming across this account it is really difficult to resist repeating it here):

He collected fifty buckets of human urine, which he then allowed to evaporate and putrefy until they 'bred worms'. This he then boiled until there was a pasty residue. When he left this in the cellar for some months he found it had fermented and turned black. [...] Brand proceeded to heat the black fermented urine concentrate with double its weight of sand in a retort, whose long neck was plunged into a beaker containing water. The final distillate collected under water in the beaker was a transparent waxy substance. When removed from the water it glowed in the dark, and sometimes even spontaneously ignited, giving off dense white fumes. He decided to name this new substance phosphorus, from the Greek *phos* ('light') and *phorus* ('bringing'). (Strathern 2001: 188)

Of course, Brand was not looking for anything like phosphorus; it was gold that he was after. He took his clues, first, from the early sixteenth-century alchemist and physician Paracelsus, who claimed that everything that in its natural state has the colour of gold probably contains in it the actual substance, as well as from ancient alchemical lore which held that the philosophers' stone for making gold was in the human body. Brand put the two together and the answer was obvious: urine. Such was the state of chemistry in 1669, over a quarter of a century after Galileo's death and the year Newton was appointed Lucasian Professor of Mathematics at the University of Cambridge. The ancient scheme of the four elements (with Paracelsus' mercury, salt and sulphur sometimes thrown in for good measure) still had much currency in chemical speculations; and the phlogiston theory was still to come.

Lavoisier is credited for bringing some order into this disparate world. He put to rest the phlogiston theory, demonstrated that water is not an element, recognised and named oxygen and hydrogen, and reformed chemical nomenclature. A few decades later the Swedish chemist Jöns Berzelius invented chemistry's modern universal language which substituted Lavoisier's descriptive nomenclature with formulations expressing quantities and proportions of elements taking part in chemical reactions. In Lavoisier, we would read that zinc + hydrochloric acid = zinc chloride + hydrogen; in Berzelius's formula this would be presented as $Zn + 2HCl = ZnCl_2 + H_2$.[16] This was the first entry of mathematics into chemistry, albeit somewhat modest, and used only as a descriptive tool. It begins to play a different role in Mendeleyev's work on the periodic table, which was first published in 1871 (that is, two centuries after the discovery of phosphorus). This publication, in

Bachelard's estimation, contains 'some of the most philosophical pages in science' (MR 91).

Mendeleyev's work was the crowning of a series of attempts to classify the known chemical elements.[17] Before his lifetime, the number of discovered elements was growing (Lavoisier listed thirty-three simple substances, Mendeleyev had to contend with over sixty), but no one could find a way of classifying them that would provide a coherent overview. Every commentator on this most notable breakthrough points out that Mendeleyev left gaps in the table, thus positing the existence of elements that were still undiscovered. Bachelard analysed in some detail how Mendeleyev arrived at this decision. Previous attempts at classification employed linear concepts: elements were aligned according to their chemical characteristics in combination with their atomic weight. Johann Wolfgang Döbereiner arranged them in triads, John Alexander Reina Newlands in octaves, but these solutions were not satisfactory. Mendeleyev established a grid that coordinated the atomic weights and the valence of the atoms and in this way he could establish a law of periodicity. This he found when he realised that when arranged in the order of their atomic weight the elements' valence ascended and then descended displaying a periodic pattern. It is important to point out that Mendeleyev did not think he was proposing merely a method of classifying the elements: to him the law of periodicity was a 'new law of matter, resting on a solid base that can embrace facts which have not yet been generalised' (in PCCM 96–7). From the beginning Mendeleyev had absolute confidence in the reality of his table, and it was this that allowed him to predict the properties of the as yet undiscovered elements. His confidence was justified. The existence of one of the elements that the periodic table predicted was placed between aluminium and uranium; Mendeleyev called it eka-aluminium. In 1875, four years after he made this prediction, the French chemist Paul Émile Lecoq de Boisbaudran found the element. However, his initial analyses indicated that the properties of the element did not quite match Mendeleyev's predictions. Lecoq wrote about this to the illustrious Russian only to be advised to do a proper analysis again and check the results; indeed, the predictions turned out to be correct. Another element, eka-silicon, placed between silicon and tin, was discovered five years later by the German chemist Clemence Winkler.

What Bachelard underlines is that the existence of these

elements, including their properties, was predicted by a rational effort before they were detected by common-sensical means. And although some of them were not seen at the time they were more real then the four elements of the early naïve constructs: they constituted the first genuinely scientific materialistic keyboard.

Mendeleyev could predict the existence of unknown elements. However, only in the twentieth century, when the structure of the atom was penetrated, was it possible to understand why Mendeleyev's table actually worked. With the understanding of the inner structure of the atom and the help of new technology, the last missing elements were found. The number of naturally existing elements was known to be ninety-two, uranium being the heaviest, but some of them could not be found. Element 43 was created in 1937 by bombarding element 42, molybdenum, with deuterons in a nuclear reactor. It was given the name *technetium* in recognition of the way it was obtained. Nevertheless, it is a natural element which has since been detected in some stars; it can be produced in sizable quantities (kilograms) in the fission products of uranium and it is used in medicine for certain diagnostic techniques. Francium 87, Prometium 61 and Astatine 85 were also found in nuclear reactions.

In this account of the developments in chemistry Bachelard charts a progression from knowledge based on the senses to a creativity which, to him, originates in a rational activity and ends with producing realities that are not available to the senses or traditional empirical methods. The periodic table moved away from grouping the elements by comparing their qualities, or their weights, to finding the relation between properties and weights on a mathematical level; the existence, and the properties of the as yet unknown elements were derived from mathematical calculations. These had to be based on the right type of mathematics. Mendeleyev states:

> The periodic law should not be represented with the aid of geometrical figures, which always suppose a continuity, but by a procedure similar to the use that is employed in the theory of numbers [...] it is more rational to try to express the dependency between the properties of simple bodies and their atomic weight [by *trigonometric functions*], because this dependence is periodic as functions of trigonometric lines. (In PCCM 92–3)

Mathematical calculations therefore predict the existence of as yet unknown elements and, furthermore, they exclude the possibility of finding intermediary elements, one between iron (atomic number 26) and cobalt (27), for example. It is not that Mendeleyev drew up his table and then 'saw' squares with missing elements. The whole grid was a mathematical calculation.[18] The conviction of its realness was such that if the element could not be found (technetium, for example) the scientists set up special technological conditions in order to create it. And because of the exactness of the calculations they knew very well what they were looking for.

The table turned out to be more than just a coherent classification; it was also a base for further experiments. Once the existence of all the naturally occurring elements was established there was no theoretical reason why one could not go beyond what nature offers and attempt to create further elements.

There is one further story to tell about the developments in the history of the periodic table that is quite remarkable; it concerns the interplay between the atomic 'number' and the atomic 'weight'. Mendeleyev arranged his table in order of atomic weights. However, in two instances the periodic rhythm of the ascending and descending valences was broken. This rhythm Mendeleyev considered a physical law that governed the table, and to preserve it he decided to change the order and place tellurium (atomic weight 127.6) ahead of the lighter iodine (126.9); similarly, the order of cobalt (58.9) and nickel (58.7) was reversed. Consequently, there was a degree of mismatch between the two orderings of weight and number in the table. At first, the atomic number was seen as representing no more than merely an element's place in the periodic table and was not thought to be associated with any measureable physical quantity. However, once the sub-atomic structure was understood it was possible to study the lines of the X-ray spectra of the elements. This work was carried out in 1913 by Henry Moseley (who died in the battle of Gallipoli two years later). These X-ray spectra, once photographed, showed a staccato progression of the elements and their order went by their atomic number, not weight. It further transpired that the atomic number is the same as the number of protons in the atom's nuclei. The properties of an atom depend solely on the number of its protons which themselves do not have any chemical properties. This is what is remarkable about this story, as Bachelard comments: it is as though the pagination of a book determined its contents (PCCM 135).

To sum up as succinctly as possible: A chemical substance cannot be of a uniform and inert structure, a holder of properties determined in themselves. A substance is an ex-tance, a 'multi-resonant system, a group of resonances, a sort of collection of rhythms capable of absorbing and emitting certain gamuts of rays'; these groups of resonances and rhythms are organised mathematically.

Pythagorism (and further thoughts on *la phénoménotechnique*)

Seeing such radical anti-substantialism coupled with the importance that is accorded to mathematics it is impossible not to conclude that we are dealing with some form of Pythagorean thinking, if not in letter then at least in spirit. And indeed, we find scattered throughout Bachelard's writings statements of a Pythagorean sentiment: 'The hidden world that a contemporary physicist is telling us about is mathematical in essence [. . .] Mathematics rule the real' (E 17–18); 'a chemical substance is but a shadow of a number' (NES 86, 84).

> In brief, the poetic art of Physics is done with numbers, with groups, with spins, to the exclusion of monotonous distributions, repetitive quanta, so nothing that functions is impeded. What poet will arise to sing this panpythagorism, this synthetic arithmetic which begins by giving to every existent thing its four quanta, its four figure number as if the simplest, the poorest, the most abstract of electrons already had of necessity a thousand faces. It matters little that there are only a few electrons in an atom of helium or lithium, each gets its serial number in four figures; a squad of electrons is as complicated as a regiment of infantrymen. (PN 39–40, 32–3)

However, to speak of a Pythagorean 'sentiment' or its 'poetic art' is not sufficient, something a little more concrete has to be said on the matter. A few aspects of Pythagorean thought are relevant here. The first one obviously concerns their mathematical discoveries. The Pythagoreans had strong mystical leanings, forming societies or brotherhoods. They were somewhat secretive about their mathematical work as they attached a mystical meaning to numbers. 'Mathematics was a religious occupation and the Decad a holy symbol' (Guthrie 1962: 153); it was not knowledge to be shared with outsiders. A certain Hippasus was expelled from the sect for revealing to the world some of its geometrical secrets. Empedocles, too, was banned from their meetings because he divulged their teachings in his poem; 'when Empedocles himself made them [Pythagorean views] public property by his poem, they made a law that they should not be imparted to any poet' (Diogenes Laertius, *Lives*, IX, 60). They were secretive (Pythagoras left no written works and nothing certain is known of any written works from the Older Pythagoreans either), nevertheless, their findings eventually became known. The discovery of the incommensurability of the diagonal of a square with its sides is known as the 'theorem of Pythagoras', and the work on the irrationals that followed from this discovery came from the Pythagoreans. However, these are no more than events in the development of mathematics, which did no doubt interest Bachelard, but this does not make him a Pythagorean.

The next aspect to be considered is the Pythagoreans' speculative numerical cosmology. The system was built from four principal objects: point, line, plane and volume; these were assigned the numbers 1, 2, 3, 4, which when added up give the number 10, the sacred number, the Decad, which was represented graphically as a triangle made of ten points (nine forming the triangle and the tenth in the middle), called the *tetractys*. These numbers constitute the essence of our *kosmos*. They evolve around Limit (*peras*) and Unlimited (*apeiron*); the stars wheeling in eternal circular motion are the symbol of perfection. The elements in the *kosmos* are arranged according to ratios of musical harmony. The cosmic music can be heard, or it was claimed that Pythagoras could hear it, although not through 'ordinary' hearing. (Plato was attracted to this idea, and the mediaeval 'music of the spheres' was probably an echo of it, as was Johannes Kepler's 1661 *Harmonices Mundi* where he thought he had established that musical harmonies exist intrinsically within the spacing of the planets.)

Aristotle already expressed bafflement about some of the Pythagorean ideas, which did not sit easily with his orderly logical mind: 'The "Pythagoreans" treat of principles and elements stranger than those of physical philosophers (the reason is that they got the principles from non-sensible things, for the objects of mathematics, except those of astronomy, are of the class of things without movement); yet their discussions and investigations are all about nature' (*Metaphysics* 989b). And a contemporary scholar had this to say: 'No one can claim even to have plumbed what a modern scholar despondently called "the bottomless pit" of research on the Pythagoreans' (Guthrie 1962: 146). But it is not necessary for our purposes to go into great detail. What was influential was the principal idea that the world is given order and held together by mathematics; it greatly influenced Plato and it has been a constant theme since the advent of modern scientific thinking: Galileo, Laplace and scores of others have been convinced that mathematics is the ultimate essence of reality. Bachelard would seem to hold the same view: 'It is through mathematics that one can really explore the real to the depth of its substances and in all the breadth of its diversity. Contemporary science is drawing the mathematical panorama of matter' (PCCM 231).

However, if we were to take Bachelard to ascribe to a Pythagorean world-view then a number of points would need to be raised. The Pythagorean scheme leads to the concept of a closed determinate world held tightly together by mathematics. Bachelard could not hold such a view for the important reason that to him mathematics is not a closed system; it is thought that evolves; consequently, the world evolves with it. And further, mathematics produces discontinuities; therefore, we would be led to conclude that there cannot be one world, but many. And, in fact, Bachelard did express himself in a similar vein: 'If we evoke a Pythagorism it must be an extended Pythagorism, drawn out, a philosophy that bases itself on a coherent and numerous assembly, in a rationalism of a coherent multiplicity' (MR 84). But Bachelard had no taste for cosmological speculations and expressed a lack of interest in or even dislike for the idea of the 'Universe', since it smuggles in the concept of unicity which he is against. He remarks that whenever there is talk of a universe it always carries the name of its inventor – Einstein, De Sitter, Eddington – like an engineer's patent (EngR 105). Finally, Bachelard's world is intermittent rather than an ever present presence. A chemical substance may well be a shadow of a number, but that substance may well also have been an artificial isotope, so unstable that it barely had time to exist.

One discovery that is attributed to Pythagoras deserves particular attention however: it is the seminal discovery that musical tones could be understood in terms of mathematical ratios, thus establishing the laws of musical harmony. The following rule was discovered: If the ratio of two strings is 1:2 the tones are an octave apart; the ratio 3:2 gives the fifth, 4:3 the fourth. The pitch is determined by the length of the string; half a length of that string will give an octave, tones with a different pitch will be consonant with it when they come at very precise intervals that can be established mathematically. The whole scale is thus a progression of sounds that is mathematically determined. At one stroke, a bridge between the visible and the audible, arithmetic and geometry is apparent. One is tempted to say that we are dealing with something akin to the Bachelardian world in so far as we see phenomena which depend on mathematical considerations, albeit not in the realm of microphysics. Of course, music is universal; it seems to be present in all cultures, so it is obvious that it was produced before the mathematics of harmony were worked out (although the octave was known early on in most musical traditions). However, once the mathematical basis of harmony was understood we can see a progressive mathematisation or rationalisation of music (but not of *all* music, needless to say). A great deal of formal activity and experimentation lies behind musical innovations.

Now, it is one thing to write a musical score, it is another thing to produce music; for which instruments are necessary. (Although the voice is in all probability the first means by which humans made music, for obvious reasons the focus here is on the question of musical instruments.) The construction of a musical instrument must obey mathematical rules of harmony otherwise the instrument will produce discordant sounds; the length of the strings on a lute, the placing of frets on a guitar neck, the dimension of the flute and placing of the holes in it have to be all manufactured to very high precision so the effect produced will correspond to the music that the player intends to perform. These observations on music (which could of course be developed) are offered because they seem to chime with Bachelard's analyses of scientific activities; we have the noumenal activity (writing down mathematically determined musical annotation), the *phénoménotechnique* (instruments), and the phenomena (sounds). In brief, a musical instrument would seem like a *phénoménotechnique*.

The rationalist element may at first appear meagre but, in fact, the mathematical dimension of music has developed. The phenomenotechnical side has also grown. Natural sound comes when things vibrate and produce waves of a frequency within the audible range (this aspect of sound was probably not known to Pythagoras, and even if he did have an inkling of it he would have had no means of measuring the vibrations' frequencies). Instruments are constructed to produce such waves (vibrating strings, the air in a flute or trumpet, etc.). They are called acoustic instruments as they produce sound through acoustic means. But electronic instruments also exist today. These new instruments produce sounds without first producing a physical vibration. Synthesized sounds only exist as voltages, digital numbers or analog oscillators which go into the construction of these instruments. All these are based on complex mathematical formulas. Kinds of sounds can be created which would not be possible by acoustic means, in other words, they are 'free' from the natural world; they are surreal.

And there is another intriguing development in the role of mathematics in music. Algorithms that can compose music are now written, which means that the rationalist dimension has grown to the point of fully eliminating the subjective element from the process of composing.

Furthermore, sounds are phenomena that exist in the temporal order only; they cannot become objects. They cannot be represented as images. Tellingly, musical terminology is practically completely devoid of spatial images; an odd term like 'bridge' or 'rondo' has found its way in; the timbre can be held inside a sort of 'envelope', it is thought; sounds can be represented visually in an acoustic spectrogram (but while a symphonic piece can be written down in a mathematically governed code that any professional conductor can more or less immediately 'see', it is hard to conceive of a spectrogram of a full symphony that would look intelligible). But these visual images are rare; music as such cannot be made to 'look' like something. It cannot be enclosed; it has an infinite variability of superimposed frequencies, timbres, overtones. This accounts for the inexhaustibility of music which at times seems such a marvel.

In what way would this differ from Bachelard's account of scientific activities? One difference is that the effects produced by these rationalist/phenomeno-technical procedures are accessible to the common mind as they produce music, unlike the physical domain of the effects of Raman or Compton which only a well trained physicist can understand (algorithmically created music may also be to the taste of only a few; although this may change as these are early days). But if this is the only difference then transposing, so to speak, Bachelard's thought into the familiar realm of music makes his thought more accessible. Is it legitimate? Well, if Bachelard gave the example of the invention of a sewing machine as an instance of how scientific inventiveness needs to break away from common practice rather than imitate it (the action of hand sewing, in this case), then thinking of musical instruments as examples of a *phénoménotechnique* should be permissible. Furthermore, music can also have a double effect, akin to the double joy that Bachelard spoke of when he described his reaction to seeing the photographic plates of the Fontainebleau forest taken by Gabriel Lippmann as a 'strange mixture of the joy of the eyes and the joy of the mind'. A piece of music can give sensuous pleasure, but for a listener who knows something about music, it can also allow an appreciation of the composition's structure, the sequence of chords, the use of counter-point, for example, or some other formal aspects; in a word, we appreciate the thought that went into the music.

This is not to argue that a *phénoménotechnique* was already present in the first musical instrument and that therefore Bachelard is a sort of Pythagorean, which would be silly; rather, if we accept a slightly wider definition of the *phénoménotechnique*, that is, as un-natural phenomena produced by devices constructed mathematically, then we will conclude that, eighty years after Bachelard presented the concept, urban life is infused with realities that began their lives as mathematical formulas. What in his time were rare phenomena emerging as results of the hard-edge of scientific experimentation are today more common than the steam engine.[19]

Some Concluding Remarks

In concluding the reflections that make up this chapter we should reiterate the view that Bachelard's analyses ought to be seen as a philosophy of scientific rationality rather than philosophy of science. In Bachelard's rendering rationality is the mind at work, a surrationality; it proceeds by dialectising concepts; it develops a philosophy of no. It is a creative force; it constructs a *phénoménotechnique* in order to turn the mathematically possible into the physically real. This would seem to be Bachelard's most original insight concerning the scientific domain specifically.

Two other notions also stand out, as they extend beyond the problematic of scientific rationality and pertain to a wider philosophical context.

Substance/matter

One should stress that although Bachelard developed arguments against the classical concept of substance and displays a pronounced Pythagorean streak he is not advocating some extreme immaterialism. Quite the opposite. It has been said of Bachelard that he is a 'lover of matter' (Quillet 1964: 28). This, however, was said in the context of his fascination with the thinking of alchemists. But the question of matter is also very present in the epistemological writings. The fact that he devoted so much of his work to studying developments in chemistry, while most of his generation stayed with the queen of sciences, physics, indicates that he was much attracted to matter. It is a question of an ontological reorganisation that he is advocating; the classical conception of unitary matter is no longer tenable. Thus we find formulations such as 'statistical ontology of substances' (NES 82, 80), 'laminated [*feuilletée*] reality' (PN 55, 46), or read that 'a substance is a family of cases. It is essentially, in its unity, a coherent pluralism' (PN 90, 76).

> For, after all, it would be rather too pat to withdraw into a total unitary realism all over again and to answer: everything is real, the electron, the nucleus, the atom, the molecule, the colloidal particle, the mineral, the planet, the star, the nebula. In our estimation everything is not real in the same way, substance does not have at all levels the same coherence; *existence is not a one-toned function*; it cannot affirm itself, everywhere and in the same tone, all the time. (PN 54, 46)

In *Le Matérialisme rationnel*, Bachelard's last major text on epistemology, we find a more elaborate account of what his materialism amounted to. The work is complex and would merit an extensive commentary; here only a few basic points can be signalled. Bachelard rejects idealism as 'too removed from the centre of action of scientific thought to appreciate the reciprocal role of methods of enquiry and the experiments of verification' (MR 76). However, the old immobilised materialism, an easy target for idealist thinking, is an outdated phantom.

> Compared with actual knowledge of diverse instances of scientific materialism (mechanical, physical, chemical, electrical instances) one can say that the traditional philosophical materialism is a *materialism*

without matter, a materialism all metaphoric [...] It seems necessary to us to study closely *the materialism of matter*, a materialism instructed by the enormous plurality of different matters, experimental materialism, real, progressive, humanely instructive. (MR 3–4)

These statements, which come in the opening pages of the book, outline quite clearly the kind of materialism that Bachelard espoused. Two things need to be underlined. First, matter is not some abstract concept that just 'exists' passively; it manifests itself in mechanical, physical, chemical, electrical instances; second, materialism is an experimental programme which makes apparent the plurality of different matters.

Discontinuity

Elsewhere acts no more on *here* than *times past* [*jadis*] act on *now*. (II 60)

This succinct sentence refers to discontinuity in two senses. *Elsewhere* and *here* pertain to spatial discontinuity. It is not space in the literal geometrical sense; rather, it is the space of rationality in which we find a plurality of co-existing *episteme*. However, discontinuity is not simply a consequence of scientific developments, i.e., that new scientific theories turn out to be incommensurable with other theories, resulting in discontinuities. It is the dialectical activity of rationality itself that progresses by discontinuing. Discontinuity is the force that makes science reorganise its activities; new theoretical bases give new epistemological regions. This proliferation is not unified by some universal method or rationality; it evolves.

Times past and *now* pertain to temporal discontinuity. Bachelard's analyses lead to a view which opposes the one advanced by Duhem according to which tracing the history of a concept is equivalent to doing a logical analysis of it. Bachelard questions the pertinence of a great deal of historical research, dismissing it as palaeontology, an obsession with origins that does not elucidate anything about the contemporary scientific mind-set.

Bachelard argues that science evolves but does not have a *history* – history in the sense of *historicity* which is burdened by metaphysics. The development of scientific rationality presents a collection of stories of some forgotten theories, others that marked the progress of rationality, and today we witness surrationalist actions that carve out new realities. But these are not linked by the substance of historical time.

The argument that the scientific past has relatively little relevance for an epistemologist may come as a surprise. But when we realise that very many scientists know absolutely nothing about the history of their discipline, and that this ignorance does not in the least hamper their work, then Bachelard's point becomes clearer. An epistemologist wants to follow and be close to the scientist rather than the past of his science; what is the point of studying the science of the eighteenth century if in Bachelard's own words this science was 'not a life, not even a metier' (FES 34)? Nevertheless, these remarks may seem odd since Bachelard's views are often referred to as a 'historical epistemology' thus making it sound as if epistemology has been welded with the historian's craft. This derives from the title of Dominique Lecourt's book *L'Épistémologie historique de Gaston Bachelard*, first published in 1969 and which has gone through a good number of editions since (eleven by 2002). Lecourt's text itself does not leave one with this impression, but more people have seen the title than have read the book, and the term 'historical epistemology' has become a label conflated into a popular image, a stereotype that refers to our habitual, and often unconscious, ways of thinking about history. But here are a few other comments on history that Bachelard makes, this time in relation to Louis de Broglie's wave mechanics; they are quite revealing: 'Wave mechanics seem to us to be one of the greatest scientific syntheses of all time. It is really a *historical synthesis*. It is in effect a synthesis of culture which implies bringing together several centuries of culture.' However:

> But here is a paradox: one would be gravely mistaken in believing that this historical synthesis was historically prepared, if one were to say, following the habitual expression of historians who want to give history body, that this discovery was 'in the air'. [. . .] No historical reason pushed science down the road to this synthesis. Only a sort of aspiration for an *aesthetics of hypotheses* could open the double perspective of thought that characterises the mechanics founded by Louis de Broglie. (ARPC 32–3)

These are quite clear and unequivicol pronouncements. History does not have a 'body', it is not a substance; it is not going anywhere, it is not endowed with reason. These pertain to our conception of history and clearly have a wider resonance than merely in the realm of scientific rationality. The question of time and history runs through Bachelard's work as an oft repeated theme; his rejection of continuous historical time is a considerable challenge to our intellectual habits. The label 'historical epistemology' when used to refer to Bachelard's work thus needs to be hedged with so many qualifications that it is perhaps wiser not to use it. In this context, it should also be noted that in Bachelard's first text – the long and complex *Essai sur la connaissance approchée*, which can be seen as an outline for further epistemological investigations as most of the themes tackled in this work are elaborated further in subsequent books – the question of history is absent. Bachelard's awareness of science's history is evident; on one or two ocassions his remarks make this clear, as shown for example in his comments on the question of precision in measurement in science as it evolved from the seventeenth century (ECA 60–1). But they are brief and there is no trace of a suggestion that history is of particular concern to an epistemologist. In one of the closing sentences we read: 'We will not explain thought by doing an inventory of its acquisitions, it is necessary to be aware of a force that runs through it' (ECA 300). This does not sound like a call to do history. *Essai sur la connaissance approchée* was Bachelard's principal doctoral thesis. His supplementary thesis, *Étude sur l'évolution d'un problème de physique: la propagation thermique dans les solides*, is by contrast a historical text that studies one specific problem in physics (the propagation of heat in solids) as it evolved throughout the eighteenth and nineteenth centuries. Both these texts were published in the same year (1928) by the Parisian publisher Vrin, but in different series, the first in *Bibliothèque des textes philosophiques*, the second in *L'Histoire des sciences: textes et études*. Otherwise, only the 1933 *Les Intuitions atomistiques* is of a principally historical dimension. Subsequently, Bachelard seemed to develop something of a dislike of history, at least in many of its aspects, as becomes apparent in *La Formation de l'esprit scientifique*.

And here is Bachelard's very last word on the question of science and history, coming on the penultimate page of his final work on epistemology, *Le Matérialisme rationnel*: '[O]nce we know the real nature of the molecule of ozone, we realise that right ideas are formed *despite history* or at least in a dialectical spirit which knows how to oppose, at certain points of a historical development, lazy traditions' (MR 223). This seems to recapitulate Bachelard's views. Once history is stripped of its metaphysical baggage – direction, *telos*, inevitability, reason, finality – once the fiction of historicity has been rejected, we are left with what we ordinarilly refer to as tradition. Tradition may call for adherence and observance but it cannot give rise to a creative act; every such act, every advance, be it in science, art, architecture or literature, is a break with tradition.

But one question still needs to be posed: If Bachelard is mistrustful, even hostile, to the concept of history then why did he so often draw examples from science's past? Was he inconsistent, or was it a certain weakness that he had for all these fascinating stories that can be found in the development of science? Bachelard may well have had this weakness but he needed examples from science's past as they were necessary to illustrate one of his central contentions: rationality evolves; it mutates through discontinuities. Only by looking closely at the structures of rationality that dominated science in earlier epochs can these discontinuities and mutations be made apparent; but these stories do not elucidate anything about contemporary rationality. The difference between history and Bachelard's view of epistemology is their relation to time: the historian's gaze is fixed on the past; the epistemologist is on the look-out for the new.

Bachelard's account of science and the lessons he draws from it are paradoxical. He follows one of the oldest obsessions of our Western tradition – a rejection of perception and common sense, which began with Parmenides – but he somehow arrives at conclusions which are completely opposite. The Parmenidean (and later Platonic) discourse rejects sensations and advocates a unified and immutable conception of knowledge and truth. Bachelard however is animated by a very pronounced anti-Parmenidean streak, which is evident in his quite unequivocal conviction that scientific rationality works against unicity:

> scientific progress marks its clearest stages in abandoning the facile philosophical factors of unification such as the unity of the action of the Creator, the unity on the plane of Nature, logical unity. In fact, these factors of unicity, still active in the pre-scientific thought of the eighteenth century, are never appealed to. We would find it pretentious if a contemporary scientist tried to unite cosmology and theology. (FES 16)

So, what is the reason for this paradox? Bachelard believes that it is sensations that give us the first intimation of the notion of substance. Why should he be so opposed to the idea of substance? Because it is through the intuition of substance that the notion of the One is kept within philosophical discourse. The notion of a unitary substance is one of the most entrenched concepts in scientific as well as philosophical thinking and Bachelard thinks, without really justifying it or demonstrating it, that this notion has its source in the sensory experience.

However, Bachelard's 'new scientific spirit' breaks with sensations not only because they lead to the notion of unitary substance but also because although they are very diverse, they are nevertheless too limiting; and, furthermore, sensations cannot be subject to a dialectical process. The world of sensations can only present us with what is already given: in other words, it can only give us a passive world. Sensations cannot give rise to the creative urge, the urge to surpass the given reality. By contrast, the new scientific spirit creates a surrationality that in turn creates a surreality. It is material proof of human thought at its most exceptional; it is thought that makes things.

Appendix to Chapter 1: 'Surrationalism' by Gaston Bachelard

(This text was first published in 1936 in a review *Inquisitions*, and was reprinted in *L'Engagement rationaliste*, pp. 7–12.)

We almost always confuse decisive acts of reason with a monotonous resort to the certainties of memory. What we know well, what we have experienced several times, what we repeat loyally, easily, warmly, gives the impression of an objective and rational coherence. So rationalism acquires a taste of school. It is easy and tiresome, cheerful as a prison gate, welcoming like a tradition. It lives 'underground', as in a spiritual prison that Dostoyevsky could have described, without recognising the true meaning of vigorous reason: 'Reason only knows what it has managed to learn.' And yet, for us to think, many things have to be unlearnt first.

Therefore, to turn the rationalism of the past into the rationalism of the spirit's future, from memory to endeavour, from the elementary to the complex, from logic to superlogic, these are the indispensable tasks of a spiritual revolution.

For this, it is necessary, through subtle endeavours, to lead reason not only to doubt its own work but also to divide itself systematically in all its activities. In short, *it is necessary to allow human reason its function of turbulence and aggressiveness*. This way one will contribute towards a foundation for surrationalism which will multiply the occasions for thought. When surrationalism eventually finds its doctrine it will be possible to put it in relation with surrealism as fluidity will be restored to sensibility and reason. The physical world will be experienced in new ways. We will understand differently and feel differently. We will establish an *experimental form of reason* which will be equipped to organise surrationally the real in the way Tristan Tzara's *experimental dream* organises poetic freedom surrealistically. We can, therefore, foresee two orders of spiritual tasks which are already beginning to be visible, in their early stages, in scientific developments of our time: reason will divide itself through an internal dialectic – reason will be divided by experimental obstacle through an external dialectic. The intervention of these two dialectics will determine in the third place the *surempiricisms* of a strange mobility and of a strange innovative force.

Let us quickly trace the programmes of these three surrationalist constructions.

The fully internal dialectic of rational thought only appears in the nineteenth century. It appears at the same time in philosophy and in science without, however, either exerting any influence upon the other: in putting dialectic into geometrical thought Lobachevsky is unaware of Hegel, Hegel putting dialectic into metaphysical thought is naturally unaware of Lobachevsky; he did not know anything about mathematics. However big the temptation to attach dialectic rationalism to Hegelian themes, it must be rejected. The Hegelian dialectic confronts us with an *a priori* dialectic, with a dialectic where the spirit's freedom is too unconditioned, too like a *desert*. This dialectic might perhaps lead to a general morality and politics; it cannot lead to a daily exercise of the freedom of the spirit, detailed and renascent. *It fits societies without life where one is free to do anything but where there is nothing to do. Therefore, one is free to think but there is nothing to think about.* Superior is the dialectic instituted at the level of specific concepts, *a posteriori*, after chance or history have brought about an idea, which remains contingent. From the day that Lobachevsky put dialectics into the notion of parallels he invited the human spirit to dialectically complete fundamental notions. An essential mobility, psychic effervescence, a spiritual joy found themselves associated with the activity of reason. In applying the spirit of finesse to the geometrical spirit, Lobachevsky created geometrical humour, *he promoted polemical reason to the rank of constituting reason*; in making supple the principle of contradiction, he founded the freedom of reason in relation to itself.

Unfortunately, no positive, real, surrealist usage has been made of this liberty, which could have renewed all the notions by completing them dialectically; the logicians and formalists arrived. Instead of realising, surrealising the rational liberty which the spirit experienced in these precise and fragmentary dialectics, the logicians and formalists, quite to the contrary, de-realised, de-psychologised the new spiritual conquest. Alas! after this formalising operation, devoid of all thought, after this relentless work of sub-realism [*sous-réalisme*], the spirit has not become more alert and alive but more tired and disenchanted.

What therefore is the task of surrationalism? It is to take forms again, even if purified and economically arranged by logicians, and to fill them psychologically, to put them again into movement and life. The quickest method for this would be through teaching multiple geometries, which are left in the shadow by official pragmatic teaching. *In teaching a revolution of reason we will multiply reasons for spiritual revolutions*. This way we will contribute to giving singularity to diverse rationalist philosophies, to give again individuality to reason. Here you have in front of you a hardened rationalist spirit that repeats the eternal example given in every school philosophy textbook by all philosophers who block rationalism with elementary scientific culture: the sum of the angles of a triangle equals two right angles. You will reply calmly: 'It depends'. In fact, it depends on the choice of axioms. With a smile, you will disconcert this elementary reason that gives itself the right of absolute ownership of the elements. You will give suppleness to dogmatic reason by making it play with axioms. You will teach it to unlearn to better understand. What variety in this disorganisation of a sclerotic rationalism! And, reciprocally, what variations on surrational themes; what brusque mutations for the suddenly dialectised minds!

As regards the experiment in physics, rationalism has now adopted a clearly and happily ambiguous attitude. It has abandoned the rigidity of the *a priori* and has taken on as its essential function the welcoming of the *a posteriori*. One can therefore pose as the general principle of experimental rationalism the necessity of reforming the first immediate experience: all surrational forms must be produced by intellectual reforms.

In effect, we have assumed too quickly our first experiences to be fundamental experiences. We have organised a scientific spirit on simple premises, on historical premises, forgetting that scientific history is, like all history, a story of the unhappiness of reason, of illusory fights against illusions. In order to advance, it was necessary to abandon the acquired experiences, to go against reigning ideas. Beginning with this conception of a continuous historical development, the individual scientific culture was presented as essentially accumulative [*capitalisante*]: still young, we received the general and indestructible frames, to enrich an intellectual patrimony. The remainder of the studies comprised in filling these frames, in enriching the collections and herbaria, in deducing from time to time some secondary theorems. The experimental pluralism respected the unity of the principles of reason. *Reason was a tradition.*

The times of this monotonous enrichment seem over. We now need less to discover things, to discover ideas. The experiment is split. Simplicity changes sides. It is the massive and shapeless that is simple; the element is composed. The elementary form reveals itself to be polymorph and shimmering while the massive form tends towards the amorphous. Suddenly, unity sparkles.

What should we sacrifice, our crude pragmatic securities or the new uncertain and useless knowledge? No hesitation: one has to go over to the side where one thinks more, where the experiment is the most artificial, where ideas are least viscous, where reason likes to be in danger. *If, in an experiment, we do not put reason at play, the experiment is not worth undertaking.*

Besides, the risk of reason must be total. Its specific character is to be total; all or nothing. If the experiment is successful I know it will change my spirit from its depth to its height. I carry out a physical experiment to affect my spirit. What more will I make of an experiment that has just confirmed what I already know and, consequently, who I already am? Every real discovery determines a new method and should destroy the prior method. *To put it differently, in the kingdom of thought, imprudence is a method.* Only imprudence can be successful. It is necessary to move as quickly as possible into the regions of intellectual imprudence. Nietzsche recognised the both tardy and methodological character of healthy transmutations, 'the most precious views are the last ones, but the most precious insights are methods' (Nietzsche, *The Antichrist*, §13). Knowledge that is slowly accumulated, patiently juxtaposed, greedily conserved is suspect. It displays the bad sign of prudence, of conformism, constancy and slowness.

We are therefore confronting a redoubled ambiguity. The initial dialectics of *a priori* notions confront the final dialectics of experimental notions. The unlinked reality is the echo of the freedom of our spirit. Nothing can any longer oppress us. Reality is no longer there to prove us wrong. Its irrationalism is only massive if we approach it with a reason working in a bad rhythm [*raison mal rythmée*].
  We should not feel triumphant too quickly. Rational pluralism touches metaphysical domains so different that one cannot hope to give it coherence through a simple synthesis of opposites. But should we seek this static coherence which would correspond to a metaphysical system closed in on itself? Is there not a place, in reason in evolution, for a dynamic coherence in a certain manner which would regulate even the mobility of the psyche? A psychic revolution has come about in this century; human reason has been un-anchored, the spiritual voyage has begun and knowledge has quit the shores of the immediately real. Is it not anachronistic to cultivate the taste for the haven, the certainty of a system? Should we continue to judge all things by their origin, by the source, the base, by cause, by reason, in brief, by their antecedents? It is enough to accumulate these questions to realise that despite the diversity of applications they are the result of a will for a monotonous spirituality. It is enough, on the contrary, to get rid of this ideal of identification for movement to suddenly get hold of rational dialectics. Therefore, closed rationalism gives way to open rationalism. Reason happily incomplete can no longer fall asleep in a tradition; it can no longer count on memory to recite its tautologies. It must ceaselessly prove and put itself to a test. It struggles with others, but first of all with itself. This time, there is some guarantee that it will be incisive and young.

2

The Imaginary

The Turn

In 1938, a decade into his epistemological studies, Bachelard brought out *La Psychanalyse du feu*. The work was intended as a continuation of the theme which he had been developing in *La Formation de l'esprit scientifique*, published earlier in the same year. There he argued that the first contact with the object of scientific inquiry is determined by a cluster of old unconscious assumptions. These produce vague, confused, naïve notions which stand in the way of the rationalist activity; they are epistemological obstacles. If the scientific mind is to keep its discourse in good order it has to clear away these first pre-scientific intuitions. Bachelard found, particularly in relation to fire, that old texts abound in fantastic ideas, and if one wants to understand them their archaic origins must be first traced. Once understood they can then be removed from the scientific mind-set. Here are some statements from the Introduction to the book, which set the tone of the work:

> The pedagogy of scientific instruction would be improved if we could demonstrate clearly how the fascination exerted by the object *distorts inductions*. It would not be difficult to write about water, air, earth, salt, wine and blood in the same way we have dealt with fire in this brief outline. To tell the truth, these substances which receive an immediate emotional value and lead objective research to the study of non-general themes are less clearly double, less clearly subjective and objective than fire; but nevertheless they too bear a false stamp, the false weight of unquestioned values. [...] One would have no trouble in discovering that underlying such notions is a system of heterogeneous values, indirect but of an undeniable affective nature. In all these

> examples one would find beneath the theories, more or less readily accepted by scientists and philosophers, convictions that are often quite ingenious. These bedevil the proper illumination that the mind must build up in any project of the discursive reason. (PF 15–16, 5–6)

So, to bring out the essence of this passage: 'the false weight of unquestioned values ... bedevil[s] the proper illumination ... of the discursive reason'. And in the same vein:

> But since for us, the past represents ignorance just as reverie represents futility, our aim will be as follows: to cure the mind of its happy illusions, to free it from the narcissism caused by the first contact with the object, to give it assurances other than mere possession, and powers of conviction other than mere warmth and enthusiasm, in short, to give the mind proofs that are not as unsubstantial as flames! (PF 14, 4–5)

The exposition of how reveries and dreams of fire distort scientific thought was to be the major thesis of *La Psychanalyse du feu*. And then, in the last chapter and in the Conclusion of the book, there is a marked change. The mocking tone gives way to comments on the joy that fire induces and the first allusions to the coherence of the poetic imagination appear.

Towards the end of the book, Bachelard tells of an experience from his youth in Champagne. He recounts how *brûlot*, an *eau-de-vie* made of brandy and burned sugar, was prepared. In the middle of a bowl filled with brandy a few pieces of sugar were set alight. After a while the flame would begin to flick all over, and the memory of seeing it leaping freely prompts Bachelard to write: 'this is the true mobile fire, the fire which plays over the surface of being, which plays with its own substance, liberated from itself' (PF 141, 85). It is here, in the warmth of such memories that the imaginative power wakes up.

The change is remarkable. While earlier Bachelard condemns fire for giving rise to futile reveries that stand in the way of scientific rationality, now he holds that fire opens a route of discovery and that we have to 'extricate the alert dialectics that give reverie its real freedom and its real function of a creative psyche' (PF 184, 112). The difference is such that the Introduction and the Conclusion of the book seem to come from different works. In between these two, a change of themes takes place: from science to poetry, from objectivity to reverie, from reason to imagination.

On the one hand, it seems that this new direction appeared to Bachelard unexpectedly without him quite realising that he was beginning a very new venture; on the other hand, an indication of another route, other than the one indicated by scientific rationality, can already be found in the earlier *L'Intuition de l'instant* and particularly in *La Dialectique de la durée* where Bachelard wonders about a possible 'poetic destiny' of a human life (DD xi, 22).

Bachelard never referred to this change in his writings, but the following account of his is quoted by Quillet:

> As I was engaged in the practice and teaching the sciences in philosophy I never felt as fully happy as I had hoped. I searched in vain the reasons for my dissatisfaction until one day, when in the familiar surroundings of practical works [*travaux pratiques*], at the faculty at Dijon I heard a student speak of my 'pasteurised universe'. This was a revelation to me. There it was, a man cannot be happy in a sterilised world . . . I ran to the poets and put myself in the school of imagination. (In Quillet 1964: 21)[1]

This is one explanation for the turn. Epistemological investigations left Bachelard in a quandary. He rejected all the naïve experience of the material world for quantum physics' ambiguous reality, insubstantial substance and mathematical constructs. But although these constructs satisfied his philosophical convictions they did not give a world he could live in. This makes sense. Bachelard's epistemological researches are about the creative side of science, but the imaginary also opens a quest for well-being which, despite utterances about the liberating power of surrationalism, is ultimately missing from the scientific realm, and cannot be articulated in this realm.

There was also something in the way alchemists conceptualised their researches that intrigued Bachelard. There he found an intuition of an element which was altogether different from what he earlier called naïve substantialism. The naïve attitude may give rise to the idea of substance as a unitary solid (although, as we have seen, Bachelard never demonstrated how this comes about), but for the alchemist the study of the elements was something different: it was the study of transmutation. In addition, and this is what makes the greatest difference between the earlier work on epistemological problems and the later on the poetic imagination,

Bachelard learned something new from the alchemists: the value of admiration. The alchemist's attitude differs from the scientist's, at least as far as Bachelard's account goes,[2] principally in that he is gripped by a fervour and love of the substance that he is attempting to transform. He injects values and aesthetics into his research:

> In fact, it is always by a *beautiful colour* that an alchemist describes a *happy substance*. [. . .] Paracelsus calcinated mercury 'until it showed itself in its beautiful red colour', or as other adepts would say, in *its beautiful red tunic*. [. . .] From this point of view, scientific thought has no aesthetic tonality. (TR 44–5)

Bachelard's writings on imagination never cease to underline the need to admire the object of enquiry: 'admiration is the first and passionate form of knowledge, it is knowledge which praises its objects, which gives them value' (TR 47). Here lies another difference between the Introduction and the Conclusion of *La Psychanalyse du feu*. The work begins with a cold and measured attitude which aims to eradicate the images of fire from the scientific discourse; in the end fire is praised.

The changes are many but in one respect – ontological, it could be said – Bachelard remained consistent. In his epistemological writings he vehemently opposed the concept of substance; in his works on the poetic image he could freely speak about the imaginary and the elements because it is clear that an element (in the first instance fire) is *not* the same as substance. Fire, as he put it, plays with its own substance, it is free from it. The same goes for the other elements. Bachelard's loose and not always consistent terminology will rather confuse this point; he will go on using such terms as 'matter', 'substance', 'elements', interchangeably, he will call some aspects of imagination which issue from the elements *material imagination*, but, nonetheless, it is clear that the elements are not the same as the notion of unitary substance, which he endlessly argued against in his epistemological writings. The variety of images that we find in Bachelard's works is so great that it is impossible to ascribe to the elements some unified characteristic; it is just as impossible to think of breaking them down into simple units, or particles of elements, as it were. The element is always complex and in this sense it satisfied Bachelard's intellectual temperament.

Now, Bachelard maintains that the world, before it is conceived in well-defined forms, shows itself through imagination which is shaped by the elements. This imaginary world, so diametrically different from the conceptualisations of the scientists, is what his subsequent writings on water, air and earth explore. The fact that the elements are not substance, of the kind that lies beneath 'pre-scientific' constructions, enables Bachelard to explore this world without contradicting himself; the idea of the elements is quite compatible with the openness that the new sciences offer. But this necessitates one more change which is of capital importance: Bachelard sheds his prejudice against the so-called first naïve experience, the prejudice which was so manifest in *La Formation de l'esprit scientifique*. This change is sudden and it constitutes what could be described as Bachelard's 'turn'. The turn to the elements is a turn towards naïvety, it marks a second beginning; it opens another pole of the creative psyche. So while in the earlier writings naïvety was a pejorative term, now, it becomes something to be praised. This changes the mode of Bachelard's scale, it is a shift from major to minor, from *dur* to *moll* . . . it is the condition for well-being.

The Imagining Faculty

Bachelard points out that due to an etymological confusion we think that imagination feeds off images of things perceived – in other words, that it depends on sensory activity. It is thought that we perceive and 'have' images of things which are then the stuff of imagination. But the 'basic word in the lexicon of imagination is not *image*, but the *imaginary*. The value of an image is measured by the extent of its *imaginary* aura. Thanks to the *imaginary*, imagination is essentially *open* and *elusive*. It is the human psyche's experience of *openness* and *novelty*' (AS 7, 1). Bachelard here draws attention to the fact that although etymologically they are linked the words *image* and *imaginary* mean quite different things. The Oxford Dictionary, for example, tells us that the term *image* denotes 'an artificial imitation or representation of the external form of any object', while *imaginary* is something 'existing only in imagination; having no real existence. (Opposed to *real, actual*)'. One should note that this definition of the imaginary has two parts. In the first part we read that the image exists as a representation of an external object, and in the second that the imaginary has no real existence. This dual meaning already appeared in antiquity with the words *fantasia* and *fantasma*, the first denoting the imagining faculty, the second the imagined object. In Bachelard's rendering the imaginary is the imagining faculty:

> It is the faculty for forming images of reality, which *sing* reality. It is a superhuman faculty. A man is a man to the extent that he is a superman. A man should be defined by the sum of those tendencies which impel him to surpass the *human condition*. A psychology of the mind in action is automatically the psychology of an exceptional mind, of a mind tempted by the exception, the new image grafted onto the old. Imagination invents more than objects and dramas: it invents new life, a new spirit; it opens eyes which hold new types of visions. (ER 25, 16)

Imagination aids the eye which is not tied to well defined objects; it is open and elusive, it cannot be enclosed in a conceptual framework; it does not ensue from perception, it is independent of memory, that is, it is not recollection; it makes no reference to reality, it develops without obligation to the laws of forms and logic; it makes no reference to the real, it is not subject to verification. This is a departure from yet another view which Bachelard held during the period of work on the philosophy of science. At that time he thought that imagination was no more than an extension of the sensory activity, 'one imagines with the retina. One cannot transcend the retinal condition of imagination' (E 39), 'imagination takes us no further than sensation' (NES 136, 132). But some years later Bachelard wrote: 'The eye itself, the pure vision, becomes tired of looking at solids. It needs to dream of deforming' (ER 123, 106). The eye of 'pure vision' no longer simply sees, it dreams. It dreams of deforming solids. 'Forms in themselves are clothes; nudity that is too well defined is frigid, closed, and enclosed within its lines' (ER 147, 128). The eye wants to see things before they are dressed in forms, it can see solids and forms but it seeks intimacy, it wants the things' nudity and it wants to know their habitat. When the eye dreams it rejects the postulate that things should be clear and distinct. It undresses, deforms and dissolves the lines which enclose objects into separateness. This eye is no longer limited by the retina as it has the openness of imagination. The element liberates itself from its own substance and the imaginary liberates itself from perception.

To explore the imaginary Bachelard will turn to literature,

mythology, the works of alchemists, poetry, old scientific treatises, the writings of Jacob Boehme, Paracelsus, as well as countless poets who give instances of images which are striking and new, images which defy logic and cannot be confronted by reality and yet have a strong affective power.

Imagination and Violence

Although in *La Psychanalyse du feu* Bachelard seemed to be announcing a study on the imaginary and the elements, it was not the famous monographs on water, air and earth that followed. Bachelard's first work on imagination proper was in fact very different. It turned out to be a little book, *Lautréamont*. It does not sit easily within Bachelard's *oeuvre*. Unlike all of his other writings on the poetic imagination, which explore different themes through various texts, this book concentrates on a single literary work – Lautréamont's *Les Chants de Maldoror*. And there is not a word in it about the elements. This is a work which deals with poetic will, energy, force and violence.

Les Chants de Maldoror, the one work finished and published by Lautréamont, first appeared in Brussels in 1869. It remained for a long time relatively unknown, until the Surrealists in the early twentieth century gave it a *cause célèbre* status. It has remained a regular reference ever since, if for no other reason than that it must still count as one of the most violent literary offerings of our modern culture. *Maldoror* repels and disturbs. It is a stream of violent images written in poetic prose, a stream so disquieting that some have thought it to be a work of insanity. Bachelard himself says that 'Lautréamont has written an inhuman fable' (L 11, 3). Lautréamont's own declaration of intent is summed up succinctly in this passage:

> My poetry will consist exclusively of attacks on man, that wild beast, and the Creator, who ought never to have bred such vermin. Volume after volume will accumulate, till the end of my life; yet this single idea will only be found, ever present in my mind. (Lautréamont 1970: 73–4)

Bachelard gives a brief sketch of Lautréamont's life. Little is known about him. His real name was Isidore Ducasse. He was born in Montevideo, Uruguay, in 1846. From the age of thirteen he was in a lycée in France. He published the first *Chant* when he was twenty-two, and a year later the complete *Les Chants de Maldoror* was printed in book form. The following year, in 1870, at the height of the siege of Paris, Ducasse died. Apart from a few details about Ducasse's time at school this is more or less all that is known about his life. Bachelard recounts these few facts in what was his only venture into biographical remarks. This was not a sudden indulgence; he took it as an opportunity to reject biographical and psychological interpretations of poetry, and with it the charge that Lautréamont was insane. These few biographical scraps do not tell us anything that suggests madness; Bachelard remarks that there is not one single known event in Ducasse's life which is strange, the only thing that stands out being the violence of his writing. (Not much more has been found out about Lautréamont since the time Bachelard wrote his book, the one notable discovery being a photograph of the mysterious author: a snapshot of a face (nothing deranged about it) that can now be put next to the name and the text.) Bachelard also argues that *Maldoror* cannot be a work of madness because the true alienation of madness cannot be conveyed; madness is too disjointed and singular to create a work of such intense power. The poetic coherence of art cannot have its roots in a deranged mind.

> We must pay tribute to the verbal assuredness of the work, to its resonant coherence. Without the help of rhyme, without the guardrail of strict meter, sounds are linked as though driven by a natural force. [...] Never has a violent piece of writing been less scattered. One could say that in its very aberration it is not aberrant. It is a madness lacking in insanity, a system of violent energy that fractures the real in order to live out its *achievement* without scruple or embarrassment. Lautréamont personifies a kind of *fulfilment principle* [*function réalisante*] that renders the *reality principle* [*function du réel*] ponderous by its passivity, pale by comparison. (L 83–4, 47)

To contrast the *fulfilment principle* with the ponderous, passive *reality principle* is to state, if in a different context, what Bachelard insists on throughout his authorship: to live in some 'unison' with 'reality' is to submit to passivity. But he goes further; to go beyond reality calls for violence which has a poetic coherence; this poetic power will open a new surreality.

Maldoror abounds in images from the animal world which are filled with violence, the most common being the fast and decisive acts of a predator:

> The Lautréamont complex is defined in the tooth, the jaw, and the beak. Something crackles and groans when the owl 'in his oblique flight [bears] a rat or a frog in his beak, sweet, living food for his young'. Likewise, the dogs grind up the toads with a snap of their jaws in a simple but complete and successful movement. (L 31–2, 16)

Bachelard drew up a bestiary of the poem and according to his count, 185 animals appear in *Maldoror*. A great variety of animals but the violence is virtually always the same: it is pure and instantaneous, constantly pouncing, tearing and crushing; it does not tolerate delay. It is violence which has not been slowed down by reason.

> This pure violence is not human; human forms would slow down, impede, and rationalise it. When ideas, vengeance and hatred become the explanations for violence, it loses its instantaneous, unquestionable intoxication, its shrill cry. (L 15, 5)

The Lautréamontian metamorphoses are fast enactments of a will-to-attack, an orgy of force. This pure energy, the unhindered speed, the single-minded drive for action, not restrained and sublimated by reason, hesitation, or deliberation is a world where, according to Bachelard, 'the Word is violence, Genesis is Gehenna, creation is brutality' (L 43, 23). But given that this violence is so pure it gives the work its poetic unity. Violence has a metamorphosing power because it destroys forms.

> We must fight against the mediocrity of our psychological life; we must break down images and behaviour to find the *res novae* within and without us. [. . .] The past of the real, the past of perception, of memory, the world and dreams gives us only images to be destroyed and smashed. Imagination then becomes equal to a future. [. . .] Imagination must avoid having formal causes follow the catagenic fate that somehow allows forms through some inertia to stiffen, to grow dull, and wear out like tufa eroded by moss, betrayed within by its porous and loose substance. [. . .] The past, the real, the dream itself give us only a closed imagination, since they have at their disposal only a group of predetermined images. But with open imagination there appears a sort of *myth of hope* that is symmetrical with the *myth of*

The Imaginary 91

memory. Pure imagination [...] delights naturally in imagining, thus changing forms. Metamorphosis thus becomes the specific function of imagination. Imagination cannot comprehend a form except by transforming it. (L 149–53, 87–9)

All this tearing, pouncing and crushing without delay and hesitation is a vertiginous violence, a sort of vertigo in an inverted form; rather than a fall to death, it is an accelerating descent that aims to destroy. It is a vertigo which is so alive that it can undertake the destruction of life, 'a work of genius is an antithesis of life' (L 102, 58).

The violence of *Maldoror* is pure and instantaneous. It destroys fossilised forms and opens new realities which are free from the constraints of logic, of narratives and all other ruses of intelligence; it is an inhuman violence that serves human freedom.

In the chapter 'Lautréamont: poet of muscles and cries' Bachelard traces a route, a series of transformations, which lead from this instantaneous animal-like violence to poetry. It begins with an awakening of the body, the tensing of the muscle: 'With Lautréamont the consciousness of having a body does not remain a vague awareness, a conscious slumbering in happy warmth. On the contrary, it is elucidated violently in the certainty of having a muscle, it is projected into an animal gesture men have long since forgotten' (L 107, 61). Out of this bodily excitement comes the first primal sound, a shrill cry. Then, the first word is uttered and, finally, through the most mysterious transformation, the word evolves into poetic syntax. The transformation is somewhat mysterious because Bachelard seemed to be seeking an answer to the question of poetic syntax in mathematics.

> The distortion of images must point in a strictly mathematical manner to a *group* of metaphors. As soon as the various *groups* of metaphors in a particular poetry can be specified, we perceive that certain metaphors fail because they have been tacked on, despite the coherence of the whole group. Naturally a mind sensitive to poetry will react on its own to these mistaken additions without need of this pedantic apparatus. But it is still true that a metapoetics must undertake a classification of metaphors and sooner or later adopt the only procedure essential for classification: the identifying of groups. (L 55, 29–30)

This is the second time that Bachelard hints at some possible rapprochement between new scientific thinking and poetic creativity.

Earlier he argued that scientific procedures would more and more resemble the way Surrealists compose their poetry. Here the new poetic syntax, free from narratives, could be understood through employing mathematical procedures. There is a point at which science and poetry do indeed converge, at least in Bachelard's account, in the sense that they have both purged 'reality' from their realm. In fact, Bachelard seems to be suggesting that the work of scientific reason and of poetic violence have the same source. 'This aggression, controlled by a Ducassian instant, can be found both in the instinct and in intelligence [...] intelligence must be *corrosive*. It attacks a problem. [...] Sooner or later it must wound. Intelligence is also a factor of surprise, a stratagem. It is a hypocritical force. If it attacks resolutely, it is only after a thousand ruses' (L 145–6, 85). Just as intelligence needs to destroy old ideas in order to develop new concepts, the imaginary first needs to destroy to find the *res novae*.

In the very last pages of the book a note of hesitation appears. For the Ducassean aggression to be an open metamorphosis it has to have a delay, it has to go through repose so it does not become agitation. And it seems that Bachelard may have been somewhat taken aback by the virulence of Lautréamont's poem; it is unstoppable. Earlier in the text, he pointedly remarks that 'the will-to-attack picks up speed, a will-to-attack which is diminishing is an absurdity' (L 17, 7). That is to say that in the universe of Lautréamont there is no place for repose.

Bachelard never returned to the theme of the imaginary as violence. In a later book, *La Terre et les rêveries du repos*, he took up the question of imagination and will, which while not the same as violence is nevertheless a force. There, will is induced by the earth element and therefore it has nothing frenetic about it. Bachelard also states that 'without the reveries of will [i.e. a will that is shaped by the reveries of earth], will is not really a human force, it is brutality' (TV 93), and from this point of view Lautréamont's *Les Chants de Maldoror* is just that.

Narcissism

After *Lautréamont* came the writings on imagination and the elements. They form the quartet of monographs: *L'Eau et les rêves*, *L'Air et les songes*, *La Terre et les rêveries de la volonté*

The Imaginary 93

and *La Terre et les rêveries du repos*. Published between 1942 and 1948 they are the outcome of a sustained period of work, both in terms of the time involved and the singularity of the subject. Four books but only three elements; fire is the subject of the earlier *La Psychanalyse du feu* and two late works, *La Flamme d'une chandelle* and the posthumously published *Fragments d'une poétique du feu*. But the four books on water, on air, and on earth constitute a complete cycle, a long and consistent meditation, of a unique kind, coming as they do from the pen of a philosopher (or any other pen, for that matter).

The first book is about water and the very first theme that Bachelard meditates on is narcissism. Narcissism is one of the key concepts in psychoanalysis and there cannot be much doubt that Bachelard was in a way responding to the Freudian theory, although he does not make any explicit references to it. In Freud's rendering narcissism is the first organisation of sexuality. I love myself before I know or perceive anything else; I am my first innate object of desire. This is sexuality conceived as a form of solipsism. One development in the psychoanalytical theory which opened Freud's sexual monad was Jacques Lacan's concept of the mirror stage. According to Lacan, in coming to terms with its mirror's double the child gains its first intimation of identity (Lacan 1977). Bachelard takes up the issue of narcissism around the problem of the mirror (although he does not refer to Lacan). But he looks at the question from a different and unusual angle: he first wants to look at *what* gives the reflection and concentrates on the properties of the mirror. He says:

> The human face is above all an instrument of seduction, man prepares, stimulates, polishes this face, this gaze, all these tools of seduction. The mirror is a *Kriegspiel* of aggressive love, [. . .] the mirror is too civilised, too geometrical, an object too easily handled. (ER 31, 21)

Bachelard quotes a similar observation that he found in Louis Lavell's *L'Erreur de Narcisse*:

> If we imagine Narcissus in front of a mirror, the resistance of glass and metal sets up a barrier to his ventures. His forehead and fists collide with it; and if he goes around it he finds nothing. A mirror imprisons within itself a second world which escapes him, in which he sees himself without being able to touch himself, and which is separated

from him by a false distance which he can shorten but cannot cross over. On the other hand, a fountain is an open road for him. (ER 32, 21)

Narcissus cannot find out who he is in the hardness of the mirror, he is trapped in its cold rigid geometry. Bachelard goes on to point out that the Greek legend tells us that Narcissus saw his reflection in water and 'in the presence of water, Narcissus receives the revelation of his identity and of his duality [...] and, above all, the revelation of his reality and his ideality' (ER 33, 23). Water does not give a reflection the way the mirror does: it reveals a double which is the ideal. In what is obviously a reference to psychoanalysis, Bachelard states:

> Narcissism does not always produce neurosis [...] Sublimation is not always the denial of a desire; it is not always introduced as a sublimation *against* instincts. It can be sublimation *for* an ideal. Then Narcissus no longer says: 'I love myself the way I am'; he says: 'I am the way I love myself.' I live exuberantly because I love myself fervently. I want to show up well; thus I must increase my adornment. (ER 33–4, 23)

In this reading of the legend we get a picture that is radically different from the one we find in Freud. Freud's interpretation is steeped in the conviction that there is a definable entity which is the centre of identity. This entity is closed off and it is generated by its own internal economy of energy. Since identity is sexuality, the first act of this centre of identity (and whether this act is conscious or unconscious is in this context irrelevant) is to recognise its own sexuality. And as the only word that this entity knows is 'I' it can only say 'I love myself', or better 'I sexualise myself'. The meditation on identity and sexuality never leaves the realm of the psychic interiority. In this account the original germ of identity engenders perversion, guilt and punishment. My sexuality enacts itself in sinful Oedipal fantasies. I fear castration because I fear my own instinctual savagery; my primary narcissism means that I am both the instigator and the victim.[3]

Bachelard moves into an entirely different world. To him narcissism is an exuberant opening, it opens a flower. Narcissus is a flower, and narcissism is a flowering which is the first consciousness of beauty: mine, and the world's. Water shows Narcissus his ideal double which is other than the enclosed substance of the self, be it Cartesian, be it Freudian. This double opens to the elements, it opens to their workings and there finds its own expression, the poetic expression.

> [A]t the fountain Narcissus has not given himself over exclusively to the contemplation of himself. His own image is the centre of the world. With and for Narcissus, the whole forest is mirrored, the whole sky approached to take cognisance of its grandiose image. (ER 35, 24)

One should perhaps point out that, in fact, Bachelard's reading of the myth is less 'correct' than Freud's. The psychoanalysts' interpretation is nearer to the spirit of the legend since the pool in which Narcissus saw his reflection was not an ordinary pool. This is how it is described in Ovid: 'There was a clear pool with silvery bright water, to which no shepherds ever came, or she-goats feeding on the mountain side, or any other cattle; whose smooth surface neither bird nor beast nor falling bough ever ruffled' (Ovid, *Metamorphoses*, bk III 407–10). This is unlike any other pool. It is stagnant, undisturbed by life. It is a dead pool. With its silvery surface which is never ruffled it cannot be anything else but a mirror. In front of it Narcissus is seduced to death. But in Bachelard's world water is an element which cannot remain static and immobile. Water changes; its surface shimmers, it has depth, currents and flows. It is unpredictable. It may be calm or violent; sometimes it is crystal clear, sometimes murky and heavy. Water is movement. Water that is perfectly still, sterile and enclosed is the water of death.

This meditation on narcissism is one of Bachelard's first in the books on the elements. The movement of water, the mobility of the images that water gives, strips off the veil with which we constitute the ego boundary, that persistent illusion of a clear demarcation between the I and the world, the illusion that there is a clear, distinct and stable ego.

The Body, Hylozoism

The imaginary of the elements is not played out through the activities of rationality; it is not memory or an extension of the sensory world. The *seat* of the imaginary is in the body: 'It is in the flesh and organs that the first material images are born' (ER 16, 8);

'only sensual values offer "correspondences", sensory values give only translations' (ER 30, 20).

Already in *Lautréamont*, Bachelard spoke of the awakening body, of the muscle out of which grows the violence of *Maldaror*. In the later books, the muscle is slower as the elements have taken out of it its violent streak. The muscle now caresses and moulds the elements. But the body remains an active force and it itself creates the imaginary.

> The hand also has its dreams [. . .] (ER 124, 107)

> [. . .] as the fingers lay themselves into the softness of a perfect pastry, as they make themselves into fingers, consciousness of fingers, dreams of fingers, infinite and free. One is however not astonished if one can see that fingers imagine, if one can sense that the hand creates its own images. (TV 81)

The hand, because it makes things, occupies a privileged place. Bachelard will write about the blacksmith, the carpenter, the sculptor and a number of others who work with their hands; the hand activates the principle of movement. 'Clay produces the *dynamic hand* which is almost the antithesis of the *geometric hand* of Bergson's *homo faber*. It is an organ of energy and no longer merely of form. The dynamic hand symbolises the imagination of force' (ER 125, 108). A full inventory of the images which are corporeal would be very extensive, but Bachelard did not develop a theory of the corporeality of the imaginary, it is rather that in an unmediated form he enters it and from there, as it were, explores it. And, as the body always breathes, poetry is also breath.

> In its simple, natural, primitive form, far from any aesthetic ambition or any metaphysics, poetry is a joy of breath, an evident happiness in breathing. [. . .] If we were to pay more attention to *poetic exuberance* and to all the forms that the joy of speaking takes, speaking quietly, rapidly, shouting, whispering, intoning . . . we would discover an incredible multiplicity of poetic breathing. In its strength and in its gentleness, in its poetic wrath as in its poetic tenderness, we would see an economy of breathing at work. We would find a wonderful control of air that speaks. Such, at least, are the poems that *breathe well*; such are the poems that are the beautiful dynamic forms created by the act of breathing. (AS 271, 239)

Utterances about breath in connection to poetry, language, speech and the soul appear in other texts. 'It is regularity of breathing that a philosophy of repose must endeavour to achieve before all else' (DD 146, 150). And this is how Bachelard ends a few pages of meditation on breath in the later *La Poétique de la rêverie*:

> And how can one live anywhere but at the summit of the synthesis when the air of the world makes both the tree and the man speak, mixing all the forests, those of the vegetable kingdom along with those of the poets? [. . .] In poetic reverie, the triumph of calm, the summit of the confidence in the world, one breathes well. (PR 156, 181–2)

The imaginary is the body, muscle and breath, and it dwells in a hylozoic world, a world in which all matter is intrinsically alive. Bachelard may insist that poetic images are not derived from our perceptions, and yet, they foster a sensitivity that awakens the world around us. When he wrote about the four elements, he made it clear that these images are not drawn at random, or that a particular element for some unfathomable reason exerts a particularly strong influence on the imagining psyche – the sensitivity to the elements is born at home: 'The region we call home [*pays natal*] is less expanse than matter; it is granite or soil, wind or dryness, water or light. It is in it that we materialise our reveries; through it our dream seizes upon its true substance. From it we solicit our fundamental colour' (ER 15, 8). The elements are a living force, they have their own dynamic and volition, *'in the realm of imagination, everything that shines is a gaze'* (AS 210, 183), 'everything I look at looks at me' (PR 159, 185). The abyss of fire 'tempts' Empedocles, the elements 'engage the whole soul'; they create perturbations and ambivalences. This is a peculiar form of hylozoism. It is not of a type advanced by the Ionians as Bachelard is not concerned with speculations about the structure of the universe: what he suggests is that the elements shape the imaginary. That he in some way felt that the elements have a direct effect on the psyche is clear. He went as far as to state that the element can be so alive that it can have a bearing on the human of quite deep dimensions: 'the summons of the material elements is sometimes so strong that it can help us determine certain types of suicide. It then seems as though matter helps us determine human destiny' (ER 95, 80). However, it must be emphasised that Bachelard does not say that an element may *cause* suicide, since that would be contrary to their nature. This is a cardinal point: 'the first *duty* of every revered element [...] is to serve man *directly*' (ER 173, 152).

The elements act in two distinct ways: on the one hand, they have volition and force; on the other hand, they temper the violent tendencies of the muscle, they slow it down, opening up the rhythm of reverie.

A Psychoanalysis of a Philosophical Mind

In science we have therefore a disembodied rationalism and in the imaginary a derationalised embodiment: in the scientific world, water is a chemical compound and subject to a rationalist analysis; the world of elements opens the body, 'Linking the world to man's need, Franz von Baader wrote: "The only possible proof of the existence of water, the most convincing and the most intimately true proof, is thirst"' (PR 153, 178). This, in a way, completes the opposition between scientific rationality and the imagining psyche.

In *Lautréamont* we still find a resonance between the imaginary and the intelligence that constructs scientific concepts; in this sense it is a transitional work. *Les Chants de Maldoror* is about the imaginary violently bringing about metamorphosis: the imaginary needs to destroy to find the *res novae*. The scientific mind also has this sting, it 'attacks a problem'; intelligence needs to destroy old habits to formulate new concepts. And just as in *La Formation de l'esprit scientifique* we read that 'the interests that life presents are supplanted by the interests that the mind presents' (FES 251), Bachelard will say in *Lautréamont* that 'a work of genius is an antithesis of life' (L 102, 58). The poetics that Bachelard was developing in *Lautréamont* was subsequently abandoned; the notion of metamorphosis which is central to the text disappears from later works in which the imaginary loses its sting of aggressiveness, and in this it also loses its last resemblance to rationality. Bachelard may still say that the eye dreams of deforming but it dreams rather than attacks; never again will the imaginary be virulent.

But most of all, Bachelard sheds his prejudice against the naïve. While the term 'naïve' in his earlier epistemological writings often equals 'pernicious' he will later 'obediently put himself in the school of naïvety' (FC 88). How can such a change come about? Since prejudice is not a philosophical question but a psychological one, it would seem appropriate to try to understand this in psychological terms. A little psychoanalysis might help us with this.

Bachelard's prejudice against the naïve is most pronounced in *La Formation de l'esprit scientifique* where, as we have seen, old science is described as a 'museum of horrors' (FES 21) with texts which are full of 'infantile regressions' (FES 36), displaying the 'sclerotic state' (FES 60) of Baconian methods, where they show the 'detestable solidarity of erudition and science, of opinion and experiment' (FES 63), and display a 'primitive consideration of the privileged object which is our body' (FES 149). Some of the book titles alone give an idea of the kind of questions that preoccupied the scientific treatises of the time (these, for example, are quite colourful: *Révélations cabalistiques d'une médicine universelle tiré du vin avec une manière d'extraire le sel de rosée et une dissertation sur les lampes sépulcrales*, published in 1735, and *Le Triomphe Hermétique ou la Pierre Philosophale Victorieuse, Traité plus complet et plus intelligible qu'il y a eu jusques ici, touchant le magister herméneutique* of 1710 (in FES 144 and 186)). The question is: how did a man immersed in the lessons coming from Einstein's relativity theory, quantum physics and the mathematisation of chemistry find the patience and time to read countless volumes of this nonsense? The simple answer would seem to be that he was genuinely drawn to this fantastic world of speculations and that he really delighted in it. And indeed, some of the old scientific stories that he tells are fascinating (theories of spontaneous combustion, for example, as well as many others), and Bachelard read them all with relish. But because of his conviction that science had to be viewed through the prism of the 'progress of rationality' he committed himself to a harsh rejection of these 'naïve' imaginings. The virulence of this rejection suggests that we are dealing here with a repressed love; the world of the imaginary was always very dear to Bachelard.

That his own imagination was quite fertile we can see in his commentary on Democritus' atomism in the first chapter of *Les Intuitions atomistiques*, 'La métaphysique de la poussière'. Bachelard begins by observing, surprised, that the historian Kurd Lasswitz, who wrote an important monograph on atomism, did not include in his 'minute index' the entry 'dust', while we find there amber, mercury and smoke, for example (IA 19). Then he proceeds to analyse the various phenomena associated with dust – pulverisation, calcination, granulation – he speaks of powder, talc, flour, ashes, rust, and about the child's marvel when seeing a sand-clock. The world of dust is rich and Bachelard conjures up many images, but this has little to do with Democritus. It is true that legend had it that Leucippus hit upon the idea of atoms on seeing motes of dust dancing in a shaft of light coming into a dark room, but not a single fragment of Democritus makes a reference to dust and not a single commentator on Democritus (and Leucippus), from Aristotle onwards, has mentioned dust let alone attached any importance to it.

Bachelard excluded the imaginary from the scientific realm but love cannot be repressed indefinitely and it all burst open, at first in the riot of violent instants of *Lautréamont*. Then, Bachelard's first book proper on the imagination and the elements, *L'Eau et les rêves*, begins with an invocation of childhood and the memory of time spent in Champagne's valleys beside running streams, 'I was born in a land of streams and rivers . . .' (ER 15, 7). From then on, the imaginary is never again equated with violence. So, when precisely did Bachelard open himself to the workings of the elements? We find, with a degree of amusement, that it happened in the earlier *La Psychanalyse du feu* in the chapter devoted to the experience of alcohol. It is then, his body awakened by the warmth of wine, that Bachelard lets go of the rationality of scientific thought which detests the naïve experience and lets himself be carried away by the experience of fire. Images are born in the flesh.

The reconciliation begins; and a true reconciliation it is. Bachelard does not change his views: he still holds that scientific activities are radically apart from the workings of the imaginary and that the concept and the image cannot feed off each other. However, there are no more rants against the naïve experience, and in *Le Matérialisme rationnel* we read: 'Nature wanting to really do chemistry finally created a chemist' (MR 33). *Le Matérialisme rationnel* was published in 1953 and was Bachelard's last major work on problems of science, but a sentence like this in his earlier epistemological output is unthinkable.

(End of psychoanalytical digression.)

The Four Elements

The imaginary is rooted in the four elements; they are the imaginary's habitat. Here we find openness; 'Forms reach completion. Matter [i.e. the elements] never. Matter is the rough sketch for unrestricted dreams' (ER 131, 113).

In the conclusion to *La Psychanalyse du feu* Bachelard mentions a poetic diagram. Such a diagram would show how the poet integrates all the images 'exactly as the diagram of a flower fixes the meaning and symmetries of its floral action' (PF 179, 109). These, like archetypal structures, reveal themselves in literary work, and they are organised around the elements:

> Reverie has four domains, four points from which it soars into infinite space. To surprise the secret of a poet who is faithful to his original language and is deaf to the discordant echoes of sensuous eclecticism, which would like to play on his senses, one word is sufficient: 'Tell me what your favourite phantom is. Is it the gnome, the salamander, the sylph, or the undine?' (PF 148, 90)

> Tell me which infinity attracts you, and I will know the meaning of your world. Is it the infinity of the sea, or the sky, or the depths of the earth, or the one found in the pyre? (AS 12, 5)

> The four elements [are] like hormones of the imagination. (AS 19, 11)

And, as has already been mentioned, the elements are not solid and substantial in nature: 'We are not dealing here with matter, but with orientation. It is not the question of being rooted in a particular substance, but of tendencies, of poetic exaltation' (PF 148, 90). Yet there is something palpable, so to speak, about the elements, 'matter is our energetic *mirror* [...] a hard body which disperses all the blows is a *convex mirror* of our energy, while a soft body is a *concave mirror*' (TV 23–4). The elements are poetic energies, rhythms, resonances, frequencies.

For all his disagreements with psychoanalysis Bachelard also continues to borrow from it when it suits his needs. The diagrams around which poetic images are grouped he often refers to as complexes. So, for example, the Novalis complex centres around the poetic attempt to re-live the primitive fire; the Hoffman complex ensues from the combination of fire and water, the experience of alcohol; the Charon complex shows images which relate water with the death voyage; the Ophelia complex is about water and suicide; the Jonas complex arises from the fact that earth gives images of enclosure. These complexes are only artificially similar to the Freudian Oedipus complex (or other complexes that psychoanalysts attempted to establish): they do not describe psychological mechanisms, nor are they part of some general metapsychology; they are not conceived as universal in character and Bachelard did not present them in a particularly systematic fashion either; in the book on air, for example, we do not find a single description of a complex. The complexes enable Bachelard to show the various ways in which the poetic imagination finds its coherence.

The differences between these poetic orientations is well illustrated by the two books on earth: two, because earth, according to Bachelard, evokes two very different meanings for the imaginary. First, earth is hard and it resists, and so it is the element around which the imaginary of will evolves; second, earth gives support, one can rest against it, therefore, it also gives rise to the imaginary of repose. These are two very different realms for the imaginary and, consequently, the lexicons are very different. In *La Terre et les rêveries de la volonté* Bachelard writes about the imaginary of combat, duel, anger, hostility, defiance, heaviness, pride, scorn; earth invites and shapes human will. In this order 'soft' is at the origin of 'yes' and 'hard' at the origin of 'no' (TV 18). In *La Terre et les rêveries du repos* we read about the imaginary of refuge, enrootedness, protection, hiddenness, shelter, enclosure; here earth is the mother. Other elements also abound in dualities. Water is the river Styx, but it is also purity and the giver of life, it is elemental milk; air opens the imaginary of the sky, of the abyss, of ascent and fall; fire (in the last unfinished *Fragments d'une poétique du feu*) is masculine destructiveness and feminine warmth.

The imaginary is principally oriented towards one element. There may exist unions between two elements, but never three, and, '*a fortiori*, no image can incorporate all four elements' (ER 111, 95). The particular element towards which imagination gravitates is more than just a particular orientation for the imagining being; it is also a seed of tensions, contradictions, conflicts, opposites:

> Material imagination learns from fundamental substances; profound and lasting ambivalences are bound up in them. This psychological property is so constant that we can set forth its opposite as a primordial law of imagination: *a matter to which imagination cannot give a dual existence cannot play this psychological role of fundamental matter*. Matter that does not provide the opportunity for a psychological ambivalence cannot find a *poetic double* which allows endless transpositions. For the material element to engage the whole soul there

> must be a *dual participation* of desire and fear, a participation of good and evil, a peaceful participation of black and white. (ER 19, 11–12)

> Every element has its abyss. Fire is the abyss that tempts Empedocles. For the dreamer a whirlpool is a Maelstrom. (TV 352)

Ambivalence is at the heart of the poetic imaginary. A complex, which is the poetic orientation towards an element, 'is always a hinge of ambivalence' (ER 189, 167). The elements and the imaginary are the two poles around which transformations and transpositions take place. Two wills, two forces moulding each other in countless variations. The elements open creative discord. The following extended quote shows what Bachelard has in mind:

> We want to show that the dream of hostility can acquire such an intimate dynamic that, in a paradoxical fashion, it entails the division of the simple, the division of the element. Within all substance imagination of materialised anger arouses the image of a counter-substance. It then seems that substance has to hold its own against a hostile substance, even within its own being. The alchemist who substantialises all these dreams and who also *realises* well their setbacks and hopes, has thus formed true anti-elements. Such a dialectic is no longer satisfied with the Aristotelian opposites of qualities, it wants a dialectic of forces which is bound with substances. To put it differently, continuing the initial dreams, dialectic imagination is no longer satisfied with the oppositions of water and fire; it wants a deeper discord, a discord between the substances and their qualities. The material images of a *cold fire*, of a *dry water*, a *black sun* are images which we come across quite often when reading works on alchemy. (TR 74)

The Imaginary and Philosophy

In his earlier writings Bachelard sought arguments for his conception of rationality in the works of scientists. Perhaps there was something wilful in his refusal to contemplate any of the philosophical conceptions of rationality abundant in our tradition, but in the case of imagination there is little to draw on in our philosophical heritage. The imaginary cannot question either 'Being' as reason does, or 'appearance' as the senses do, and cannot therefore lead to any approximation of truth, so in this realm it cannot be of any value. One would expect imagination to figure prominently in the philosophical meditations on art, but it does not. When it came to art, the notions that the Greeks privileged were beauty, proportion, the form, the ideal. They did recognise the importance of the imaginary in the affective life, most notably in the idea that it leads to *catharsis* and with it to an emotion of an emancipating power, but this did not have any appreciable philosophical consequences. This is just as true for modern philosophy. For a different view of the imaginary it is necessary to look at the heterodox philosophers, the 'marginals', the likes of Giordano Bruno, Paracelsus, Jacob Boehme. To them imagination is the highest and supreme faculty; it is the inner sun which gives reality vitality. The Romantics also saw the imaginary as an expression of our spiritual life. Consequently, the mere representation of reality is in effect a betrayal of the spiritual life. In modern times the almost direct inheritors of this view were the Surrealists. To them the imaginary was a vital organ in our relation to the world, which was very much the view adopted by Bachelard.[4]

Bachelard does not discuss the question of the place of imagination in our philosophical tradition but he does make occasional comments on how a philosopher's mind is ill-equipped to deal with the realm of the imaginary. For example, it will distort the findings about the antagonistic forces played out in imagination; these forces acquire a different destiny in the hands of a philosopher. The oppositions, contradictions and tensions which the elements generate are translated by the philosopher into a dialectics of strife. In such a dialectics imagination:

> finds pleasure in such images of radical opposition, [it] plants within itself the ambivalence of sadism and masochism. [. . .] This imagination starts an *ontology of struggle* where being articulates itself in a *counter-self*, all embraced in a torturer and the victim, a torturer who has not the time to revel in his sadism, a victim who is not allowed to take pleasure in his masochism. Repose is denied forever. There, there is no place for matter itself. One affirms an intimate agitation. The being which follows such images knows then a dynamic state which does not function without drunkenness: it is agitation *pure*; it is a *pure ant-hill*. (TR 75)

A dialectic which gorges on the opposition where a self articulates itself in a counter-self and which describes the master-slave dialectic may be a reference to Hegel; it could also be to Sartre (*La Terre et les rêveries du repos* was published a few years after Sartre's *Being and Nothingness*). Such a dialectic abandons the wisdom of the elements. The ambivalence of the elements opens a creative tension, but the element will not produce a dialectic of mortal strife because it softens and tempers the wilful pole of ambivalence. If imagination does not listen to the elements it becomes frenetic; 'without the reveries of will, will is not really a human force, it is brutality' (TV 93).

Then, in *Lautréamont*, Bachelard articulates another charge against philosophy. In this text, imagination is a pure force and speed that forges a creative opening, and here the philosopher is accused of slowing it down, filtering it through reason, enclosing it in the realm of philosophical ideas and thus turning it into a malevolent force.

> For a philosopher, to understand violence, in a permissible way, in a minor key, within the already airy life of ideas, is to practice it. To *understand* violence is to give it the moral guarantee of idealism. One thus discovers a Platonism of violence, a *Platonic violence*, stranger still than Platonic love. (L 135, 78)

But whether conceived as pure destructive force or repose, two features of the imaginary remain: its mobility and freedom. This mobility and freedom are protected by eliminating philosophy from it as philosophy only gives us '*categories* of understanding that are forms of intellectual prudence made concrete, fossilised states of intellectual repression' (L 155, 90).

Overcoming Pain, Overcoming Death

The four books on imagination and the elements display a stupendous confidence in the workings of the imaginary. The imaginary heals the hostile separateness between the I and the non-I. But they are not just a simple feast of joyful imagery. The poet Edmond Jaloux made this comment on *L'Eau et les rêves*:

> These symphonies, these sonatas, these quartets they tell of nothing else but a perpetual movement of a man running towards the world, towards tenderness, towards love, towards nature, towards heroism; a perpetual breaking, the bitterness of a heart which is repelled by everything, and then a prodigious entry onto the scene of a conquering will,

of an inspiring liberty, of a power to conquer the demons and which organises around itself an immense feast of joy, to which it invites all the humanity which did not want him. (In Lescure 1983: 69)

This is a comment on the pattern of the book. *L'Eau et les rêves* begins with an invocation of childhood dominated by the streams of the valley in which Bachelard was brought up. Water is to him the most personal of elements, 'the nameless waters know all my secrets' (ER 15, 8). It is also an invocation of death – the dead water of Edgar Allan Poe, Ophelia's complex, the last voyage on Charon's boat. Then, more or less half way through the book, a change occurs – first there is Xerxes' fury, followed by maternal and feminine water, by pure water; and finally, the solution – listening to the elements we shall learn to speak. Speech that grows from the elements overcomes memory, it opens the poetic life; it heals. The closing sentences of the book read:

> Come, oh my friends, on a clear morning to sing the stream's vowels. What is our first suffering? We hesitated to speak ... It was born in the hours when we hoarded within ourselves things left unsaid. Even so, the stream will teach you to speak; in spite of the pain and memories, it will teach you euphoria through euphuism, energy through the poem. It will say anew, with each instant, some beautiful word, all round that rolls over the stones. (ER 218, 195)

It must be said that neither *L'Eau et les rêves* nor any of the other books from the elements quartet are *about* death, rather, they read like an effort of the imaginary to overcome death. Even this is putting it too strongly as there is no direct meditation on this: rather we find it in the pattern and rhythm of these monographs and the concluding remarks which close each of them.

L'Air et les songes is, amongst other things, a study about ascending and descending, about the nausea and horror of the fall, and about not being able to rise. Again, the theme of death emerges, and again in reading Edgar Allan Poe: 'In a horrible caress, Death places her heavy shroud upon all things' (AS 121, 103). And just as in *L'Eau et les rêves*, the concluding sentence is an invocation of the power of language:

> A philosophy concerned with human destiny must not only admit its images, but adapt to them and continue their flow. It must be

an openly living language. It must study the *literary* man candidly, because the literary man is the culmination of meditation and expression, the culmination of thought and of dream. (AS 302, 266)

The first book on the imaginary of earth, *La Terre et les rêveries de la volonté*, ends with a meditation on the fall, the abyss, the night. The final sentence reads: 'in a fall which is completed the poet will find the *black*. So "the black and the void" are inseparably united. The fall has ended. Death begins' (TV 402). Although the end of a book, it is in fact only the end of the first part of the study of the imaginary of earth. The second part, *La Terre et les rêveries du repos*, concludes with the chapter 'The Wine and the Vine of Alchemists', and at the end we read the following:

> And who will sing us, for example, the wines of the look: tenderness and malice, the wine which teases in loving, oh, wine of my home. [...] Wine is really a *universal* which knows how to make itself *singular*, only if it finds, however, a philosopher who knows how to drink it. (TR 332)

Each time Bachelard explores an element he evokes death and he also gives an answer. The first tells us about the healing power of speech, which is how the studies on water and air are concluded; the books on earth end with a praise of wine. Bachelard is telling us, very much in a Dionysian spirit, that when faced with the shadow of death, the answer is poetry and wine.

Topophilia

In 1957, some ten years after the project on the four elements had been completed and during which period Bachelard wrote his last three epistemological monographs, he returned to the question of poetic imaginary with the work *La Poétique de l'espace*. This was another beginning. In the opening sentences of the book Bachelard declares a need to unlearn all the philosophical habits that he had acquired during his work on scientific epistemologies. This is necessary as the poetic image opens the naïve consciousness which cannot be apprehended through the philosophical apparatus of the earlier work. The poetic image must be studied without the mediation of a coordinated philosophy. What is required is a 'direct ontology' which can seize the essential novelty of the poetic image that is the origin of a speaking being.

Bachelard also spells out in the introduction the basic convictions that will guide his researches. The image is an event that announces at the same time the subject and the object without, however, representing anything, neither the world we perceive nor the psychic interior. As an event, the image is mobile and variable, independent and new, a point of departure with no antecedents: 'the philosophy of poetry must acknowledge that the poetic act has no past, at least no recent past, in which its preparation and appearance could be followed. [...] The poetic image is not subject to an inner thrust, it is not an echo of the past' (PE 1, xi–xii). In the writings on the imaginary of the four elements Bachelard spoke of diagrams around which he sought to organise the poetic images. This was not just because these images are attached to one of the elements which unifies them. In *Lautréamont*, the work which has nothing to do with the elements, Bachelard thought images could be held together following procedures similar to those mathematicians use to specify groups. In *La Poétique de l'espace* Bachelard abandons all attempts to group poetic images; now the image will be studied without encumbering it with a metapoetics and it will no longer be fastened to the element. The very nature of the poetic image proscribes a method which would be constrained by an overall ontological hypothesis. Bachelard announces a phenomenology of the poetic image, which in his view means that it has to be studied in isolation.

> if there be a philosophy of poetry, it must appear and re-appear through a dominant verse, in total adherence to an isolated image [...] moreover, nothing general and coordinated can serve as a basis for a philosophy of poetry. The idea of principle or 'basis' in this case would be ruinous as it would block the essential actuality, the essential psychic novelty of the poem. (PE 1, xi)

As the imaginary does not ensue from perception so the phenomenology of imagination, though intimately attached to objects, is very different from the phenomenology of perception. The image is not attached to the object the way the act of perception is: 'we can hardly see it [the image] start and yet it always starts the same way, it flees the nearby object and right away it is far off, elsewhere, in the space of *elsewhere*' (PE 168, 183–4). The object of imagination flees; it is always in movement. That movement would form such an important part of the meditation on space makes sense as we cannot think of space without movement; we know what distance is, when we think of traversing it.

Pure perception is flat, so to speak, that is, it can focus on anything, it scans the field of perception without prejudice; imagination, on the other hand, chooses its object, attaches value to it. This is the imaginary's intentionality: 'We are not available for dreaming no matter what' (PR 143, 166). The imaginary creates a cosmos in which the object privileged by the dreamer forms its centre.

The phenomenologist of the imaginary must be faithful to the subject he is studying. Images, always alone, unhindered, abound in the unexpected; they exaggerate, they produce paradoxes, they defy the logic of organised space and linear time. This, therefore, is what the phenomenologist of the imaginary must heed: 'how should one receive an exaggerated image, if not by exaggerating it a little more, by personalising the exaggeration? The phenomenological gain appears right away: in prolonging *exaggeration* we may have the good fortune of avoiding the habit of *reduction*' (PE 197, 219). Elsewhere, commenting on two lines from a poem by Tristan Tzara, Bachelard states: 'Tzara's image was overcharged with surrealism. But if we overcharge it still more, if we increase the charge of the image, if we go beyond the barriers set up by criticism, then we really enter into the surrealistic action of a pure image' (PE 203, 227). Every poetic image must be taken on its own merit, closely studied, followed through its vagaries, inconsistencies. Then we shall see that it is always new, that every image opens a world, a space in which it dwells.

Bachelard also breaks with all affinities with psychoanalysis. This is announced in the work that followed *La Poétique de l'espace*, *La Poétique de la rêverie*. In the writings on the elements Bachelard thought that the imaginary of the day and the night's dream belong in the same zone: 'the nocturnal dream and the reverie of the morning [. . .] have here the same tonality of living creation' (TV 100), 'our oneiric being is *one*. During the day it carries on the experience of the night' (AS 31, 22). Now, Bachelard holds that there is a radical separation between the poetic reverie and the dream of the night; the depths of the nocturnal dream do not belong to our being:

[the dreamer's] space is encumbered with solids and solids always have a reserve of sure hostility. [. . .] In the dream the dreamer suffers from a hard geometry. It is in a nocturnal dream that a pointed object wounds us as soon as we see it. In the nightmares of the night objects are evil. (PR 145, 168)

So far, this is not very different from what Freud taught. But while Freud claimed that the dream opens the inner core of our being, hard, hostile and ridden with strife, Bachelard asserts the opposite:

The night dream does not belong to us. It is not our possession. With regard to us, it is an abductor, the most disconcerting of abductors: it abducts our being from us. (PR 124, 145)

The dreamer of a nocturnal dream is a shadow who has lost his self; a dreamer of reverie, if he is a bit philosophical, can formulate a *cogito* at the centre of his dreaming self. (PR 129, 150)

The dreamer's *cogito* is, needless to say, different from Descartes'. The Cartesian *cogito* is the centre of certainty and it defends itself from being deceived. The dreamer's *cogito* is based on imagination which 'never deceives itself, because imagination does not have to confront an image with objective reality' (PE 144, 152). Descartes' *cogito* is an unchanging unity, but Bachelard argues that the sentiment of having a stable *cogito* has its genesis in the diachronic order of social life.

We were several in the life we tried, in our primitive life. Only through the accounts of others have we come to know of our unity. On the thread of our history as told by the others, year by year, we end up resembling ourselves. We gather all our beings around the unity of our name. (PR 84, 99)

The imaginary diffuses that unity, 'reverie splits [*dédouble*] being' (PR 69, 80), it suspends the monolith of history and memory and opens the soul to the event. The image is an event, an enactment which renews being. In this sense we can speak of different tonalities of being.

At the level of the tonality of being a differential ontology can be proposed. The dreamer's *cogito* is less alive than the philosopher's

> *cogito*. The dreamer's being is a diffuse being. But on the other hand, this diffuse being is a being of diffusion. It escapes the punctualisation of the *hic* and the *nunc*. The dreamer's being invades what it touches, diffuses into the world. Thanks to shadows, the intermediary region which separates man from the world is a full region, of a light density fullness. The intermediary region deadens the dialectic between being and non-being. Imagination does not know non-being. Its whole being can easily pass for a non-being in the eyes of the man at work, under a pen of a metaphysician of a strong ontology. But, on the other hand, the philosopher who gives himself enough solitude to enter the region of shadows bathes in an atmosphere without obstacles where no being says no. (PR 144, 167)

The dreamer's *cogito* is achieved in reverie. It is different from a dream and it is different from daydreaming. Reverie is a state of heightened consciousness while daydreaming is the opposite, it is a diminishing consciousness. The *cogito* of the heightened consciousness can create a destiny out of acts of reverie. In order to evoke the special status of the source of the imaginary Bachelard brings in an old-fashioned term: the 'soul'.

> The language of contemporary French philosophy – and even more so, psychology – hardly uses the dual meaning of the words soul and mind. As a result, they are both somewhat deaf to certain themes that are very numerous in German philosophy, in which the distinction between mind and soul (*der Geist und die Seele*) is so clear. But since a philosophy of poetry must be given the entire force of the vocabulary, it should not simplify, not harden anything. For such a philosophy, mind and soul are not synonymous [...] The word 'soul' is an immortal word. In certain poems it cannot be effaced, for it is a word born out of breath. (PE 4, xvi)

Interestingly, and at first sight somewhat surprisingly, Bachelard speaks of a painter rather than a poet to meditate further on the question of the soul and the image, but this is probably because he wants to draw attention to the fact that images do not passively present themselves to the soul: it is more that the soul is the agency of work, it engenders the image with force. It would seem to be the imaginary's equivalent of the nougonal noumenon of rationality.

And the soul – Rouault's painting proves it – possesses an inner light, the light that an inner vision knows and expresses in the world of brilliant colours, in the world of sunlight, so that a veritable reversal of psychological perspectives is demanded of those who seek to understand, at the same time that they love Rouault's painting. They must participate in an inner light which is not a reflection of a light from the outside world. No doubt there are many facile claims to the expressions 'inner vision' and 'inner light'. But here it is a painter speaking, a *producer of light*. He knows from what heat source the light comes. He experiences the intimate meaning of the passion for red. At the core of such painting, there is a soul in combat – the fauvism is in the interior. Painting like this is therefore a phenomenon of the soul. The work must redeem an impassioned soul.

[...] [I]t is reasonable to speak of a phenomenology of the soul. In many circumstances we are obliged to acknowledge that poetry is a commitment of the soul. A consciousness associated with the soul is more in repose, less intentionalised than a consciousness associated with the phenomena of the mind. Forces are manipulated in poems that do not pass through the circuits of knowledge. (PE 5, xvii, italics added)

Words, language, speech, writing, are born from the diffuse being of reverie. Without language there would be no imaginary. The imaginary *is* language, not a picture, not a thought, but language. In the poetic imaginary language blossoms. 'By its novelty the poetic image sets in motion all the linguistic activity. The poetic image places us at the origin of the speaking being. [...] all that is specifically human is *logos*, we would not be able to meditate in a zone that precedes language' (PE 7, xix). What Bachelard sees as essential about language is the human capacity to re-new it, to constantly inject new life into it. Therefore, language, in its poetic capacity, is the root of happiness. 'What is the source of our first suffering? It lies in the fact that we hesitated to speak' (ER 218, 195). 'But for a simple poetic image, there is no project, a flicker of the soul is all that is needed. In a poetic image the soul speaks its presence' (PE 6, xviii). The soul, mobile and multiple, expresses itself in speech. In speech it finds its freedom and since speech finds its most free expression in the poetic image, this open self is poetry.

Comments on language and speech give Bachelard another argument for a separation of reverie from the dream. A phenomenologist cannot study the 'subject' who dreams at night because for Bachelard the phenomenology of the human psyche is the phenomenology of language, of speech and of writing. Psychoanalysis concentrates on the dream, but the dream of the night cannot be spoken, it can only be recounted, and as such it cannot be subjected to a phenomenological study.[5] Out of the dreams of the night we cannot create a narrative and this is why they do not belong to our being. 'Nights have no history. They are not linked one to another [...] The night has no future' (PR 124, 145). When we dream the soul is passive. It is in the speech of reverie where being is concentrated, 'The "I" of reverie is maintained in such vigilance that it can permit itself the happiness of writing' (PR 146, 169).

La Poétique de l'espace seems to be completing a parallel universe to the one explored in Bachelard's epistemological writings. In the early works, the analyses and discussions centred on, among other things, the ways scientists conceived of substance and space. So, after the studies on the four elements, the poets' substance, a book on space would seem almost inevitable.

The parallel epistemological text to *La Poétique de l'espace* is to an extent *L'Expérience de l'espace dans la physique contemporaine* written some three decades earlier. Bachelard was attracted to the new non-Euclidian geometries because of their indeterminacy, their multitude, because they 'un-box' space. The title of the earlier work is a little misleading as there is not much by way of 'experiencing' space in the work of the physicists; Bachelard dealt with their *conceptualisations* of space, and he himself, when referring to this book in the later *La Philosophie du non*, speaks of the '*space of configuration*' in contemporary science which differs from the '*represented* space' of Newtonian mechanics (PN 71–5, 60–4). In *La Poétique de l'espace* we come nearer to its experience, although to be precise it is not about the experience of space as it is given to us, so to speak, but how through the imaginary we create it.

It is not any space: 'we would like, in fact, to examine simple images, images of a *happy space*. In this sense, our quest merits the name of *topophilia*' (PE 17, xxxi). The titles of the chapters that make up *La Poétique de l'espace* already make a suggestive reading: 1. The House. From Cellar to Garret. The Significance of the Hut, 2. House and Universe, 3. Drawers, Chests and Wardrobes, 4. Nests, 5. Shells, 6. Corners, 7. Miniature, 8. Intimate Immensity,

9. The Dialectics of Outside and Inside, 10. The Phenomenology of Roundness.

In the book itself we may read that the image flees the object and is immediately in the space of elsewhere, yet his own meditations on the house, the hut, corners, wardrobes, shells, etc., awaken intimations of dwelling.

> Sometimes the house of the future is better built, lighter and larger than all the houses of the past, so that the image of the *dreamed house* is opposed to that of the childhood home. [...] Maybe it is a good thing for us to keep a few dreams of a house that we shall live in later, always later, so much later, in fact, that we shall not have time to achieve it. For a house that was *final*, symmetrical to the house we were born in, would lead to thoughts, not to dreams; serious, sad thoughts. It is better to live in a state of impermanence than in one of finality. (PE 68–9, 61)

Bachelard dreams a palpable space. It is not surprising that this book is very widely read by architects.

The space of the imaginary is intimate; intimacy with the world opens up a space and 'nothing that concerns intimacy can be shut in' (PE 198, 220). In the zone of intimacy formulas such as 'Being-in-the-World' or 'World-Being' are far too majestic. The dreamer's world is an intimate immensity, an entire cosmos which has no alien corner, where instead of distances that measure space, the world is a neighbourhood where 'distance' has no meaning. The lines run in curves, enveloping things and opening at the same time. Such space is dehiscent and a sign of welcome, and in such a space '[i]mages cannot be measured. And even when they speak of space, they change in size. The slightest value extends, heightens and multiplies them. The dreamer becomes the being of his image, he absorbs all its space, or he confines himself in the miniature of his images' (PE 160, 173). The inside and outside become values which are different from the clear inside/outside of classical geometry, however, 'if there exists a borderline surface between such an outside and inside, this surface is painful on both sides' (PE 196, 218). Yet, it is this surface where the imaginary finds itself, moving in, moving out, always changing the nature of its space, shifting from homogeneity to heterogeneity. 'The phenomenology of the poetic imagination allows us to explore the being of man as the being of a *surface*, of the surface that separates the region of the same from the region of the other' (PE 199, 222). The same and the other are not interchangeable with the inside and outside. Sometimes the inside is hostile and the outside welcoming, sometimes it is the reverse. Each gesture concerning space is a world of its own – 'is he who opens the door and he who closes it the same being?' (PE 201, 224). Life is a series of gestures in space in which our temporal experiences find expression.

> At times we think we know ourselves in time, when all we know is a sequence of fixations in the spaces of the being's stability, a being who does not want to melt away, and who, even in the past, when he sets out in search of things past, wants time to 'suspend' its flight. In its countless alveoli space contains compressed time. That is what space is for. (PE 27, 8)

In the world where the unity of Being has been dispersed the objects are for the imagining subject goods of the world. They are the principle of welcome and adhesion, they nourish the dreamer's being, they are 'World-Fruits'. 'Being starts with well-being' (PE 103, 104). Being begins at home, in an intimate space, and if there is no well-being to begin with there cannot be being at all.

Masculine Death, Feminine Death

In *La Poétique de la rêverie* Bachelard insists that the poetic soul is feminine, it is the *anima*; the scientific concept is masculine and belongs to the world of the *animus*.

> Between the concept and the image there is no synthesis. And there is no filiation either [...] Whoever gives himself over to the concept with all his mind, over to the image with all his soul, knows perfectly well that concepts and images develop on two divergent planes of the spiritual life. [...] [O]ne will encounter nothing but disappointments if he intends to make them cooperate. The image cannot provide matter for a concept; by giving stability to the image, the concept would stifle its life. (PR 45, 51–2)

Thus Bachelard repeats what he stated in his earlier work on scientific rationality: there is a duality that cannot be effaced. And yet, Bachelard ended *La Poétique de la rêverie* promising that in his next work he would explore the *animus*: 'But just the same, so that it may not be said that the *anima* is the being of our whole life, we would still want to write another book which, this time, would be the work of an *animus*' (PR 183, 212). This must have been an enigma, since nothing suggested that Bachelard intended to return to epistemology. In light of his earlier declaration that the poetic image belongs to *anima* and *anima* only, what this promise would hold could not have been clear. Bachelard's last two works were a return to the elements, to the one he explored in his own estimation least satisfactorily – fire. The first part of this project became a little book *La Flamme d'une chandelle*. It is a very personal work, and in it Bachelard meditates on death.

> Yes, in front of a flame the old man reads no longer. He is thinking about life. He is thinking about death. The flame is precarious and valiant. This light, one blow annihilates it, one spark lights it up. The flame is easy birth easy death. Here, life and death can be well juxtaposed. In their thought games the philosophers conduct their dialectics of being and nothingness in a simple logical tone which, faced with light which is born and dies, becomes dramatically concrete. (FC 25)

This is yet another comment in which it seems Bachelard is obliquely referring to Sartre. To him the Sartrean dialectic of being and nothingness is too hard, too concrete, and in a passage that follows he meditates on how facile the image of death can be:

> But when one dreams more profoundly this nice balance of thought between life and death vanishes. At the heart of the dreamer of the candle, what sonority in the word: *to go out* [*s'éteindre*]! [...] What is a bigger subject of the verb *to go out*? Life or the candle? Verbs that metamorphise can make bear upon most heteroclitic subjects. The verb *to go out* can make anything die, a noise as well as a heart, a love as well as an anger. But those who want the real meaning, the first meaning, should remind themselves of the death of a candle. The mythologists have taught us to read the dramas of the light in the spectacle of the sky. But in a cell of a dreamer, familiar objects become myths of the universe. The candle which goes out is a sun which dies. The candle dies more gently than the star in the sky. The wick bends, the wick grows black. Embraced by shadow, the flame has taken its opium. And the flame dies well: it dies while falling asleep. (FC 25–6)

The Imaginary   117

The interesting point that Bachelard makes is the difference between the verb 'to die' and the verb 'to go out'. What he seems to be saying is that the metaphor of death is abused. This brings to mind a remark of Empedocles: 'when the elements combine to form animals or plants, men say these are born, and when they scatter again men call it death, *wrongly*, but I comply with custom myself' (Empedocles fr. 9, italics added). And the following passage suggests something even stronger; Bachelard sees different images of death:

> I wanted to follow the dreamers of the flame most diverse, even those who meditate on the death of emeralds attracted by the light. But those are the reveries in which I do not participate. I know well the vertigo. The void attracts me and frightens me. But I do not suffer the Empedoclean vertigo. The solitude of death is too great a subject for meditation for the dreamer of solitude that I am. (FC 52)

Thus we see the two different images of death: first, the image of the flame that goes out and, second, Empedocles' leap into Etna, death *in* the flame.

In his last unfinished project, *Fragments d'une poétique du feu*, Bachelard decides to confront what he earlier declined: death in the flames, the vertigo of the crater of Etna. Here he crosses over into the territory which, as he says, is nearest to his own personal nightmare, the vertigo. (In *La Terre et les rêveries de la volonté* he recounts a story from his youth. When twenty, he climbed the tower of Strasbourg cathedral. He describes the ascent in detail and considers it inhuman, and the experience, he says, left an indelible trace: 'Climbing and descending, twice some minutes of an absolute vertigo, and there we go, a psyche marked for life' (TV 344).)

Three great poets attempted the theme of Empedocles' leap: Matthew Arnold, Hölderlin and Nietzsche. Of these three, Arnold alone was able to complete his poem, only to withdraw it from bookshops after scarcely fifty copies were sold; Hölderlin developed over the years three different versions of his work, none of them completed; Nietzsche did not progress beyond the preliminary stages. One should note that Bachelard always insisted that only the image, not the poet's biography, have meaning, yet he takes care to recount the failures of Arnold, Hölderlin and Nietzsche, a practice he otherwise never engaged in: 'after the failures of the poet to write the myth of Empedocles, the myth of death in *animus* in the flames, the lyricism of the myth of voluntary death remains to be determined' (FPF 148). But in Bachelard's own terms such a lyricism cannot be determined, *animus* is hostile to poetry. This is where writing reaches an impasse, where absence announces itself: this is the realm that Maurice Blanchot, for example, explored.[6] Bachelard may declare that he does not suffer the Empedoclean vertigo yet he attempts to turn it into a poetic principle: 'A traveller who today climbs Etna remembers Empedocles. If he throws himself into the crater, it will be a failed act. Yes, the only way of living the Empedoclean act is to write a poem' (FPF 142). This is to try to reconcile the irreconcilable. Poetry under the sign of *animus* is not possible. Bachelard seems to have known this. Underlining the failures of Hölderlin, Nietzsche and Arnold was not a facetious exercise. And *Fragments d'une poétique du feu*, the work on the poetics of the *animus*, was the work that Bachelard never completed . . .

> The death of Empedocles is the extreme point where being unburdens itself [*se décharge*] from everything it has lived, believes it has lived. The fire is there. This small point of being which is the being of man who wants to become the immensity of fire. The *Dasein* which is too sure of its roots has to become, in the immense tree of flames, a *Feursein*. [. . .] Death, finally, is the return to the Father with the spirit ablaze [*dans un flamboiement de l'esprit*]. [. . .] Faced with the crater, faced with the flame, Hölderlin celebrates 'The Spirit, the Ancient Father'. We are well in the presence of death with its *masculine prestige*. It is essentially a masculine cosmos which opens itself to the spirit which 'precisely belongs to itself' [*justement s'appartient à lui-même*], liberated from the nostalgia of feminine softness. (FPF 149–51)

The masculine death is a death in the Hegelian dialectic, of the spirit which 'precisely belongs to itself'. Death with a masculine prestige is a death which is sought and confronted, it is a vertigo where the calling of the ancestors and ancient spirits is answered in flames. The feminine death is the going out of the flame while falling asleep. Life is this flame, precarious and valiant. The flame is playful and mobile, it is liberated from its own substance. It dies well without knowing that it has to die.[7]

3

The Poetics of Time

what would I do without this world faceless incurious
where to be lasts but an instant where every instant
spills in the void the ignorance of having been
without this wave where in the end
body and shadow together are engulfed
what would I do without this silence where the murmurs die
the paintings the frenzies towards succour towards love
without this sky that soars
above its ballast dust
          (Samuel Beckett, *Six Poèmes 1947–1949*)

The Instant

Bachelard's first work on the question of time, published in 1932, carries the title *L'Intuition de l'instant*, and the text of the book reflects the title: Bachelard constructs his 'metaphysics' of time around the concept of the instant. Before entering this text it might be worth having a brief glance at what philosophy has had to say about the instant.

The first time, it would seem, that the question of the instant arises is in Zeno's arrow paradox (Zeno's argument is given to us by Aristotle (*Physics* 239b5–32)). To construct his paradox Zeno takes time to be composed of instants, and states the following: In any given instant a moving arrow must occupy a space equal to itself; it cannot extend into another instant, which is to say that at any given moment it is at the place where it is, nowhere else. But places do not move. So, if in each instant, the arrow is occupying a space equal to itself, then the arrow is not moving in that instant because it has no time in which to move; it is simply there at the place. The same holds for any other instant in what we take to be the arrow's flight. Therefore, the arrow is never moving. The question of the instant as such is not addressed directly, it seems, but what would appear to be clear is that the paradox can only be formulated if it is assumed that an instant is devoid of any duration.

Plato noted exactly the same when confronted with the question of the instant: 'This queer thing the instant [...] occupies no time at all' (*Parmenides* 156d). Plato comes to this conclusion after scrutinising the problem of change. He takes as an example a moving object coming to rest and tries to determine at which point this change takes place. But he finds that it cannot be located; the coming to rest cannot happen while the object is still in movement nor can it happen when it is already at rest. It is thus an unfathomable point which cannot be 'located' in time, 'it makes the transition instantaneously; it occupies no time in making it as at that moment it cannot be either in motion or at rest' (156e). Plato further adds that 'the same holds good of its other transitions' (157a), that is, all change happens at this timeless instant. Seemingly perplexed, Plato then drops the subject and never returns to it.

When the question of this unfathomable instant poses itself a difficulty is apparent and something paradoxical emerges. However, although philosophers have deliberated a great deal on the nature of time, it is difficult to find anything which addresses the question of the instant as such. It does appear in the thought of some mystically inclined thinkers. Meister Eckhart, for example, said that the birth of the Word in the ground of the mind must accomplish itself in an instant, in the 'eternal now'. Søren Kierkegaard is an interesting example in this context as he is drawn to the same passage in Plato's *Parmenides*. However, he inserts into the question of the instant the notion of eternity. 'The instant is that ambiguous moment in which time and eternity touch one another, thereby positing the temporal, where time is constantly intersecting eternity and eternity is constantly permeating time' (Kierkegaard 1973: 79). This is far away from a strict question about temporality as first formulated by Plato. Plato presents it as a puzzle, which can be formulated thus: change does not take place *in* time. In this sense, one should distinguish between two conceptions of the instant, one as pertaining to the problematic of temporality, the other as a mystical experience, which has its own distinct vocabulary (ecstasy, revelation, epiphany, hypostasis),[1] but which is very different from a 'queer thing that occupies no time'. Plato's insight, which would seem of intrinsic philosophical interest, has not attracted attention. This is reflected in philosophy dictionaries, practically none of which has an entry on the subject. One exception (that I am aware of) is André Lalande's *Vocabulaire technique et critique de la philosophie* where we do find the entry 'instant'; it is very brief and has two definitions. The first states that the instant is: 'Very short duration, which consciousness seizes as an all.'

This definition is at odds with the intuitions of Plato and Zeno that an instant occupies no time at all and cannot have any duration, however short. Furthermore, as we shall see below, Bachelard would certainly reject this way of defining the instant, and therefore it is better to discard it. The second is of more interest, being, by contrast, close to Bachelard's reflections on the question; it states:

> It [time] has a mark that expresses the distinct, that is the *instant*, analogous to the unity, from which it differs, however, a most important point, as unity is part of a number, the limit is not part of quantity. [. . .] The instant calls its opposite, the *lapse in time*, without which it cannot be comprehended: instants succeed each other on condition that they come one separated from another, that is to say, in brief, by being separated by an interval. (Lalande 2002: 519)

This is cited from a work by Octave Hamelin, *Essai sur les éléments principaux de la représentation*, the second edition of which came out in 1925. Bachelard does not refer to it but he must have known Hamelin's view as he makes references to his work in the earlier *Essai sur la connaissance approchée*.

Bachelard's meditations on the philosophy of time come in two works: in 1936, that is four years after *L'Intuition de l'instant*, he published *La Dialectique de la durée*. A later edition of the earlier work has an appended further short meditation on the subject dating from 1939, 'L'instant poétique et l'instant métaphysique', which develops some of the theses presented in the initial work. *L'Intuition de l'instant* is a short text running to less than a 100 pages. It is ostensibly a commentary on a little-known work by Gaston Roupnel, *Siloë* (1927), or, rather, not a commentary in the strict sense but an appraisal of Roupnel's central thesis: The instant is the first reality of time, it is time's only reality and is therefore where the meditation on temporal phenomena must begin.

> *Time has but one reality, that of an instant* [...] To put it differently, time is a reality grafted [*resserrée*] on the instant and suspended between two nothingnesses [*néants*]. (II 13)

> [The only reality that we have is] the reality that the present instant presents us with. (II 74)

> Why not accept then, as metaphysically more prudent, the equality of time with the accident, which comes to equalling time with its phenomenon? (II 33)

Instants do not have duration; they also 'cannot touch each other or, rather, they cannot dissolve into one another' (II 27). This means that the instant has no recourse to a previous instant, that is, to memory; instants 'are not fecund by virtue of memories which they can actualise' (II 86). The instant does not anticipate its future either; so it is not a *germ*, which, as Bachelard notes, is a seat of a mystery, a seed wherein are inscribed and united both matter and force, both being and becoming. The idea that potentiality evolves in a spontaneous manner into actuality, an idea that is present in Aristotle and is dear to all organicists, does not, in his view, stand up to scrutiny (II 62–3). Instants are alone, they are separated from the instants that preceded them and the ones that follow; they are temporal monads. But they are not held together by a preestablished universal harmony in the manner that Leibniz held the monads together. This concept Bachelard rejects on the grounds that it presupposes a continuity at the heart of each monad, a continuity created by its link with universal and absolute time (II 60). And finally, an instant must not be conceived of as belonging to a series of identical smallest units of 'objective' time ticking away. An instant is an act of attention that is instantaneous; it is an act that is condensed in the instantaneity of its occurrence. Thus, instants differ; depending on what reality an instant presents, the fecundity will differ; 'The more filled time is, the shorter it seems. One should give this banal observation a prime place in temporal psychology. [...] It will then be advantageous to speak of *richness* and *density* rather than duration' (DD 37, 54).

In this context, Bachelard makes an interesting observation about memory which illustrates what the intensity of an instant might mean. He begins by praising Maurice Halbwachs's *Les Cadres sociaux de la mémoire,* a remarkable 1925 text on the nature of memory. What is striking about Halbwachs's work is not just the fact that he analysed so minutely the phenomenon of collective memory but, most of all, that he contests the idea of memory as a strictly private, self-enclosed activity: 'Memory outside the social framework which men living in a society use to fix and find their souvenirs is not possible', and, therefore, 'there is no such thing as a souvenir which could be said to be purely interior, that is, that can be preserved only in individual memory' (Halbwachs 1925: 63, 196). Bachelard is impressed by Halbwachs's 'admirable' book[2] but adds a further dimension to this analysis. He observes that instants are memorable not only because they are lodged in a social context but principally because of what they have triggered, that is, instants that opened up the future are the ones we are most apt to recall:

> [...] *we remember an action much better by linking it to what followed it rather than to what preceded it.* [...] What makes the social framework of memory is not historical lessons but far more a will to a social future. All social thought is pulled towards the future. All forms of the past must, if they are to give us truly social thoughts, be translated into the language of the human future. As a result, even in individual terms, it is impossible to refer purely and simply to an innermost intuition, to knowledge that the past would write passively in our soul. (DD 45–6, 61)

The event that triggers a future may be accidental, we remember a chance meeting that led to a friendship, for example, but those that mark us most are instants in which a Decision was taken and from which fruitful action unfolded.

An instant is an event, an act, which has been tempted by the possible. But not every possibility can be accepted, that is, as Bachelard says, it is not possible to exist all the time. 'An atom radiates and exists often, it uses a great number of instants, it does not, however, use all the instants; a living cell is more miserly in its efforts, it only uses a fraction of the temporal possibilities given by its ensemble of atoms; as for thought, it uses life only in irregular flashes.' A search of lost instants will bring, together with some memories of joy, memories of interminably long hours, which did not give anything. 'The objective time is the maximum time, it contains all instants. It is made from the dense unity [*ensemble*] of the acts of the Creator' (II 47–8).

The time of the world, of appearances, of the flow of phenomena, is transitive time; it is what is often referred to as 'lived time', or 'horizontal time'. The instant that Bachelard is speaking of is a disengagement from this transitive horizontal time. In the instant of this disengagement a new act takes place. The 'temporal axis which is perpendicular to transitive time, to the time of the world and matter, is an axis where the I can develop a formal activity' (DD 98, 108). It is around these instants that we create our destinies rather than just 'live time' as it flows through us. An instant of courage can transform a life. Instants like these can be of such intensity, of such depth, that they have been 'likened to an eternity' (DD 95, 105). However, although such instants are complex and are likened to eternity, they never lose their sense of instantaneity; to put it differently, they do not become contemplation.

(It must be stressed, however, that although Bachelard says that the instant has been likened to eternity, it does not mean that he is seeking or suggesting a convergence of this instant with the instant of the mystical/religious tradition. This is clear from the way he appropriates the concept of the instant from Roupnel's *Siloë*. He says 'We have permitted ourselves to take from the book what was helpful for our spirit' (II 91), in other words, Bachelard took Roupnel's instant out of its context, and the context is indeed mystical. *Siloë* appeals to pantheism and theosophy, it is a work with deep religious leanings; these Bachelard does not share and in what seems a clear reference to this dimension of Roupnel's book, he says: 'Let each follow his own path' (II 91).)[3]

Duration

But if the only reality of time is an instant, which itself has no duration and which is radically separated from another instant, then how is it possible to have the impression of duration? Bachelard states that duration is 'made of instants without duration, as a line is made of points without dimension' (II 20), it is 'a dust of instants' (II 33). We organise instants into a duration in a manner similar to how we use perspective to arrange objects in space. Just as perspective is a construct which assures that each object has a definite location in space, duration is a construct which enables us to link up memories and organise our narratives; duration is not immediately given either in experience or by intuition, it is not like

The Poetics of Time   125

some sort of ether of time in which we place memories; duration is something we get to, it is an *achievement* of our will.

Our ability to create duration means that we can create habit and progress. They are intimately linked. 'Habit is the will to begin oneself' (II 79). Yet simple mechanical repetition will not sustain habit. 'This, which commands being, is less the circumstance necessary for subsisting but rather the sufficient cause for progressing. [...] hence the necessity of desiring progress in order to guard the efficacy of habit' (II 80). A habit will therefore only be efficient if within its scheme it can accept novelty; habit is a 'routine assimilation of novelty' (II 64). This may seem a paradoxical way of putting it, as ordinarily we do not think of routine and novelty as belonging together. But in this scheme they do, as the admission of novelty is necessary for the habit to be efficient. It is the novelty of instants that furnishes the *élan* necessary for progress. (Bachelard gives the example of practising on the piano, which indeed would seem a good illustration of this. Once a piece of music has been technically mastered comes the habit of repeatedly playing it. In each repetition the ear has to be open to the novelty of timbre or timing, if not, the repetition will become lifeless and the music will lack depth, like a tune played mechanically on a hurdy-gurdy.) This is a point which is central to Bachelard's argument: progress is accepting the repeated temptation that the novelty of instants furnishes; rather than speak as Nietzsche did of the 'eternal return' we should think habit and progress as an 'eternal repeat' [*l'eternelle reprise*]; 'it represents the continuity of courage in the discontinuity of endeavours' (II 81).

Everything that has been said so far about duration pertains to durations that we construct, to coherent actions that have been triggered by a Decision. But there are also durations that are behind us, some that we are born into, so to speak; and there are others, old ossified habits that have lost all efficiency; these durations tend to be of an automatic, passive, organic nature. The durations that we construct Bachelard refers to as *anagenic* durations; the ones that are behind us as *catagenic*.[4] Catagenic durations need to be loosened and broken. In 'Instant poétique et instant métaphysique', the 1939 addendum to *L'Intuition de l'instant*, Bachelard speaks of three types of duration that need to be shaken off.

And, therefore, there are three orders of successive experiences which should unlink our being that is chained to horizontal time:
1. To gain the habit of not referring one's proper time to the time of others – to break the social frame of duration.
2. To gain the habit of not referring one's proper time to the time of things – to break the phenomenal frame of duration.
3. To gain the habit – hard exercise – of not referring one's proper time to the time of life – to no longer know if the heart beats, if joy propels – to break the time of the organic frame of duration. (II 106)

How one should go about acquiring these new habits Bachelard does not spell out, but it would seem that some meditative techniques would be necessary, and indeed in a passage in the chapter 'La rythmanalyse' of *La Dialectique de la durée* he suggests that breathing exercises, to which he found references in Indian thought, would be helpful (DD 146–7, 150). Also, in this context, we can understand better what Bachelard meant when he said in *La Formation de l'esprit scientifique* that we should think against the brain (FES 251). The brain is at the service of our bodily needs, in other words, it is the organic regulator of *catagenic* duration, and that is why it is necessary to break free from it.

In a sense, all of the past, even one's very personal past, is of a *catagenic* order; it might be benign, so to speak, in which case it will simply wither away. But one way or another it is necessary to detach oneself from the past; 'a thought is always from a certain point of view an attempt or a sketch for a new life, an attempt to live differently, to live more or even [. . .] the will to go further than life' (DD 79, 92).

The Void

Instants are alone; instants are atoms of time, they are atoms of solitude. But in *L'Intuition de l'instant* Bachelard adds: 'As soon as we accept the constitution of temporal atoms, we are led to think of them in isolation, and for metaphysical clarity of intuition, we realise that the void is necessary – whether it in fact exists or not – to imagine correctly a temporal atom' (II 27). Four years later, the equivocal words ('whether it in fact exists or not') are absent and the tone is more peremptory: 'The decisive centres of time are its discontinuities' (DD 38, 54).

These two utterances differ not only in the degree of their assertiveness but also in that they refer to somewhat different things, or to be more precise view the problem from different perspectives. This is clearer when we try to reconcile the assertion that discontinuities are the decisive centres of time with the opening premise of *L'Intuition de l'instant* that 'Time has but one reality, that of an instant' (II 13). This might seem inconsistent because if the instant is time's only reality then in what sense can discontinuity in time be the decisive centre of time? But this inconsistency is only an apparent one: in the first work Bachelard concentrates on the question of the instant and in the second he puts the notion of duration under scrutiny; and as Plato already sensed, instants and duration do not belong in the same order. From the point of view of the instant, the void is the possibility of an instant occurring and a possibility of another one following, 'the interval between two instances is nothing else but an interval of probability' (II 55). This does not mean that the probability that precedes an instant is a period of preparation. It does not link instants; what it 'does' is increase its probability. In this sense the void could be viewed as a frame around the instant. In *La Dialectique de la durée*, Bachelard examines the problem of the construction and deconstruction of durations. From this point of view, the void is an interruption, an interregnum in time, a moment when one's being is liberated from duration. We live in various durations which we have constructed but there is also a need to 'establish metaphysically [...] the existence of lacunae in duration' (DD vii, 19). The lacuna in time is necessary to open the dialectic of repose and the instantaneity of acts of will; 'repose is inscribed in the heart of being' (DD v, 17).

An agitated mind cannot think; it can re-act, but it cannot make a Decision; a Decision can only emerge from repose. In a way one could say that *L'Intuition de l'instant* is a meditation on the Decision, on how to conceive of an *'absolute beginning'* (II 66), while *La Dialectique de la durée* deals with the question of repose; the very first sentence of the book reads: 'This study will only lose its obscurity if we establish at the outset its metaphysical aim: it is intended as a propaedeutic to a philosophy of repose' (DD v, 17).

Bachelard's repose brings to mind Epicurus' *ataraxia*, freedom from mental disturbance. But one would not expect Bachelard to pose a notion, in this instance repose, that would have a single straightforward meaning. We saw that instants can be full or empty by differing in their intensity; likewise, repose is not simple disengagement, it must be understood dialectically. If it were restricted to the Epicurean description as freedom from mental disturbance, we would be left with a state defined merely by an absence. This would be an empty instant, just simply empty *catagenic* repose from which nothing can emerge. But there is also repose that rests on time that vibrates; it is a vigilance, it is 'pure consciousness that will be revealed as the capacity for waiting and for watchfulness, as the freedom and the will to do nothing' (DD vi, 18). Out of this repose, new beginnings emerge.

> Being a poet means multiplying the temporal dialectic and refusing the easy continuity of sensation and deduction; it means refusing catagenic repose and welcoming a repose that vibrates, a psyche that vibrates. (DD 125, 132)

> By placing human life in the framework of these great natural rhythms we are determining happiness rather than thought. (DD 148, 152)

To summarise: the first and only reality is the instant. The instant 'in itself' is an unfathomable absolute, an apodictic moment which has to be posited because it is impossible to think of an act of attention independently of the instantaneity of its occurrence. From the progression of discontinued instants that we live, through their bundling together comes the impression of duration. This impression of duration of time is akin to the impression of perspective in space; it is not a primary reality but something created. We create duration, habit and progress through choosing from a range of available possibilities. Apart from creating habits, which are necessary for survival, we create an ethical life out of willed time. We detach our temporality from the phenomena that link transitive horizontal time into a *catagenic* duration. However, although all that time gives us are instants and intervals there is a thread woven through this discontinued temporality; without this thread there would be no such thing as 'identity', there would be no story to tell. The thread is woven by will and desire. It is will that seizes an instant turning it into an efficient one and it is will that holds the instants together: 'we are bit by bit led to clearly separate, from the functional point of view, the will that triggers off an act and the will that continues it' (DD 40, 57). Will gives the courage to get on with creating durations, continuities and narratives; it gives us the impression of having been and of a future stretching out in front of us. The desire for renewal is what constitutes the soul. It is, therefore, as Bachelard puts it, necessary to recognise the 'supremacy of willed time over lived time' (DD 42, 58).

Rhythm and Vibration

Only a tiny fraction of instants is brought into conscious living and, therefore, there is a *'temporal alternative* [...] either in this instant nothing is happening, or in this instant something is happening' (DD 25, 44), there is 'the time that one refuses and the time that one uses, on the one hand, the inefficient time, dispersed into a dust of disparate instants, on the other hand, the time cohered, organised and consolidated into a duration' (DD 78, 91). This organisation and consolidation takes place through resonance, timbre and frequency, all of which are of course musical metaphors. 'A habit is a certain order of instants chosen from the base of the ensemble of the instants of time; it plays with a determined height and with a particular timbre' (II 74).

Bachelard accords a central role to the question of rhythm, and it is far more than a metaphor since rhythm (and vibration) has an ontological dimension in Bachelard's universe. This is already apparent in his epistemological writings, and it clarifies in more detail some questions that the notions of substance, objects and rhythms raise.

> [T]he most stable patterns owe their stability to rhythmic discord. They are statistical patterns of a temporal disorder, and nothing more than this. Our houses are built with an anarchy of vibrations. We walk on an anarchy of vibrations. [...] [T]he initial problem is not so much to ask how matter vibrates but to ask how vibration can take on material aspects. (DD 131–2, 137–8)

This last sentence is more than mere rhetoric, a question of reversing the formula. First of all, one should point out that matter that does not vibrate does not exist; on the other hand, there are vibrations that do not manifest themselves as matter. Therefore, strictly speaking, to say that matter vibrates is meaningless as it would imply a possibility of matter not vibrating; in effect, to say that matter vibrates is to utter a pleonasm (akin to saying that water is wet). Matter is vibration that materialises itself. Bachelard's own words are quite clear: 'If a particle ceased to vibrate, it would cease to be. It is now impossible to conceive the *existence* of an element of matter without adding to that element a specific frequency. We can therefore say that vibratory energy is the *energy of existence*' (DD 131, 138). However, it is not only the question of avoiding a pleonasm. To posit vibration, that is, movement, as prior to matter, is to underline the impossibility of a state of inertness.

The concluding chapter of *La Dialectique de la durée*, the remarkable 'La rythmanalyse', sifts through the dialectics of rhythm. Bachelard bases his reflections on the theses from a book, *La Rythmanalyse*, by a certain Portuguese author Lucio Alberto Pinheiro dos Santos. It feels like a phantom book because no one has managed to trace a copy of it. Since Bachelard says that he is presenting the theses of Pinheiro dos Santos by 'turning them slightly' (DD xi, 22) for his own purposes, one must be careful in assuming that Bachelard's account is a fair representation of the contents of the book, just as, for example, nothing in the text of *L'Intuition de l'instant* hints that Roupnel's *Siloë* is a mystical text (although one might guess as much from the title of the book).

Bachelard describes Pinheiro dos Santos's work as a 'phenomenology of rhythm'. This rhythm is studied from three points of view: 'material, biological, and psychological' (DD 129, 136). What Bachelard takes to be the basic thrust of the work is contained in Pinheiro dos Santos's sentence 'matter and radiation exist only in and through rhythm' (in DD 132, 138), the continuous oscillation between matter and radiation instils a vibrating duality at all levels of life.

Taking his clues from the work of Pinheiro dos Santos, Bachelard offers some comments on the question of homeopathy. He seems to be intrigued by the concept of homeopathy because of its basic contention that the greater the dilution of the curative substance, the higher its potency, and he draws some interesting lessons from it.

> In a massive form, [...] substance would in a way absorb its own rhythms; it would start resonating with itself, without fulfilling its role as a stimulus external to itself. It would escape indispensable destruction and fail to play with nothingness. It would re-appropriate itself. Indeed, radiation physics does show that substances act above all through what is on the surface and that radiations from what lies deep are absorbed by radiant matter itself. The dilution of homeopathic matter is thus a condition of its vibratory action. (DD 135, 141)

The question of the plausibility of homeopathic treatments is not of concern to us (although some dilutions are so extremely high that it is difficult not to be puzzled). What is of interest is that Bachelard reiterates in this context lessons drawn from his reflections on the relation between substance, rhythm and radiation. Furthermore, this is another way of explaining why some objects, mountains, for example, might appear to be immutable and eternal, which for all human intents and purposes they are. Bachelard gives different formulas for what constitutes an object; at one point he suggests that it is 'merely an arrested phenomenon' (PN 109, 94), elsewhere that 'to believe in the permanence of things is to open eyes always to the same phase of their rhythm' (DD 64, 78). But these will not quite do if we are facing a mountain that we have seen and climbed a number of times over a period of some decades. We can understand its relative permanence as the mountain fails to play with nothingness because all its radiations, cacophonies and anarchic vibrations are trapped inside their own immense mass.

Above all, in fact, the teachings of rhythmanalysis and homeopathic principles open up the question of embodiment and dispel the impression that we are dealing with an empty shell held together by the force of will like the knight in Italo Calvino's *The Nonexistent Knight*. These are teachings that lead to a good life since rhythm 'is the base of the dynamics of life as well as the dynamics of the psyche' (DD 128, 134):

> For a deep Epicureanism, ambrosia and divine alcohols are the first necessities. Wisely dosed, these marvellous 'tinctures' bring us the rare and multiple essences of the plant world. They are the source of an exalting homeopathy that guides us to an enhanced life. (DD 136, 142)

Against Bergson

In both *L'Intuition de l'instant* and *La Dialectique de la durée* Bachelard presented his arguments for a temporal discontinuity in the frame of a polemic: they are an explicit engagement against the philosophy of Henri Bergson.

Bergson presented his doctrine of temporality in his first major work *Essai sur les données immédiates de la conscience*, published in 1889, and he never significantly altered it. His thinking is distinct in that it rejects the Aristotelian scheme in which time is linked with movement and measurement. To Bergson time is a strictly inner process; its experience, the feeling of succession, is a flow of sensations. These are characterised by quality and intensity, they merge with one another and therefore cannot be separated and made clearly distinct. It follows that the experience of time has nothing to do with measurable quantity. It is duration, a single and continually changing flux; it forms our personal *élan vital*, a life force that pushes us along, so to speak. The world outside us is spatially organised and comprises objects, which, unlike the experiences that make up our inner world, are extended and distinct; their ordering is that of simultaneity and not succession. In consciousness we find states that succeed one another without being distinguished; in space we find distinct objects which are simultaneous without succeeding one another. Our idea of succession in the external world comes from the projection of the succession of the acts of consciousness that we experience; the idea of the distinctness of our acts of consciousness is due to the mistaken assumption that our consciousness can be conceived in spatial terms.

Time, to repeat, is an inner process, independent of the objects of the external world. The distinction is so sharp that Bergson divides the 'I' into a 'profound I' (*le moi profond*) and a 'superficial I' (*le moi superficiel*) (Bergson 1889: 93). The superficial I is under the influence of the external world and thus is characterised by a lack of the freedom which emanates from the *élan vital* of the 'profound I'. Time flows, uninterrupted. Memory, or the past, in a manner of one unbreakable block, exerts a continuous pressure on the future. And although Bergson claimed that time cannot be represented in geometrical terms, nevertheless, it is akin to substance; it increases, it swells and it marches on. We read in *L'Évolution créatrice* that 'The state of my soul, in advancing along the road of time, continuously swells [*s'enfle*] with duration that it collects; it is, so to speak, a snowball with itself'. It also, in advancing, 'consumes' what is in front of it: duration is a 'continuous progress of the past which consumes the future and which swells [*gonfle*] in its advancement' (Bergson 1908: 2, 5).

(One should note that this is an almost exact repetition of the formula of St Augustine of Hippo that we find in his *Confessions*: 'And thus passeth it on, until the present intent conveys over the future into the past; the past increasing by the diminution of the future, until by the consumption of the future, all is past' (bk XI, 36).)

Bachelard expresses a deep disagreement with this view of time and his objections are numerous. He contends that contrary to Bergson's assertion we do not and cannot have an immediate experience of duration. Attention, the sharper it is, will reveal the instantaneity of all thought, images, ideas; the sentiment of duration can only accompany inattention. Bergson, states Bachelard,

> little by little effaces events, or the consciousness of events; so he will wait for a time without events, or the consciousness of pure duration. We, on the contrary, only know how to feel time by multiplying conscious instants. [. . .] For us the consciousness of time is always the consciousness of the use of *instants*, it is always active, never passive. (II 88)

Further, Bachelard disagrees with the idea that time is an interior experience independent of external reality: 'we must attach our time to things for it to be effective and real' (DD 38, 55). To attach an instant to a thing means to act. An instant is an act, a verb, and 'it would be futile to *lengthen verbs*' (DD 19, 38), he remarks. According to the doctrine of the instant, a series of events, which constitutes a continuous repetition, is an 'every time', it is a process of multiplying acts, which follows a numeric pattern; in the continuist theory, such a series is an 'always'.

Another of Bachelard's objections: if duration was the first temporal reality we could not have the experience of novelty. Novelty, argues Bachelard, is essentially instantaneous. The philosophy of duration and *élan vital* promotes a philosophy of inactivity, of laziness. In this world-view 'our life is so full that it acts when we are not doing anything' (DD 1, 23). The scheme of *élan vital* gives us assurances of fullness and richness whatever we might be engaged in.

> In a way there is always something behind us; life behind our life, the *élan vital* beneath our impulses. Our entire past is awake behind our present, and it is because my I is old and deep and rich and full that it can truly act. Its originality comes from its origin. It is recollection and not at all a find. We are linked to ourselves and our present action cannot be disconnected [*décousue*] and gratuitous; it has to be that it expresses our I the way a quality expresses a substance. In this respect

> Bergsonism has the facility of all substantialism, the ease and charm of all doctrines of interiority. [...] in no circumstance can the soul detach itself from time; it is always like all the happy ones of this world, possessed by what it possesses. (DD 1–2, 23–4)

Bachelard is implacable in his opposition to Bergson, to the point of referring to Bergsonians as his 'adversaries' (II 61). The sustained polemic, unusual in Bachelard's *oeuvre*, serves to make clear the aspirations that govern his choices.

> We see that all his [Bergson's] theses do not get to the metaphysical essence of risk. The philosopher has not written anything on risk and for risk, on risk that is absolute and total, on risk that has no aim or reason, on this strange and moving game that leads us to destroy our security, our happiness and love, on the vertigo which draws us towards danger, towards newness, towards death and nothingness. Consequently, the philosophy of the *élan vital* could not give the full meaning of what we shall call a purely ontological success of being, that is the renewed creation of being by itself, in a spiritual act in its completely gratuitous form, as resistance to the call of suicide, as triumph over the seduction of nothingness. (DD 6, 27)

The 'ontological success of being', the 'metaphysical essence of the risk', the ability to renew, to create, is, in Bachelard's view, only comprehensible if we accept time as having its first and only reality as an instant, and if we learn ways of breaking duration.

In one of Bachelard's most often quoted statements he declares: 'Of Bergsonism we accept almost everything except duration' (DD 7, 28–9). How are we to understand this? In a way it does not make much sense. It is akin to saying that one agrees with everything in Freud's theory except his notion of the unconscious. To disagree with the notion of duration is to take out of Bergson his fundamental concept and leave so little that there is almost nothing to accept. The frequent snipes at Bergson that appear in many of Bachelard's books would suggest that he is simply being ironic and what he says should not be taken at face value. But perhaps there is another way of answering the question. First, Bachelard only states that he accepts 'almost everything', which can really mean anything (and the list of things he would not accept, like the idea of the 'profound I', for example, would be quite long). But we can very confidently assume that he accepts Bergson's preoccupation with creative evolution and mobility, and the sense of freedom that emanates from his work, as well as the elevated place he accords to imagination. (One should point out that Bachelard never quite conveys the richness of Bergson's thought, he only engages with what he sees to be Bergson's central thesis. This is not a sign of disrespect. He likewise takes from Roupnel's *Siloë* the notion of the instant but we learn nothing about the content of the book; and we do not discover much about Pinheiro dos Santos's *La Rythmanalyse* either.) One can perhaps put it this way: Bachelard accepts all the aspirations of Bergson's work but he rejects duration as an adequate metaphysical concept in which to realise these aspirations. And he more or less says as much: he accepts almost everything but adds, 'We would like to develop an essay on discontinued Bergsonism, in showing the necessity of arithmetising the Bergsonian duration to give it more fluidity, more numbers, and also more accuracy in the correspondences that are present between the phenomena that thought presents and the quantum characteristics of reality' (DD 7, 29).

And finally, the two conceptions of time that Bachelard and Bergson espoused bring to mind two temporal concepts of ancient Greece. The image of time as a past swelling and consuming the future is an exact metaphysical representation of the cruel version of time where *chronos* turns into the savage god Kronos who devours his own children; time is Father Time, an old man with a scythe. We are at the mercy of time's relentless progress, we are imprisoned in a substance that will never loosen its grip, not even for a moment, and will always defeat us; time's progress has one and only one end, death, when all is past and there is no one left to remember. Bachelard's conception of the instant brings to mind another Greek notion with a temporal meaning: *kairos*. *Kairos* is best translated as an auspicious moment, the opportune time; it is opportunity (in the sense of being opportune rather than expedient). Aristotle evokes it in his discussion of *phronesis* or prudence (*Nicomachean Ethics*, bk VI). He states that a good act must be performed at the right moment and being able to identify the good moment for action is part of *phronesis*. The Sophists, Gorgias in particular, were sensitive to the importance of *kairos* in the art of rhetoric. (Although it was also said that 'No one, not even Gorgias who first wrote on the subject, has defined the art of "the right moment"' (Gorgias fr. 13).) The conception of time as an auspicious moment can be found in today's English in such expressions as 'an opening' or 'in the nick of time' (Onians 1988: 347). *Kairos* is about seizing the opportune moment, holding on to it and from there creating one's own unique destiny.

The Void and Nothingness

The notion of discontinuous time has never entered our philosophical heritage, in fact, it seems a rather alien concept in our tradition. However, when we cast our eyes to the Orient, we find arguments for the discontinuity of time and the primordiality of the instant discussed with great finesse. These were put forward most forcefully by the Buddhist thinkers, in particular those from the school of Dignāga and Dharmakīrti in the sixth and seventh centuries, the last period when Buddhism flourished in India. In the overall picture of Buddhist thought the Dignāga school is not the most prominent; it has however attracted a number of commentaries because of the immensely rigorous logic and epistemology that its thinkers developed (Stcherbatsky 1970, Chinchore 1995, Mookerjee 2006). It is the most 'philosophical' (that is, least religious) of the many Buddhist schools. Lilian Silburn's *Instant et cause: Le discontinu dans la pensée philosophique de l'Inde* (1989), deserves particular attention here, and for a number of reasons. First, while the other commentaries focus on the logical and epistemological developments, Silburn concentrates mostly on the importance that the school accorded to the intuition of the instant. Second, it deals at length with the conflict between the partisans of duration, which is characteristic of Brahmin thought, and the partisans of discontinuity, characteristic of Buddhist thinkers, and their disagreements are much the same as those voiced by Bachelard in relation to Bergson. One difference should be noted however: the Brahmins do not conceive of time as some primary given, something akin to the immanent flowing *élan vital*, but consider it as evolving from an act, just like the Buddhists. But while the Brahmin strives to create stable duration to the point where he renounces the act and passes to ultimate eternal being, the Buddhists hold the opposite view: they advocate the doctrine of the instantaneity of the act and aim to destroy duration. Finally, reading Silburn's work, especially Chapter VIII on the logicians of the Dignāga school, one is struck by the similarities between

Bachelard's thinking and what we find to be the Buddhist position. It is also intriguing to note that when Silburn presented the text as a doctoral thesis in 1948, Bachelard was one of the members of the jury, the only non-Orientalist, and he is the only Occidental philosopher referred to in Silburn's text. He must have found many echoes between his own meditation on time published over a decade earlier and Silburn's exposition. Also, in the *Avant-propos* to the 1989 reprint of her book, Silburn notes that developments in modern science, notably intuitions about time and causality, should make the thinking of the ancient Indian sages less strange. (And indeed, from the point of view of contemporary physics there is nothing strange in claiming that 'a mountain, this unique thing, durable and immutable *par excellence*, and which does not seem to be subject to differentiation by time, space or form is [. . .] an aggregate of diverse and instantaneous atoms' (Silburn 1989: 299).) Finally, reading Silburn's work helped me to better understand Bachelard's texts. Her work is rich in detail; for example, the debates between the Brahmins and Buddhists are very carefully presented with great attention to detail; in brief, when viewed through the lens of Silburn's work, Bachelard's thought seems to become clearer. (For example, the difference between *anagenic* and *catagenic* duration is spelt out in detail in Silburn's text (1989: 304–9, 314).) It should be added that the few comments offered so far and the citations that will follow do not do even the remotest justice to the richness and subtlety of Silburn's magnificent work which is so much wider and deeper in scope, the citations being chosen to convey only the resonances between Bachelard's thinking and the Buddhist doctrine. It should be emphasised however that these citations are not marginal or taken out of context to fit the purpose of this presentation; they are in fact at the heart of the thought of these Buddhist thinkers. Here is a short collage taken from Silburn's work (page numbers given in brackets; the various Sanskrit terms inserted in the text have been omitted; one sentence in the collage and a few more further in the text are in italics as they are translations of Silburn's French renderings of the original Sanskrit texts and not her own words):

> A philosophy of time will be derived from a philosophy of the act, there is no time only the construction of time (1). The time that interests the ancient priests is not the time broken into pieces and, consequently, inefficient, but the time that realises an activity, a time articulated

piece by piece, linking one utterance [*articulation*] to another (2). A thought that is not rooted in desire cannot organise and elaborate a duration (4). For the one who knows things 'as they are' everything is discontinuous and it is our activity, influenced by desire, that forges continuity and duration (5). The Buddhists reject the triple infiltration of continuity, either appearing as a permanent I, or disguised in the aspect of the distinction of a substance and its attributes, or, finally, it persists subtly in the form of the real existence of past and future epochs (231). The point-instant of efficiency becomes the ultimate base of reality, all the rest being but a construction of imagination. Reality is defined by efficiency and only instantaneous things are efficient (276). *The Instant is an acquisition of the proper nature immediately perishing* (277). It is the thing in itself, inexpressible, indivisible, beyond all determination, absolutely separated from all other things, without spatial extension and without duration; pure existence, pure efficiency, this is in one word the instant as point [*instant ponctiforme*] (280). It is not the object which creates knowledge but it is knowledge which creates the object (283). The instant is the sole reality which serves as the foundation of all constructions (285). One does not perceive a substance which would underlie successive modes, one cannot, therefore, consider substance as real (298). In place of flowing with transitive time, thought stands up to escape time (320). The monk knows how to choose creative instants and how to link them into supple rhythms. He becomes the master of time (324). Man being but a succession of heterogeneous thoughts, of momentary impressions and not of a substantial soul, is never linked with himself; nor is he a slave of his past (326). *Āsevanā* and *paṭisevana* can be translated by the term 'habit' with the condition that these are conscious habits, dynamic with an infinitely supple and free play. It is habit that is devoid of all routine and it implies less persistence and permanence than perseverance and progress; these habits are controlled by a vigilant thought that never slackens (329). Causes form independent series; each of these series has its proper temporal rhythm: the temporal series which we name metaphorically cause or more precisely a seed is but a series amongst others and it is only a correlation of these numerous series that will make an effect emerge. It follows that all that exists are efficient instances, instances of the coincidences between series. No duration links efficiently an effect and its causes. (353)

To underline the exact stakes that are in play in these meditations on temporality, Silburn sets the stage early on in her comments on the Vedic texts. Following these texts, the Brahmin priests evolved sacrificial rites; 'The Brahmins, being preoccupied with acts and rites, are only interested in long life or immortality' (113), 'the sacrifice appears as a vast construction which launches an assault to gain non-death' (19). The metaphysics that accompany this aim include the following: '*There is no contentment but in infinity or plenitude; there is no contentment in finitude [. . .] he who is plenitude is immortal; he who is final is mortal. The plenitude does not rest on anything, it is ultimate; it is all that exists*' (155). But, Silburn remarks:

> The enormous elaboration of stability and of continuity to which during centuries the Brahmin priests devoted their efforts was not sufficient to assure confidence and security. [. . .] death was not conquered. Much to the contrary, it is in the very desire for duration that we find the root of anguish. (403)

The Buddhist answer is: '*To escape the king of death one should consider the world as a void and remain perpetually vigilant. When one has destroyed the erroneous belief in the I, one can surmount death*' (154). The exchange between the Brahmins and the Buddhists that Silburn highlights in her commentary helps us to understand better an isolated passage in *La Dialectique de la durée* that at first reading seems a little cryptic:

> To have an impression that one has duration, an impression that is always singularly imprecise, we have to put back our memories, as real events, into the milieu of hope and anxiety, into a dialectical undulation. No memory without this trembling of time, without this affective shudder. Even in this past, which we believe to be full, the recalling, the account, the secret replace the void of inactive time. In remembering we endlessly blend useless and inefficient time with time which served and gave. The dialectic of happiness and pain is never so captivating as when it is in accordance with the temporal dialectic. So one knows the time that takes and a time that gives. One suddenly becomes aware that time will take again. To relive the time, which has disappeared, is therefore to learn the anxiety of our death. (DD 33, 50–1)

Bachelard's words are much the same as those of the Buddhist: if we think that memory constitutes time as lived duration we will create an entrance for the anticipation of death; that is, to link past, present and future into a continuous flux is paramount to bringing death into the experience of time. Only if we accept that time is discontinuous and that the sole reality that confronts us is the reality of the lived instant will we eliminate the fear of death.

Could this be the principal reason Bachelard so vehemently opposed Bergson's notion of duration? After all, the debate he launched against Bergson was the only one he entered into in his entire *oeuvre*, no other philosopher was a specific target for an attack; and at times it is trenchant. Whether this was the reason one cannot be certain, but one lesson can be drawn: the notion of time as duration renders death a philosophically legitimate theme.[5]

The exchange between the Brahmins and the Buddhists also gives us a clue as to how to go about differentiating between the void and the troubling 'nothingness' that can be found in our philosophical tradition, troubling because it evokes death. This differentiation is necessary because 'nothingness' is too close in appearance to the notion of the gaps between instances, the intervals of time. One could argue that these gaps, the void, are a variation on nothingness, which then becomes the abyss, and then death. But the void is not death. Death acquires philosophical meaning in the Bergsonian scheme of duration but also in a metaphysics which operates with the distinction between the absolute and the contingent, between infinity and finitude. The discourse on Nothingness is complex; it often has a theological dimension, so here only a few signposts can be indicated. One can begin with Blaise Pascal who said:

> He who regards himself in this light will be afraid of himself, and observing himself sustained in the body given him by nature between those two abysses of the Infinite and Nothing, will tremble at the sight of these marvels; and I think that, as his curiosity changes into admiration, he will be more disposed to contemplate them in silence than to examine them with presumption.
>
> For in fact what is man in nature? A Nothing in comparison with the Infinite, an All in comparison with the Nothing, a mean between nothing and everything. Since he is infinitely removed from comprehending the extremes, the end of things and their beginning are hopelessly hidden from him in an impenetrable secret; he is equally incapable of seeing the Nothing from which he was made, and the Infinite in which he is swallowed up. (Pascal 1958: II, 72)

The Poetics of Time 141

Man is a Nothing in comparison with the Infinite and he comes from Nothing. What remains is respect for Death. It is in respect of this that Pascal reproaches Montaigne (for whom he harboured a deep dislike):

> One can excuse his rather free and licentious opinions on some relations of life; but one cannot excuse his thoroughly pagan views on death, for a man must renounce piety altogether, if he does not at least wish to die like a Christian. Now, through the whole of his book his only conception of death is a cowardly and effeminate one. (Pascal 1958: II, 63)

The tone for subsequent meditations of this kind was set by Kierkegaard's work *The Concept of Dread* (Kierkegaard 1973). Dread is a mood that cannot be attached to anything; it is a free-floating anxiety, unlike fear, for example, which is always a fear 'of' something. Since dread is not provoked by anything that can be identified it follows that it reveals nothingness; we know nothingness through those moods and emotions that do not seem to be attached to anything. Kierkegaard's reflections greatly influenced Martin Heidegger (he 'has gone farthest in analysing the phenomenon of anxiety'), who himself says in *Being and Time* that 'Anxiety is anxious in the face of the "nothing" of the world' (Heidegger 1973: 393). In Sartre's *Being and Nothingness* we find the following: 'Nothingness lies coiled in the heart of being – like a worm' (Sartre 1956: 21). And this in Emmanuel Levinas: 'The fear of nothingness is but the measure of our involvement in Being' (Levinas 1978: 20).

Bachelard expressed a deep dislike for this conception of Nothingness.

> The philosopher heeds to the absolute. He mistrusts images; he has no need of images. For him ideas are enough. There are some ideas that are so quick that they are no longer active ideas. Such is the idea of nothingness. The philosopher applies it to everything without realising that the 'application' of each idea is the sole measure of its reality, of its efficacy. Thus Nothingness [*Néant*], Emptiness, Nothing [*Rien*], No, are handled like torn paper. Negation is immediately in operation. It permits the thinker a turn around in the realm of his ideas. It makes the *other* cheap, without effort, without responsibility, with a stroke of his pen. The philosopher – this king without a kingdom – reigns

through his negativity. But to destroy is a different labour than to negate. One never knows if the work is finished, if the world retains a trace of what one has destroyed. And above all, one is never at peace when one has a soul of a destroyer. Destruction has to destroy the one who destroys. The ruin is in us. (FPF 11)

But a question needs to be asked: why would we experience anxiety, dread or fear when confronted with nothingness? Anxiety, dread and fear are states that signal a menace to the I, when the sense of selfhood is under threat. They are premonitions of the nothingness of death; they echo the groundlessness of human existence. The Buddhists retort: '*When one has destroyed the erroneous belief in the I, one can surmount death*', and there is therefore no need for anxiety, dread or fear to arise; this is when the void gives. 'The first clear thought is the thought of nothingness' Bachelard insists in *La Dialectique de la durée* (DD 9, 30). This nothingness does not provoke dread, it entices an act, 'every creation springs from a sort of psychic nirvana' (PR 137, 159). The Buddhists, it is interesting to note, distinguished two types of the void. There is the void out of which instants emerge but there is also a 'void of passion, void of existence, void of bonds of pleasure, and from this void, they make clear, things are not born' (Silburn 1989: 154). (And we learn from Silburn's text that in Sanskrit these two are denoted by different words which, one can easily see, have different roots, *suñña* would be the void, *ākiñcañña* the barren nothingness.)[6]

The interregna in time are the principle of intermittency. They affirm as they break the deadening inertia of duration, they are the principle of change and difference, they open the possibility of the new. Death effaces, discontinuity affirms. Poetry is born in the lacunae of duration, where there is absence. This absence is not the annihilating nothingness, the black hole from which there is no escape, it is a 'not now' a 'not here', a mode of the intermittent being; the vanity of the heroic confrontation with Nothingness is alien to it.

No, something better must be found, a better reason, for this to stop, another word, a better idea, to put in the negative, a new no, to cancel all the others, all the old noes that buried me down here, deep in this place which is not one, which is merely a moment for the time being eternal, which is called here, and in this being which is called me and is not me, and in this impossible voice, all the old noes dangling in the dark and swaying in a ladder of smoke, yes, a new no, that none says twice, whose drop will fall and let me down, shadow and babble, to an absence less vain than inexistence.

        (Samuel Beckett, *Texts for Nothing*)

Concluding Remarks

I

What is most striking about Bachelard is the utter singularity of his project. As Étienne Gilson remarked in his Foreword to the English translation of *La Poétique de l'espace*, 'he was a free mind, unfettered by any conventions either in his choice of the problems he wanted to handle or in his way of handling them'. In the process he drew a philosophical landscape of great originality but nevertheless he very much belonged in his milieu, he was widely read and his work had a considerable impact on his contemporaries.[1]

The most lasting and tangible presence of Bachelard is without doubt to be found in French philosophy of science. But it is also his epistemological views that have provoked opposition. There is a point in returning to this question and to the sentence cited earlier that contains in a nutshell the reason for the negative reaction: 'one can see that the interests that life presents are supplanted by the interests that the mind presents' (FES 251). Isabelle Stengers objected specifically to the idea that one can distinguish interests in this way and from her point of view (and in fact from any) it does hit a disagreeable nerve. However, before rushing to rash conclusions it might be better to hold back and look calmly at Bachelard's pronouncement. Bachelard speaks of the interests that life presents and not of the interests *of* life, *intérêt à la vie* rather than *intérêts de la vie*; which is unfortunately how Stengers misquotes Bachelard (Stengers 1995: 34). He is not pitching scientific activities against the interests of life, and it is difficult to imagine that he would accept such activities as legitimate let alone desirable. One should say that there is something rather abstract about what he is saying: Bachelard treats scientific (phenomenotechnical) activities as an outcome of rationalist efforts, much in the way a work of art is seen as result of artistic effort. But he does not give any consideration to the impact that scientific activities might have on the world we live in. This might seem a little strange but one should remember that this was not an identified concern in his generation;[2] would he be more sensitive to these questions if he were active today?

Also, Bachelard is displaying what seems to be part of a surrealist make-up, namely, a disdain for everyday reality, for the common, for the mundane; typically, art that represents reality was of no interest to the Surrealists (Breton disliked Renaissance art so intensely that he never travelled to Italy). In the post-four elements writings Bachelard distanced himself from his earlier views and the surrealist contempt for the common and everyday is no longer evident; it is doubtful whether he would voice the same opinion in his later period. Still, the sentence is there: the distinction is made between life and reason and one can see why it might leave a bad taste in the mouth . . .

But there is also another reason for bringing up this question. Viewing the matter from a different perspective, one could say that Bachelard is pointing out (inadvertently, it would seem) a rather unpalatable truth about scientific rationality – its intrinsic amorality. Driven by an insatiable hunger for the new, scientific rationality detaches itself from the interests of life, and this means that scientific rationality is immune from ethical considerations. Rationality may have an aesthetics, but it does not have an ethics. Further, if we take on the consequences of Bachelard's distinction between the interests that life presents and those of reason then we are bound to conclude that science is too important and has too much of an impact on everyday life to be left in the hands of scientists alone. If we want a new contract with nature, as argued by Serres and Stengers, we cannot expect scientists themselves to forge this contract. This is one of the points that Feyerabend argues so forcefully in *Against Method* (Feyerabend 1993) and in his subsequent writings. (Bachelard himself did not seem to see this consequence as deriving from his own distinction between reason and life; if he had, he would not have advanced the idea of a *Cité Scientifique*, where the cream of scientific minds would gather to think up ways of constructing new surrealities. It is not clear whether this idea is indeed desirable, although it is consistent with the separation of common knowledge and scientific rationality that Bachelard argues for, and with the fact that scientific activities are always collective. Yet it is also a somewhat odd idea in Bachelard's universe as it comes across as something that could lead to an elitist society, and elitism is not a feature of his thought. As it happens, it is a rather marginal idea, only mentioned fleetingly.)

But Bachelard's thought needs to be put in a wider context. It is useful to begin by following Foucault's observation that, for all its diversity of themes, French contemporary philosophy has two dominant currents:

> While fully aware of the distinctions that have, during these last years and since the end of the war, opposed Marxists and non-Marxists, Freudians and non-Freudians, one-discipline specialists and philosophers, academics and non-academics, theoreticians and those involved in politics, it seems to me that one could find another line of separation that runs through all these oppositions. It is the line that separates a philosophy of experience, of the sense, of the subject and a philosophy of knowledge, of rationality and of the concept. On the one side it is the filiation from Sartre and Merleau-Ponty; and on the other side from Cavaillès, Bachelard, Koyré and Canguilhem. (Foucault 1994: 764)

Cavaillès, Koyré, Canguilhem and Foucault himself were mostly involved in questions of science, so we are in the epistemological circle.[3] Further names could be added: Léon Brunschvicg, Émile Meyerson, Abel Rey, Pierre Duhem preceded Bachelard; François Dagognet and Gilbert Simondon followed quite closely in his footsteps. This is an illustrious list and Bachelard's place in it is very prominent. We can further underline this prominence by quoting one commentator's remark that Bachelard's first work, *Essai sur la connaissance approchée*, was the 'birth of twentieth century epistemology' (Quillet 1964: 17). But, paradoxically, the more Bachelard's prominence in French epistemology is highlighted the more of a disservice is done to him. Today this illustrious lineage is a Tradition, and raised on a high pedestal within it is not where Bachelard would want to be; his dislike for the tradition was quite real.

Bachelard's impact on thinking about science can be made tangible and is well recognised, but clearly his purview is much larger – the fact that figures like Lyotard, Starobinski, Blanchot,

Minkowski and Hyppolite wrote texts on him attests to this. Bearing in mind how widely Bachelard was read by his contemporaries many echoes, if not strong influences, can be found in their writings. It is something about Bachelard's style of thinking that has had an impact. This 'style of thinking' can be characterised by the following precepts: the rejection of the notion of transcendence or any other overarching metaphysical unifying principle; the rejection of the notion of Truth which is approximated by efforts of rationality; the rejection of the concept of the subject or identity as a stable autonomous agent. One of the consequences of these initial premises is a penchant for breaking up discourses and an advocacy for a pluralist view; for arguing that facts are human constructs; for underlining the importance of error in epistemological thought. Such notions as discontinuity, break, gap, interruption and rupture have entered the philosophical vocabulary. It is probably this that makes the French philosophers of that generation so distinct. Many of these themes feature prominently in Bachelard's writings; in fact, he was the first to articulate them with full force and to draw from them philosophical consequences that are so striking in their originality and depth.

Foucault singles out the question of discontinuity as the most important and distinctive of the concepts that came from Bachelard. However, it is not discontinuity for its own sake, and certainly not simply an original way of 'doing history'. Discontinuity is the possibility of breaking with the past; it announces the possibility of the new, of the surreal. In this Bachelard in a sense opened a new philosophical space. When he entered the fray the world of philosophy consisted of Reality, Truth, the World, and a metaphysical scaffolding of Essence, Existence, Being, Transcendence, *Telos*, History, Hermeneutics and various *a priori* postulates. This was a closed world, as Bachelard saw it: 'philosophies posit their principles as intangible, their primary truths as total and complete. [They] glory in their *closedness*' (PN 7, 7); philosophy only gives us '*categories* of understanding that are forms of intellectual prudence made concrete, fossilised states of intellectual repression' (L 155, 90). To offer (and perhaps abuse a little) an analogy: Bachelard's thought is akin to breaking out of the closed Newtonian world. However, his way of breaking out was simply to ignore his philosophical heritage, just as he ignored traditional concepts of rationality, formalism and logic.

'It is the new that is fundamental' (MR 7). This is Bachelard's credo; it is one of the most important notes on his scale, and the whole thrust of his thought is animated by it. While the immense originality of his epistemological writings is undeniable, to concentrate excessively on this aspect is to overlook another layer in his thought. One way of putting it is to say that what matters about Bachelard's work is not so much the necessity of understanding what he tells us about scientific developments – *la phénoménotechnique*, for example, although obviously this is important – but the ever present aspiration of his thought: how to render intelligible the emergence of the new. This is what should perhaps be heeded most: his exhortation to think the new. It was pointed out in the Introduction that one of Bachelard's principal concerns is to make philosophically understandable a mind that is at work. A mind at work is defined by the way it is in time; it is a mind that is drawn by the future, tempted by the new. This is a theme that runs through his writings on rationality, imagination and, naturally, those on time. A mind that is at work accepts the risk that comes from refusing the safe haven of tradition; it also requires the 'capacity for waiting and for watchfulness' (DD vi, 18).

2

> A man is a man to the extent that he is a superman. A man should be defined by those tendencies which impel him to surpass the *human condition*. (ER 25, 16)

These words have a Nietzschean ring to them and one could try to establish a stronger bond between the thought of Bachelard and Nietzsche. It is difficult not to be touched by the latter's distinct and powerful voice, and Bachelard himself certainly was; he does, in fact, make frequent references to him. Nevertheless, one should not rush into declaring him a Nietzschean (as some of my friends and colleagues have suggested to me), even though there are a good number of similarities in some of their ways of thinking. Bachelard would have known about Nietzsche's rejection of the concept of substance and about his views on the Cartesian 'ego' ('It is a falsification of the facts of the case to say that the subject "I" is the condition of the predicate "think". *It* thinks; but that this "it" is precisely the famous old "ego" is, to put it mildly, only a supposition, an assertion, and assuredly not an "immediate certainty"' (Nietzsche 1968: 214)). But the following declaration, taken from *The Gay Science*, makes one hesitate about thinking of Bachelard as Nietzschean:

> I want to learn more and more to see as beautiful what is necessary in things; then I shall be one of those who make things beautiful. *Amor fati*: let that be my love henceforth! I do not want to wage war against what is ugly. I do not want to accuse; I do not even want to accuse those who accuse. *Looking away* shall be my only negation. And all in all and on the whole: some day I wish to be only a Yes-sayer. (Nietzsche 1974: Section 274)

One could say that *La Poétique de l'espace* is written in this spirit so no objection to it as such can be voiced. What is at issue however is not an objection to this statement itself; it is that Nietzsche himself never adhered to this resolution and allowed himself to be haunted by the ghost of Callicles.

However, an important question that Nietzsche's name brings to mind needs to be addressed: the question of will – the 'will to power', after all, must be one of the most recognisably Nietzschean expressions. The question of will is quite prominent in Bachelard's thought (which is why it has been suggested to me that he is Nietzschean). In his epistemological writings he spoke of a nougonal noumenon that engenders the noumenon with a capacity to invent and transform concepts; in *La Poétique de l'espace* we read that the soul generates poetic images; and in his writings on time Bachelard argues for the superiority of willed time over lived time. So, the question is: is Bachelard's philosophy a philosophy of the will, some kind of voluntarism? To put it differently, are these just different ways of speaking about the conatus or vitality? Bachelard himself did not address this question directly, and the way he expressed himself leaves the matter a little unclear. He speaks about the 'inner light' in Rouault's soul which produces light in his paintings, and says that 'the fauvism is in the interior' (PE 5, xvii). Elsewhere, criticising the traditional conception of the atom he declares that the atom has a 'zone of *influence* rather than zone of *existence*', which could lead one to think of there being atomic points of energy in the manner of the energetic atomism of the eighteenth-century ontology of Ruder Boscovich and that similarly some kind of inner seed could be posited from which the will (which is force and energy) emanates. But this would not seem to be the right inference. Before any arguments are presented two remarks of a general nature need to be made. First, as just mentioned, Bachelard never addressed this question directly, and since rigour was not of uppermost concern to him, we sometimes find in his writings statements that should not be taken too literally; second, in our habits of speech in which verbs such as 'to want', 'to wish' and 'to desire', when preceded by an 'I', suggest an agency, there is an assumption of some kind of autonomous acting will and this assumption becomes a habit of thought.

However, the idea of an autonomous agency that would be the seat of the will is alien to Bachelard's thinking. To begin with, there is no substantive ego in which this will could be located, so to speak; Bachelard quite explicitly rejected the Cartesian ego. Further, just as he argues that a chemical substance should be viewed as an ex-tance, the ego is also extantially determined. To an extent, we are following here a line of reasoning similar to that of Halbwachs's on the nature of memory, which has already been referred to in Chapter 3. He argued that there is no such thing as a strictly private, self-enclosed memory: 'Memory outside the social framework which men living in a society use to fix and find their souvenirs is not possible'; therefore, 'there is no such thing as a souvenir which could be said to be purely interior, that is that can be preserved only in individual memory' (Halbwachs 1925: 63, 196). Likewise, will is relational; it is not something emanating from an isolated 'I'; it cannot do so, since 'the unique has no properties'. This point must never be forgotten.[4]

So far so good, but this only tells us what the source of the will is not, and clearly something of a more positive content is needed because while memory might be thought of as 'resting' in a social frame, some form of intensity must be identified that could account for the emergence of will. Since the idea that the ego itself can be the source of this intensity has been rejected, one might be therefore tempted to revisit the notion of some vital force, but recourse to this is barred in the Bachelardian universe. The introduction of the notion of 'belonging' should help with the task of thinking through this problem.

Belonging exists as a noun – the cumbersome 'belongingness'; it also has a verb form and, tellingly, unlike 'I want', 'I wish', etc., the phrase 'I belong' does not announce an 'I' as an agency; rather, it opens a field, which announces that to which I belong. This field will act on me, it will make me act; it will determine reasons for acting and the form it takes. The sense of belonging need not be

Concluding Remarks   151

conscious but it is an engine of behaviour, a great deal of which is quite irrational from the strictly individual/ego point of view, like going to a funeral for example. Some complex emotions, such as embarrassment or empathy, are products of belonging. And a common observation tells us that a crowd can whip up in its members a frenzy which could never be theirs when alone.

Belonging is not unique to humans. In biology, behaviour which indicates collective identity, that is, that can only be accounted for by the sense of belonging, has been attributed to viruses. Viruses are the borderline between the inanimate and animate world and it seems that the notion of belonging can be legitimately extended into the inanimate world. This is justified upon realisation that no form of activity is a necessary requirement for belonging (belonging to a family, for example). Belonging may manifest itself in numberless ways; but it can also be conceived in various ways. Things can belong to a logical category, to a series; ideas belong in a chain of reasoning, etc. Reflecting on this further one can conclude that belonging can be posited as a basic ontological principle: *Everything that exists belongs; to exist and not belong is not possible.* (This could be a good starting point for thinking of hylozoism.)

Bachelard never expressed himself in this way but it would seem very much in the spirit of his thought, since he endlessly stressed that phenomena viewed in isolation make no sense. In *Le Rationalisme appliqué* he discussed at some length the question of inter-subjectivity in science and the circulation of ideas and definitions within scientific discourse: it is their inter-relation that gives them meaning (RA 31–64).

> The determination of an essence can only be made relatively to a body of notions in the ordering of correlative essences. There is no punctual rationality, it is necessary to envisage a developed rationality in solidarity with an inclusive rationality. An idea is clear because of the clarity of the associated ideas. Even at the level of a well defined idea there is in play a sort of extroverted character of the definition. Essentialism, in a philosophy of rational relations, is an extrinsicism [*extrinséquisme*]. Thus an isolated idea is not a casket-essence [*essence-cassette*]. Its richness comes from its circulation, from its conversions of values, from its relations with other ideas, from its more and more numerous engagements in constructions, either technical, either theoretical, but always rational. [. . .] Existential thought is here joined by co-existential thought. (RA 33–4)

And Bachelard adds further:

> For there to be co-existence, in the sense that we are using it, there is need of a mind that makes entities co-exist and, of course, this mind must be active, it must be a *determined activity*. Therefore this co-existence requires a focalisation of the subject. But we will soon see that this focalisation of the subject is accompanied by an inter-subjectivity which gives culture a special sign of objectivity. (RA 41)

It is not entirely clear how the 'focalisation of the subject is *accompanied* by an inter-subjectivity'. In other words, can we have an experience of inter-subjectivity? And, further, can we experience inter-subjectivity and yet retain the sense of the 'I'? Once we replace the notion of the experience of inter-subjectivity with that of belonging somehow it seems this difficulty does not present itself anymore.

Had Bachelard become attracted to the question of belongingness, which is not improbable, he would no doubt be tempted to dialectise it and perhaps speak of a *catagenic* belonging and an *anagenic* belonging, but we cannot pursue here this hypothetical line of thought which would rapidly become rather complex and take us away from the *propos* of this study. What needs retaining in this context is the contention that it is belonging that can generate the intensity that makes possible the emergence of the will, it is not a property of the agency of 'I', nor is it some vital force.[5]

There is another important dimension in Bachelardian will that needs to be considered. This Bachelard had already articulated in relation to Halbwachs and in various other contexts. It is of a temporal order: the mind and the soul are driven by a will for the future; their intentionality is not directed at already existing objects of the world but by what is yet to come. Therefore, while belonging generates the necessary intensity from which the will can emerge, it is the promise of the new that is the axis of will and desire. And the following must be stressed: belonging makes the emergence of will possible, but an act of will, a real act of will, is a solitary act; it is an instant in which some disengagement from belonging (which is a form of duration) takes place.

3

Bachelard began his intellectual adventure exploring the mind and rationality as it expresses itself in scientific activities. In *L'Intuition de l'instant* and *La Dialectique de la durée* the path of the soul and well-being, the path that led to the poetic image, is opened. 'By placing human life in the framework of these great natural rhythms we are determining happiness rather than thought' (DD 148, 152). Bachelard followed both these paths most of his philosophical life. But he did not remain faithful to both to the end. His last years were exclusively devoted to the poetic image and his interest in epistemology seemed to wane. Why? The answer is not difficult to formulate. The surrationalist Odyssey did not bring the hoped-for fruit: the spiritual renewal that Bachelard expected, and announced in 'Le Surrationalisme', was not fulfilled, and he eventually committed himself to the imaginary. Let us quote again the apparent reason:

> As I was engaged in the practice and teaching the sciences in philosophy I never felt as fully happy as I had hoped. I searched in vain the reasons for my dissatisfaction until one day, when in the familiar surroundings of practical works [*travaux pratiques*] at the faculty at Dijon I heard a student speak of my 'pasteurised universe'. This was a revelation to me. There it was: a man cannot be happy in a sterilised world ... I ran to the poets and put myself in the school of imagination. (In Quillet 1964: 21)

Can we be more precise about this? We can begin by looking at an interesting observation from Schrödinger:

> I believe it to be true that I actually do cut out my mind when I construct the real world around me. I am not aware of this cutting out. And then I am very astonished that the scientific picture of the real world around me is very deficient. It gives a lot of factual information, puts all our experience in a magnificently consistent order, but it is ghastly silent about all and sundry that is really near to our heart, that really matters to us. It cannot tell us a word about red and blue, bitter and sweet, physical pain and physical delight; it knows nothing of beautiful and ugly, good or bad, God and eternity. Science sometimes pretends to answer questions in these domains, but the answers are very often so silly that we are not inclined to take them seriously. So, in

brief, we do not belong to this material world that science constructs for us. (Schrödinger 1996: 95)

The one difference that stands out is that while Schrödinger says that scientists are not aware of cutting themselves out of the world in which they operate, Bachelard was very conscious of this process; moreover, he even turned it into a virtue. And yet, he also found himself astonished to see that in his epistemological writings he was propagating a sterilised universe. In the comment above we learn that this happened in Dijon in the 1930s. So Bachelard did not immediately run to the poets, and he certainly did not abandon his research on epistemology. But things did change. Somewhat unexpectedly, this can be seen more clearly in the writings on the imaginary. In the early *Lautréamont* Bachelard pronounces the need to destroy the everyday view of the world in order to create a space for the poetic imaginary, 'we must break down images and behaviour to find the *res novae* within and without us. [. . .] The past of the real, the past of perception, of memory, the world and dreams give us only images to be destroyed and smashed' (L 149, 87). This is not very different from his sometimes belligerent attitude towards common knowledge in *La Formation de l'esprit scientifique*. This does not compare with the mood of *La Poétique de l'espace* where we read that the image 'always starts the same way, it flees the nearby object and right away it is far off, elsewhere, in the space of *elsewhere*' (PE 168, 183–4). The imaginary no longer destroys; it flees to find its freedom. And in *Fragments d'une poétique du feu* Bachelard makes this statement:

> The poetic Reign is no longer in continuity with the Reign of signification. It establishes itself above the oscillation of the signifier and signified which the psychoanalyst must restrict himself to in order to disentangle enigmas. Sometimes the poetic image does violence to signification. The Surrealists have given many examples of this violence. It was a polemical necessity so the liberty of imagining could be awakened. But now, poetry having gained its right to verticality, a simple aerial exaltation of language gives us this liberty. (FPF 39)

In the end Bachelard's surrealism became very tempered. This went with his change of heart about the naïve. Nevertheless, it was the surreal that continued to reign. But it was the surreal that emerges from the soul; and the interests presented by the soul,

Concluding Remarks 155

which is born from breath, cannot be distinguished from those that emanate from life.

Earlier, a word was said about Bachelard thinking like a Buddhist. This seems the place to flesh out this thought a little further. In Chapter 3 we saw a great convergence between Bachelard's meditation on time and the teachings of the school of Dignāga. But there is a far more general dimension which gives all of Bachelard's thought a Buddhist tinge. Buddhism is a broad church but all Buddhist thinkers, whether they are followers of early Theravāda or of the later Mahayana, deny that there is such a thing as the ego-substance behind our consciousness, as a concrete, ultimate and independent unit, a closed off interiority, which we call a self. It is known as the doctrine of *Anatta* or *Anatman* (in Pali and Sanskrit respectively), which we would render 'no-ego' or 'no-self'. This is exactly Bachelard's position. 'The human being is a beehive of beings' (FPF 47) we read in his last, posthumously published, *Fragments d'une poétique du feu*. We can speak of a unity of the person, but it is always concentrated in the instant, *'the unity of the person*: the unity of time grafted onto the Instant, unity of place on the Summit, unity of action concentrated on a Decision' (FPF 146). *Anatta* follows from the anti-substantialist position which is expressed in the doctrine of impermanence (*Anicca/Anitya*). This, again, is Bachelard's position. One could point out that Hume already voiced doubts about the concept of substance and the ego, but he voiced his doubts and moved on to consider other matters. Nietzsche was perhaps more inclined to accept the consequences that follow from these doubts, but Bachelard bases his entire *oeuvre* on the no-ego, no-substance principles, and he is remarkably consistent and radical, drawing all the consequences from these premises.

These remarks are not meant to turn Bachelard into a Buddhist thinker,[6] but bearing in mind that one of the stakes in his thought is to re-awaken new modes of thinking, then some sensitivity to Oriental thought, which is largely lacking in our tradition, might be helpful.[7]

Bachelard was a surrealist, and there is something of a Buddhist in his make-up, but there are some clearly recognisable philosophical themes in his work as well. He dissected the problem of substance, he made penetrating comments about the Cartesian ego and, of course, he wrote some very influential pages on the interface of science and philosophy. These are all modern themes, and his reflections on history and historicity could only be articulated by a contemporary mind. Yet, in a sense, Bachelard thought like a Presocratic philosopher. He was immensely drawn to the Pythagorean teaching but by temperament he was an Ionian. The four elements were as real to him as they were to the early Greeks; he dwelled in a hylozoic world ('everything I look at looks at me' (PR 159, 185)), and he thought like an atomist (more on this in the Appendix). And if one were to single out the most important concept against which he philosophised it would be the lifeless, motionless Parmenidean One, and the various guises in which it insinuates itself into philosophical thought; not Plato's offerings, for example, as Bachelard's was a Presocratic world before philosophers entered the arena of politics and power, before they felt the allure of the State, when philosophical thought could still be naïve.

A final thought: On reading about Bachelard's life we learn that during the First World War he spent thirty-eight months in the trenches (his principal task was restoring telecommunications systems that were constantly blown up during fighting). What this meant we can scarcely imagine today but we cannot doubt that it was an experience of sheer horror: every account of the trench war, from Erich Maria Remarque's to Siegfried Sassoon's, attests to this. Bachelard lived through over three and a half years of this horror but not a single reference to this experience can be found in his writings, not even a bare allusion; and he began his monographs on the four elements during the Second World War. Does this mean that Bachelard was indifferent to the madness of war? This is not the answer. It rather reminds us that amidst the worst that humans are capable of there are also those who continue to write poems, paint paintings, compose music, print books and teach; they refuse to succumb to the madness. Bachelard was one of these people and this is evident in his philosophical project. In his insistence on the capital importance of well-being he echoes the beautiful words of the earlier Greeks, *athambia, euthymia, eudaimonia, euesto* (serenity, imperturbability, happiness, well-being). Well-being is the secret of naïvety. In well-being we lose the timidity that hard rules impose, we trust our associations, we find our creativity. The naïve spirit laughs. The space of naïvety is the space of welcome.

Appendix: Bachelard and Atomism

Some Opening Remarks on Democritus, Epicurus and Pierre Gassendi

Bachelard's conception of time is atomist, and he thinks like an atomist. And yet, on the several occasions when I raised this point with my French friends and colleagues the response would usually be one of bafflement: Bachelard? atomist? This is strange since the atomist thought in his writings would appear evident: his two books on time have a clear atomist dimension, and in 1934 he penned *Les Intuitions atomistiques*, in which he traces the development of atomist thinking in scientific thought, from the early Democritus to the atomist universe of contemporary science. His interest never waned – the 1951 *L'Activité rationaliste de la physique contemporaine* is largely devoted to an analysis of atomist thinking in the new physics, and in the early 1950s Bachelard recorded a number of radio programmes, two of which deal with atomism. In *Les Intuitions atomistiques* we find the following appreciation of the importance of atomism:

> One can say that today's atomic science lights up all philosophical perspectives and that contemporary atomism is the most prodigious of metaphysics. Never has such a swarm of ideas been so alive around things, never has the seizure of the real been prepared from so far away as in our conquest of the infinitely small. So we will be right not to neglect any of the philosophical paths which we have retraced in this work. It will be necessary to find means of establishing correspondences between different philosophies to manage to really *think* the atom. (IA 155)

So why the bafflement when atomism is mentioned in relation to Bachelard? When one goes back to the early days of the doctrine, namely to the thought of Democritus, and begins to examine the matter a bit more closely, one quickly discovers that we have been taught the atomist doctrine poorly, with the result that when we hear the word 'atomism' the image of billiard balls bouncing off each other immediately springs to mind like a knee-jerk reaction. This image is wrong. The thought of the Greeks was far more subtle and complex than the mechanistic world commonly associated with it, and it is of great intrinsic interest. Let us now trace some of the features of atomist thinking from the early Democritus to contemporary developments; after this, it will be clearer in what sense Bachelard is an atomist.

The hopelessly meagre fragments of Democritus that have come down to our times set a limit to what can be said with confidence about his thought.[1] Nevertheless, it is clear that Democritus' system was coherent and consistent. This was at least Aristotle's view; although he makes his disagreements plain, he shows immense respect for the man, often singling him out as the most astute. Aristotle devoted a monograph to him, which has not, however, survived to our times either. Pyrrho, too, seemed to admire Democritus (Diogenes Laertius, *Lives*, IX 67).

Plato's reaction to Democritus also deserves attention, but for a different reason. According to Diogenes Laertius a story circulated that Plato wanted to burn Democritus' writings (Diogenes Laertius, *Lives*, IX 40). Diogenes goes on to say that Plato was only dissuaded from this when it was pointed out to him that the circulation of the writings was so wide that he could not succeed in destroying them all. One can believe the story or not. On the one hand Diogenes takes as his source a certain Aristoxenus who was apparently notorious for spreading libellous gossip, and therefore not trustworthy; on the other hand, the sentiments that Plato expresses in the *Laws* make it plain that burning books would have been well within his range (and if it is true that this was the fate of Protagoras' books, as Diogenes Laertius tells us was the case (IX 52), the Athenians would have tolerated such a measure). What is nevertheless incontestable is that, in all his writings, Plato not even once mentions Democritus' name, and it is this that makes Diogenes think the story might be true.

What was it that Plato found so unacceptable? Clearly, a doctrine that lacked any sign of divine design must have been anathema to him. But if Democritus had argued using a primitive mechanistic atomism Plato would have had no difficulty in destroying the arguments. We know from his treatment of the Sophists that when dealing with opponents he did not shirk from conflict and was capable of underhand tactics. Why not do the same to Democritus? Diogenes thought that Plato feared having 'to match himself against the prince of philosophers' (Diogenes Laertius, *Lives*, IX 40). Maybe; but it still does not tell us anything concrete about Democritus' views (and Diogenes' own account is too brief and sketchy to be of much help). Nevertheless, everything suggests that he was a philosopher of immense depth.

Although Democritus was a contemporary of the first Sophists and Socrates, his views belonged to the earlier period; he inherited the Ionian tradition, he knew and admired the mathematical ontology of the Pythagoreans, but, most of all, his system was a response to the shackles of the doctrine of Parmenides of Elea. It is against the Parmenidean backdrop that atomism comes into full relief. These are the salient features of the Eleatic doctrine:

The goddess reveals to Parmenides the way to seek truth. It begins with a simple premise: the object of any inquiry either is or is not. The idea of inquiring into something that is not is rejected as meaningless. Therefore, what we say, think, must exist: it *is*. This something that is cannot lapse into non-being, therefore it cannot change. Following this insight and never diverting from his resolute path, Parmenides establishes a system of uniform constancy of the unchanging One. The One is a plenum that knows no void; it is continuous and complete; it is not subject to time, it does not move, it cannot change. This is the 'Way of Truth', which can only be apprehended by the mind, independently of the bodily organs. The ordinary mortals' view that the world is varied and changeable is a delusion induced by the senses: it is the false 'Way of Seeming'.

Parmenides' doctrine was the first philosophical system that made a point of violating every ordinary person's experience of the world, 'next door to madness' was Aristotle's view (*On Generation and Corruption* 325a19), and at the same stroke established a philosophical realm which can only be grasped by superior reason or, as in his case, come through divine revelation. Here we see the beginnings of a purely metaphysical path, which operates by the law of exclusion. Experience, perception, imagination, everything that enters our daily lives, is the false 'Way of Seeming' and is banished from the realm of a philosophy that enquires into Truth.

Already in antiquity Democritus' doctrine was presented as an attempt to reconcile everyday experience with Eleatic logic. The atomists did not seek an answer in divine revelation but in nature, that is, in their proper habitat. What they saw was a world that consists of an infinite variety of phenomena that are distinct and separated from each other. They assumed that the discrete reality, which gives rise to the world we perceive, should not be in principle any different. They went on to say that this discrete reality is made up of atoms that are in perpetual movement in the void. The atoms, the invisible bits of matter, are the smallest possible particles of matter; they cannot be divided any further. The atoms differed in size, shape, position, arrangement, and possibly weight.[2] In one respect the atomists' theory complied with the Parmenidean stipulation: they held that all atoms are made of the same impenetrable stuff and that they are imperishable and immutable; every atom was a miniscule One. But in another respect the theory departed from Parmenides: every single One was endowed with motion.

The doctrine of Epicurus that followed more than a century later is much better understood than the earlier doctrine, largely due to Lucretius' *De Rerum Natura* which it is thought faithfully presents Epicurus' thought. It is sufficiently different from earlier Democritean thought to speak of two distinct atomisms. Democritus was steeped in the Ionian tradition and wrote before Plato and Aristotle; Epicurus, the Athenian, was active after them. The details of their respective systems reveal considerable differences at the very basics: their concepts of the void and the movement of the atoms diverged.

While it is not clear whether Democritus attributed weight to the atoms, it is clear it did not affect the direction of their movement as he conceived them as moving in all directions; Epicurus did assign weight to atoms and as a consequence the natural movement of the atom is a downward vertical fall. However, no life would emerge if the atoms just fell in a straight line:

> One further point in this matter I desire you to understand: that while the first bodies are being carried downwards by their own weight in a straight line through the void, at times quite uncertain and uncertain places, they swerve a little from their course, just so much as you

might call a change of motion. For if they were not apt to incline, all would fall downwards like raindrops through the profound void, no collision would take place and no blow would be caused amongst the first beginnings: thus nature would never have produced anything. (Lucretius, *De Rerum*, 2.216–2.224)

This 'swerve' is known by its Latin rendering as the *clinamen* (from *clinare* – to incline); it makes atoms collide, and these collisions, in turn, form vortexes, from which various forms of life emerge. The *clinamen* was also the principle of indeterminacy in Epicurus' system:

it break[s] the decrees of fate, that cause may not follow cause from infinity, whence comes this free will in living creatures all over the earth, whence I say is this will wrested from the fates by which we proceed whither pleasure leads each, swerving also our motions not at fixed times and fixed places, but just where our mind has taken us? (Lucretius, *De Rerum*, 2.254–2.260)

Thus we have two founding images, so to speak, two starting points: dust for Democritus, rain for Epicurus. Michel Serres went a long way to argue that Epicurean atomism is a physics of fluids (Serres 2000). No such argument seems possible with Democritus, and not just due to the lack of extant texts. The two systems were genuinely very different, which incidentally makes Epicurus' claim that he learnt nothing from Democritus, which has at times puzzled scholars, perhaps a little more understandable.

In post-ancient times, atomism practically disappeared; in the intellectual climate dominated by the teachings of St Augustine there was no place for such a godless theory. It was reintroduced into scientific thought in the seventeenth century by Pierre Gassendi. Gassendi based his thinking in principal on the later Epicurean version. He 'cleaned up' the doctrine to make it acceptable to the Church (of which he was himself a loyal servant). He removed the *clinamen* and made the atoms move in all directions in conformity with Democritus' thought. He also removed the notion of multiple worlds as argued for by Epicurus and earlier advanced by Democritus.[3]

Gassendi was active as a scientist, mathematician and philosopher, but historians have a low opinion on his contribution to these domains. His great merit was to have argued the case for atomism and, most of all, for the legitimacy of the concept of the void: this he perceived as empty space, a pure physical nothingness, in which atoms moved. This new version of atomism was adopted by Newton; it was the kind of ontological hypothesis that the science of the time needed and it was on the whole accepted by the scientific community, although there was also some opposition (Ernst Mach and Wilhelm Ostwald being the most notable later examples). At the beginning of the twentieth century, the French experimentalist Jean Perrin confirmed the atomist hypothesis and it was practically universally accepted.

Democritus and Hylozoism

However, the atomism that re-emerged in the seventeenth century was a lifeless mechanics that could only be given some sense by positing an omniscient God who arranges that matter conform to a divine scheme, manifest in the immutable laws of nature. In time God was deemed unnecessary: 'Sire, I had no need of that hypothesis', the French astronomer Pierre-Simon Laplace famously declared; the laws of nature were so precise, he claimed, that in principle, if it were possible to take all the factors into account, any past or future event could be deduced from these laws.

> An intelligence knowing at a given instant all the forces in nature and the position of each entity in it, if it were powerful enough to submit all the knowledge to analysis, would be able to encompass in a single formula the motions of everything, from the largest physical bodies in the universe to the lightest atoms: nothing would escape its grasp, and the future, just like the past, would at once be present before its eyes.
> (In Pullman 1998: 272)

This was not the vision of Democritus. To begin with, on some counts he seemed to follow hylozoic principles. The picture at first may seem confusing. Heraclitus, for instance, is quite obvious; he bases constant change on a hylozoic substratum. On the other hand, a doctrine which claims at the outset that all that exists are bits of impenetrable, immutable matter and absolute void, lends itself to interpretations that lead to a theory of dead matter in mechanical motion. However, one important feature of the atomist system is hylozoic: Democritus did not conceive of any external force needed to set the atoms in motion (as did Anaxagoras whose multiple seeds were set in motion by *Nous*) or to organise the atoms and the void into a coherent world. The core premise that governed his thinking was the notion that matter is in perpetual movement and that this is its primary characteristic. (Aristotle viewed matter as essentially inert and insisted that movement was a phenomenon that needed explaining.)

Another aspect of Democritus' thought that suggests he was close to hylozoic thinking is his great interest in the question of heat and its connection with life.[4] Democritus is thought to have been the first to make a clear distinction between heat and fire; he observed that warmth (the soul) escapes gradually from the deceased body. The soul is made principally of atoms of fire. He studied other phenomena to do with temperature and heat, and advanced an explanation as to why liquids freeze. Newton's world is devoid of heat; it is not even cold, it is simply not alive.

Movement and heat, both present in Democritus' thinking, are the principal *sine qua non* ingredients of a hylozoic outlook of the early Greeks.

Furthermore, accounts of Democritus' system frequently present it as a world in which atoms are in perpetual movement, moving chaotically, bouncing off each other or hooking up into random structures. However, the account that Aristotle gives suggests a scheme that is more thoughtful:

> the differences [in the atoms] are three – shape, arrangement and position; being, they say, differs only in 'rhythm, touching and turning', of which 'rhythm' is shape, 'touching' is arrangement and 'turning' is position; for A differs from N in shape, AN from NA in arrangement, and Z from N in position [Z if turned 90 degrees becomes an N]. (*Metaphysics* A4 985b4)

Aristotle's words give a clear intimation that Democritus progressed far beyond a mindless mechanics since they suggest that he was working out a way in which the 'substantive' properties of the atoms could be represented either in terms relative to other atoms or in terms of their movement as dynamic systems but not in isolation. Most intriguing is the notion of 'rhythm'. It is a concept that came into philosophy from the Ionian thinkers and it clearly suggests some temporal dimension, but its etymology is obscure and it is difficult to be precise about its original meaning. (It is striking how

Democritus' dynamic temporal concepts are translated by Aristotle into geometrical forms, '"rhythm" is shape, "touching" is arrangement and "turning" is position'.) And here is a fragment of one of Democritus' preserved writings that casts further doubt on the seemingly random mechanistic character of his vision of the world:

> Living creatures consort with their kind, as doves with doves, and cranes with cranes, and similarly with the rest of the animal world. So it is with inanimate things, as one can see with the sieving of seeds and with the pebbles on beaches. In the former, through the circulation of the sieve, beans are separated and ranged with beans, barley-grains with barley, and wheat with wheat; in the latter, with the motion of the wave, oval pebbles are driven to the same place as oval, and round to round, as if the similarity in these things had a *sort of power over them* which had brought them together. (fr. 164, italics added)

This is the fragment from which we know about Democritus' principle of 'like tends towards like', a crucial part of his doctrine according to most commentators. The expression 'a sort of power over them' is quite striking as it suggests that atoms not only collide haphazardly, but also react to each other at a distance, or to be more precise, are drawn together by a power which is not their own (and, of course, is not of a divine nature). It is also worth noting that Democritus proceeds with his demonstration by first drawing examples from the animal world and then saying that the same happens in the inanimate realm; a mechanistic description would present the demonstration in the reverse order.

The Atom in Contemporary Thought

We shall return to Democritus, but the above observations seem sufficient to indicate that his world was quite different from the one propounded by Newton. However, another thing must be pointed out: although the ancient Greek systems and the seventeenth-century atomism differ in many respects, a fundamental element of the theory remained unaltered: in Democritus, in Epicurus and in seventeenth-century mechanics, the atom is conceived as immutable and imperishable; it is seen as a mini Parmenidean One that is a constant block in the universe's fabric. This was to change. Perrin's landmark study *L'Atome* appeared in 1913. A year later isotopes were discovered and this began to unsettle the picture as it rocked one of the basic assumptions of atomism, namely, the atom's immutability. These were developments in chemistry. Earlier, physicists began to realise that the atom has an inner structure. In 1897 Joseph John Thompson detected a negative electricity charge in the atom, which led to the discovery of the electron. Then, in fairly quick succession, the structure of the atom was penetrated, its composite structure of a nucleus and electron was established, and sub-atomic physics was born. Contrary to what might at first appear this did not change the picture in any significant way, at least in the context discussed here; however, semantic slippage allowed what is still somewhat confusingly called an atom, literally an un-cuttable, to stand for a composite body made of primary particles. These particles in fact are atoms in the strict meaning of the term as being not divisible any further. (At least, this was the view of the physicists at the time when the first elementary particles, the electron, proton and neutron, were discovered.)

At this point, one could say that there was no substantial disagreement between the new discoveries and the speculations of Democritus. The picture became more complex when attempts at determining the exact nature of the electron threw up two conflicting theories: sometimes the electron seemed to behave like a particle, sometimes like a wave. So was the electron a wave or a particle? Or was it sometimes a wave and sometimes a particle? Two solutions to the problem were proposed. One was Heisenberg's uncertainty principle, which stated that the electron's dual characteristic was due to the impossibility of determining at one and the same time the electron's position and its momentum. The second solution was Bohr's complementary principle. This stated that the different theoretical models follow from different initial hypotheses. By this Bohr meant that it is impossible to separate the observer from the observed phenomenon; the initial hypothesis determines in advance the appearance of the phenomenon because the ways of conceiving, analysing and proving are already encoded in the hypothesis. We cannot see the wave and the particle at the same time. However, Bohr further argued that this is not because of a human inability to grasp the real nature of things but because the world (or 'reality') is itself inherently ambiguous and fuzzy; to Bohr, reality was akin to a Cubist painting, the multiple moving perspectives of Cubist works greatly appealed to him and influenced his thinking.[5]

Bohr and Heisenberg's views became known as the Copenhagen interpretation of quantum physics. What is the status of the atom (i.e. electron) in this theory? It tells us that although its existence can be experimentally confirmed, strangely it is impossible to conceive of it as a simple particle; it cannot be said 'in one word' what 'one thing' an electron is; in fact, it is not possible to say that it *is*; it *behaves* either as a wave or as a particle, but it cannot be an electron pure, so to speak. Nevertheless, although their exact nature could not be determined, the particles/waves were still thought of as being out there, in the manner of imperishable units from which the universe is built. This view came to an end with the hypothesis of Paul Dirac presented in 1928. Dirac was exploring the link between mass and energy, or their equivalence; the fact that energy is manifest in different states and that it is emitted in little packets or quanta, as Max Planck called them when he first discovered this phenomenon. Through an analysis of the positive and negative energy states of the electron Dirac arrived at the conclusion that an electron must have a corresponding anti-electron. Further, Dirac speculated that on meeting, the electron and anti-electron will annihilate each other and disappear in a burst of gamma rays. Inversely, an electron and anti-electron can be created out of a sufficient amount of energy. Dirac's conclusions were later confirmed experimentally with the discovery of the positron (which was the name given to the anti-electron) by Carl D. Anderson in 1932. This brought about a startling realisation: matter is coupled with anti-matter and particles can be created and annihilated; Democritus was wrong: atoms are not imperishable. The kind of change Dirac's theory effected is best summed up in this comment from Heisenberg:

> I believe that the discovery of particles and antiparticles by Dirac has changed our whole outlook on atomic physics [...] Up to that time I think every physicist had thought of the elementary particles along the lines of the philosophy of Democritus, namely by considering these elementary particles as unchangeable units which are just given in nature and are always the same thing, they never change, they never can be transmuted into anything else. They are not dynamical systems, they just exist in themselves. After Dirac's discovery everything looked different, because one could ask, why should a proton not sometimes be a proton plus a pair of electron and positron and so on? ... Thereby the problem of dividing matter had come into a different light. (In Pagels 1986: 224)

A point that Heisenberg makes here must be underlined. Even though the exact nature of the electron seemed impossible to establish, until Dirac presented his hypothesis it was taken as certain that, much according to Democritus' idea, an electron was a constant, i.e. not subject to any change. Atoms (particles) were viewed as unchangeable units which are just given in nature and are always the same thing; they can never be transmuted into anything else. It should be borne in mind that all the thinking that led to the fall of the concept of the imperishable atom was consistent with Democritus' views, and indeed, we will not find ideas or formulations that are in conflict with the ancient atomists' thinking. Some of them, such as the new concepts of energy, or fields of force, gravitational, electro-magnetic, etc., were unknown to the Greeks; the mathematical apparatus has grown enormously; the concept of statistics is new – but, to repeat, none of these contradict the spirit of atomism. One commentator on Greek and modern science remarked: 'although [there is] hardly a single detail capable of withstanding the criticism of modern science, the ways of thinking of the ancient atomists were, none the less, essentially the same as those of our atomic theories' (Sambursky 1956: 119). This may seem a little surprising until we realise that the strength of the earlier atomists' thinking presumably lay not only in their initial assumptions, which have been largely demolished by contemporary criticism, but in the fact that their explanations did not rely on transcendental realities and/or teleological principles.

Still, a question arises: how is it that atomism in its development remained faithful to its own principles, and yet ended in abolishing one of its basic postulates, namely, that the atom is imperishable? It should be underlined that this did not come about as the result of an act of speculative daring like the questioning of Euclid's axiom about parallel lines, which led to non-Euclidian geometries. The postulate about the imperishability of the atom was never contested; it fell as a *consequence* of exploring and developing the atomist outlook. And it had to fall. Why? The answer to this question is surprisingly simple. Atomism was an attempt to break away from Parmenides. Leucippus and Democritus did it by positing an ontology of multiplicity as against Parmenides' One. However, in conceiving the atom as immutable and imperishable the atomists made a compromise: their atom was an exact replica of the Parmenidean One, albeit miniaturised and in a multiple and moving form. This one concession to Parmenides was an alien import into the system, it was atomism's principal weakness as it was exactly the notion of an everlasting primary substance that pushed atomism into a mechanistic materialism.⁶ Dirac's 'correction' of atomism's basic postulate amounts to an exorcism of the ghost of Parmenides from the atomist universe; the ballast of immutability and imperishability was thrown off and atomism could be thought anew.

One further clarification is necessary. It sounds a little too easy to say that the Parmenidean element of the atomist thinking was simply dropped. This was only possible once the doctrine had been subjected to a rigorous rationalist analysis, that is, a mathematical analysis. To do this the visual image of the atom had to be bracketed out. Dirac did not 'imagine' antimatter: he was told about it by mathematics (and was apparently at first somewhat perturbed by the message).

The Void

One might be inclined to think that this brought traditional atomism to an end, as it would seem to be demonstrably wrong; after all, the Ancients' idea of the atom turned out to be untenable and therefore the doctrine is of no more than historical interest. But this would be too hasty. Democritus' conception of the atom was only one element of the doctrine. There are other aspects of his thinking that need to be considered.

Let us look at some of Heisenberg's comments on the earlier doctrine. His nutshell summary states: 'In the beginning was the particle' (Heisenberg 1971: 133). Elsewhere, opening his reflections on the atomists, he says: 'The concept of the atom [. . .] has its origin in ancient Greek philosophy and it was in that early period the central concept of materialism as taught by Leucippus and Democritus' (Heisenberg 1990: 47). These statements may seem a fair reflection of the views of those early thinkers but, as it happens, not altogether; in fact, they are somewhat misleading. This is not the way the Ancients presented the doctrine. The most common opening formula that they used was almost always the same: Aristotle stated that 'Leucippus and his associate Democritus say that the full and the empty are the elements' (*Metaphysics* 985b); Diogenes Laertius writes: 'The All includes the empty as well as the full' (*Lives* IX, 30), and Cicero repeats the same: 'Leucippus' elements were the filled and the empty' (*Academica*, II, XXXVII; translation modified).

Appendix: Bachelard and Atomism   169

This way of presenting the doctrine suggests that these early Greeks did not begin with atoms but with a dichotomy, an oscillation between what is and what is not, between absence and presence; that is, they begin with a dialectics. But there is more to it than just a dichotomy. In Democritean terms the atom and the void are presented in three different ways, all of which cast them as opposites: aside 'the full and the empty' formula, the two elements are presented as 'the existent and the non-existent' and 'the thing and the nothing'. At least two commentators, David Sedley and Frédéric Nef, seem to have arrived independently at the conclusion that Democritus might have been conceiving of a negation of substance: 'the void is the privation or negation of the full' (Nef 2011: 113), the void is 'not empty space but the negative substance which occupies empty space' (Sedley 1982: 179).

The fragments and doxography of Democritus' thought are too scanty to permit us to go any further than these conjectures, but one thing is clear: Democritus' void is complex and certainly cannot be reduced to Newtonian empty space. And there is a further point to be made about presenting the ancient doctrine as having the atom as its central concept, as Heisenberg does: its consequence is that the void is pushed into the background. Yet it was not the idea of the atom that was the most original ingredient of the theory; it was the concept of the void. This was a contentious proposition from the beginning. It was a violation of the Eleatic world; Aristotle pronounced himself against it. The fact that the Greeks did not have the concept of zero must also have affected their thinking. (What would the Pythagorean system have looked like if it had had to incorporate zero?) Mediaeval thought rejected the void with such meaningless utterances as 'nature abhors the vacuum'. Western philosophy's agenda was dominated by the intricate scheme of the Great Chain of Being, which, following the 'principle of plenitude' (that is, that God does not allow any potentiality for being to remain unfulfilled) expressly forbade the void.[7] Tellingly, many of the scientists and philosophers who were inclined to adopt the atomist theory went along with it only as far as the concept of the atom was concerned, but they did not accept the void. It was argued that the space between the atoms had to be filled with some very subtle substance; Descartes spoke of a 'subtle matter', which was most often referred to as ether, conceived as an omnipresent medium. Newton, too, throughout his life toyed with the idea of incorporating the concept of ether into his thinking. In the event, he did not; the final scheme of Newtonian mechanics is based on solid bodies moving in empty space; the void is no more than a passive container.

The fact that the void (empty, nothing, non-existent) was consistently seen as the opposite of substance (full, thing, existent) already takes us away from the 'space the container' image of the void. The void is an element itself and thus it shares some characteristics of the 'full'; it is also capable of locomotion, for example; something that we can imagine when thinking of a moving gap between cars in traffic or a vacuum in a thermos flask that we carry around.[8] In the following comment, Aristotle indicates that the void is not passive, it is also the cause of things: '[. . .] they [Leucippus and Democritus] say being no more is than non-being [. . .] and they make these the material causes of things' (*Metaphysics* 985b5). Finally, we must consider the following:

> But people really think that there is an empty interval in which there is no sensible body [. . .] an interval, different from the bodies, either separable or actual, an interval which divides the whole body so as to break its continuity, as Democritus and Leucippus held. (*Physics* 213a27–b1)

This intimates that the void is a force, a force that 'breaks up' and 'divides'; it is because of the void that reality is discontinuous.[9] Discontinuity as a principal feature of reality is perhaps the most lasting legacy of Democritean thought; as Schrödinger said: 'quantum theory dates 24 centuries earlier, to Leucippus and Democritus. They invented the first discontinuity – isolated atoms embedded in empty space' (Schrödinger 1996: 158). The question of discontinuity is further heightened by the realisation that the void might have been conceived as the negation of the atom; discontinuity is a consequence of an act of negation. What exact form this negation took cannot be perhaps ascertained, but in this case it would seem clear that a 'no' introduces a discontinuity.

Because of the fragmentary character of the surviving writings of Democritus, it is difficult to present a secure reading of the available material. Much is left to conjecture and speculation. By contrast, thinking in the contemporary quantum world is open to full examination. It presents a complex picture with differing solutions, proposals and views, but whatever it is the void has nothing to do with the concept of passive space. The void can be conceived in several ways as 1) a field, 2) a latent state of reality (matter being its actualised state), 3) a permanent energy bank, 4) probability, 5) antimatter. The void is not emptiness, it has a mathematical structure; it is 'pregnant', so to speak; it is out of the void that matter emerges.

The Four Atomist Systems

It will be clear by now that the term 'atomism' is complex and that the seemingly simple formula 'there are only atoms and the void' has given rise to very distinct philosophical outlooks.[10] A comment on the term 'atomism' is necessary before proceeding any further. It is a seventeenth-century coinage; the Greeks did not have an equivalent term and spoke of the philosophy of Democritus (and Leucippus) or of the Epicurean system. They did not collapse them into some unified overview, as the so often used term 'Greek atomism' obviously does. How clearly the Greeks distinguished them is evident when we compare the entries for Democritus and Epicurus in Diogenes Laertius' *Lives of Eminent Philosophers*. These are two different men, from different epochs, with different temperaments, even if they do, of course, also share many convictions (materialism, the lack of a *telos* or divinity). The term 'atomism' is an obstacle in that it conjures up an initial guiding image, which shapes the thought: the problem is that when the Greeks are approached with this first image we are already on a wrong track; the image of billiard balls bouncing off each other does not do justice to Epicurus and is positively misleading with respect to Democritus. This would be an instance where Bachelard's argument about the negative value of images would be particularly pertinent.

We can overall identify four distinct systems based on the concept of atoms and the void. A brief résumé of these systems follows, showing some of the problems that each one presents and which are helpful for this specific enquiry (without presuming to be comprehensive or in any way offering a particularly authoritative reading of the early Greeks and subsequent developments in atomist thought):

1. The system of Leucippus and Democritus presents multiplicity and movement, a dialectics of the empty and the full; reality is conceived as discontinuous. Discontinuity is the source of

indeterminacy. These are the basic ontological outlines. An important epistemological consequence is the role of the dialectising negation in rationalist thought.

2. The Epicurean system also presents multiplicity and movement. We do not find in it, however, either the problem of negation or discontinuity; the indeterminate character of reality is the consequence of the workings of the unpredictable *clinamen*; deviation is the source of variety and changeability. The void is empty space. However, it is not the Newtonian homogeneous space that provides a uniform location in which physical bodies interact and that can be held within the confines of Euclidian geometry, a unity subject to metric measurement; rather, it is material, a vectorial space of networks of multiple paths, of different physical domains in which everything is local. '*Atomist physics is based much more upon a vectorial space than on a metric space*' (Serres 2000: 62).[11]

3. If Laplace is taken to be the crowning of Gassendi's atomism then we are presented with a deterministic world which is governed by immutable laws. It may be a godless universe but these laws operate much like St Augustine's doctrine of predestination, since, for example, we could in principle calculate which species are destined for extinction. Such a calculation is not in reality possible but that is what makes it so similar to predestination. The iron grip of inevitability is certain, only it remains just as inscrutable as the workings of God. This is not surprising, because the notion of a fixed immutable universal physical law has its origins in theology.

4. The post-Diracian quantum/wave universe is so complex and full of contradictions and disagreements that it does not make sense to attempt a general overview (and I do not have the necessary competence to undertake such a task). But in the context of these reflections it suffices to bear in mind that the void is conceived as being dynamic in nature; that the atom ceases to be an imperishable bit of substance as the older doctrines held; and that rather than discontinuity it would be better to speak of intermittency in order to add a temporal dimension to the scheme.

Bachelard and Atomism (Epistemology)

We can now try to locate Bachelard in this 'atomist' landscape. We will begin with his objections to the classical concept of the atom which he spelt out in some detail in *L'Activité rationaliste de la physique contemporaine*:

1. *The corpuscle is not a little body.* The corpuscle is not a fragment of a substance. It does not have properly substantial qualities. [...]
2. *The corpuscle does not have absolutely assignable dimensions*; it is only given *an order of grandeur*. This order of grandeur determines its zone of *influence* rather than zone of *existence*. [...] 3. *Correlatively, if the corpuscle does not have an assignable dimension, it does not have an assignable form*. To put it differently, the *element has no geometry*. [...] 4. *Since one cannot attribute a form to a corpuscle one can no more attribute to it a very precise place*. [...] 5. In a number of circumstances, microphysics poses, as a veritable principle, *the loss of the corpuscle's individuality*. [...] 6. Finally, the last thesis that contradicts the fundamental axiom of philosophical atomism: contemporary science admits that *the corpuscle can annihilate itself*. Thus the atom, of which the first function was to resist all intimate change and, *a fortiori*, resist destruction, no longer fulfils in contemporary science the function of absolute presence, of radical existence. The old adage: nothing gets lost, nothing is created, must be re-thought afresh. (ARPC 106–15)

Bachelard tended to lump all pre-contemporary atomist thought together because in all its variations it held the atom to be immutable and imperishable. He expressed a dislike of the Newtonian scheme: 'the Newtonian world was a spacious and lustrous abode. Newtonian physics was from the first a marvellously clear example of a closed system of thought. The only way out was by force' (NES 46, 44). As far as Bachelard was concerned, the old atomist systems were extinct. And since he was intensely interested in the developments of contemporary physics, it is also not surprising to find that he shared the new world-view. Like Bohr he stated that 'ambiguity attaches not to our knowledge of reality but to reality itself' (NES 55, 53). The revised status of the atom's existence sat well within Bachelard's anti-substantialist convictions. And here is an interesting passage from *Les Intuitions atomistiques*:

Look at this invisible world with the eyes of the spirit. Contrary to a universe where masses are stable, where the events are lazy and chained up, imagine a world that is multiple, discontinuous and of a perfect mobility, without friction and kinetic wear. Just make sure that all this is rationally possible, that is that no intimate contradiction slips into your first suppositions. Make also sure that nothing superfluous is added, in other words, that the system of postulates is complete and close. Once these preliminaries are established, close your eyes on the real and entrust yourself to intellectual intuitions. That way you will construct a rational world and you will produce unknown phenomena. (IA 150–1)

The world that Bachelard exhorts us to imagine is an atomist world, in the sense that it is multiple, discontinuous and of perfect mobility; most notably, however, the atoms as such, the ever existent entities always available to our scrutiny, are absent. It is within this atomist universe that Bachelard places scientific developments. This does not mean that he rejected the concept of the atom, only that he was of the view that it had to be re-thought. He did say in an early work that 'contemporary atomism is the most prodigious of metaphysics', and that if we were to 'really *think* the atom' (IA 155) lessons coming from the developments in contemporary physics would have to be absorbed. 'What is an atom?', which is a question about something that is assumed to have a determined existence, morphs into 'How do we think an atom?'

However, as it happens, Bachelard never carried out anything like a systematic attempt to arrive at a level of understanding where we could really *think* the atom. He did devote some pages to this question in *L'Activité rationaliste de la physique contemporaine*; at other times, he seemed to profess a sort of agnosticism on the matter: 'The atom is a mathematical society; it has not yet revealed its secret' (PN 40, 33). Most importantly, Bachelard did not systematically pursue the question because in fact this would be a task for a 'natural' philosopher, and this was not his principal interest, as has already been noted in the Introduction to this work.

The revival of atomist thought from the seventeenth century onwards took place in science, or in what could be called 'natural philosophy'; however, this new way of thinking did not so much penetrate 'pure' (so to speak) philosophical thought. Such a mechanistic world-view could not be of much interest to a philosopher, and furthermore the notion of the void remained unacceptable; Descartes rejected it, Leibniz riled against Newton's empty space, Kant also rejected the void. Bachelard's interest in atomism is not that of a 'natural' philosopher, he does not seek to acquire a better understanding of the mysteries of the universe but strives to comprehend how science can carry out a surrealist programme. The discoveries in the world of sub-atomic particles,

Appendix: Bachelard and Atomism

the conceptual breakthroughs, the developments in mathematics, all these fascinated Bachelard and he analysed them at length. But it is the laser, for example, rather than understanding the microscopic level of matter, that would have animated Bachelard more (as a young man, he did think of becoming an engineer). This device (its name stands for 'light amplification by stimulated emission of radiation') is a veritable surrealist machine, which produces an unheard of phenomenon: it is thought that lasing did not exist in the solar system before the laser was invented. It is a feat of science that demonstrates the role that mathematics plays in these developments since the possibility of producing the lasing effect was mathematically predicted in 1917 (by Einstein), some decades before the theorems could be reified into a phenomeno-technical device. At first, it was a rare physical effect produced in a far-off laboratory and nobody quite knew what use it might have; it seemed to be a solution to an as yet unidentified problem. It has since become ubiquitous.

The ontologising power of mathematics comes into full view and is put into effect in an atomist universe, in a world that is 'multiple, discontinuous and of a perfect mobility', but a world which is devoid of permanent substantial matter.

If in Bachelard's view science needs the new atomism to carry out its surrealist project this is not the only atomist feature in his thinking. Another is the very important role that discontinuity plays in his thought. Science breaks away from the natural world; there are discontinuities between different scientific *episteme*. Bachelard demonstrates these discontinuities and provides an explanation – science is discontinuous as a consequence of the atomist nature of our rationality: 'atomism does not come from material nature but on the contrary it comes from the modes of perception and intellectualisation' (IA 104). And he quotes from an 1895 text by Arthur Hannequin, *Essai critique sur l'hypothèse des atomes dans la science contemporaine*:

> Physical atomism is not imposed onto science by reality, but, rather, by our methodology and by the very nature of our knowledge. It would be wrong to believe that atomism necessarily implies the actual discontinuity of matter; it merely implies that we conceive of matter that way in order to understand it, and that mathematics as we know it introduces discontinuity while trying to describe it. (IA 104–5)[12]

This discontinuity manifests itself in rationality as a dialectics. We do not progress in science by lumping together certitudes, each certitude being a verified atom of knowledge; rationality cultivates a philosophy of no, it questions the seemingly most obvious assumptions and it will not contemplate notions which cannot be dialectised.

Bachelard and Atomism ('Metaphysics')

Bachelard never seriously took up the question of how to think the 'natural' philosopher's atom; he only catalogued all his objections to the classical view on the question. However, in *L'Intuition de l'instant*, a work that could be described as overtly atomist, the problem of the atom *is* addressed directly, except that this is not the atom of the natural world, but a temporal one: the instant.

Bachelard wrote *L'Intuition de l'instant* and *La Dialectique de la durée* in the middle of his earlier period of epistemological writings and therefore one might be tempted to think that his meditation on discontinuous time somehow evolved out of his thinking about the new sciences. There have been attempts to develop insights from contemporary science and then adapt and graft them onto a wider set of problems, such as working out a theory of consciousness based on the findings of quantum physics (as in Roger Penrose's *The Emperor's New Mind* (1990), for example). This was not Bachelard's route. He did claim that philosophy should learn from science but he meant by this that philosophy should learn from scientists' suppleness, their ability to discard old thinking and be open to the new; he did not argue that we should borrow from science concepts and solutions for other questions. He may state that 'of all the life energies, the mind energy [*l'energie spirituelle*] must be closest to quantum and wave energy' (DD 140, 145), and we will find an odd sentence of this kind here and there in his writings. On the whole, however, there are few of them and there are no sustained arguments based on scientific findings. For example, if we look at *La Dialectique de la durée*, we find that chapter II draws mostly from the psychology of Pierre Janet; chapter VII, in which Bachelard speaks of duration, resonance and rhythm, draws exclusively on writings of theoreticians of music; and the final chapter is entirely devoted to the presentation of Pinheiro dos Santos's *La Rythmanalyse*. There is only one specific reference to a contemporary scientist (Louis de Broglie).

It is not science that is the inspiration for *L'Intuition de l'instant*; this book comes from elsewhere. The very title is non-scientific and Bachelard's meditation on the instant was triggered, as he says himself, by the text of the historian Gaston Roupnel. He also picks as his adversary a philosopher, Henri Bergson, and couches his disagreements in philosophical terms; these are not questions to be settled by scientific arguments. (Tellingly, Bachelard makes no reference to Bergson's apparently unsuccessful attempt to refute Einstein in *Duration and Simultaneity*, which he probably would have done had he wanted to confront Bergson on the scientific terrain.)

L'Intuition de l'instant is a meditation on the temporal atom – the instant. Instants differ in intensity; this is so because the instant carries the Democritean duality of 'the full and the empty': there is 'a *'temporal alternative* [...] either in this instant nothing is happening, or in this instant something is happening' (DD 25, 44). Thus there are only instants; boredom is not some gluey duration, it is a succession of empty instants. Substance, life, thought are successions of instants forming through endless oscillations, vibrations, rhythms, a life of depth and mobility, a life that is tempted by the new, by the poetic instant.

While in Bachelard's epistemological writings the void manifests itself as discontinuity, it is within this temporal landscape that he poses the question of the void directly; and one should note that he does it in a language that would not be permissible in his work on science (hence the added italics): 'As soon as we accept the constitution of temporal atoms, we are led to think of them *in isolation*, and for metaphysical clarity of intuition, we realise that the void is necessary – whether it in fact exists or not – to *imagine* correctly a temporal atom' (II 27). Once the question of the void is voiced, its complexity becomes apparent. It can be articulated in two distinct ways. First, it is the principle of discontinuity, it breaks duration; it is the intermittent being. Second, it is repose; and it is out of this void, out of the psychic nirvana, that creative acts emerge.

The full and the empty, and discontinuity, are complemented by another ontological principle: movement. Movement, just like discontinuity, is omnipresent, as is also the case in the thought of Democritus and Epicurus. Bachelard speaks of the 'perfect mobility' of contemporary atomism. Already in *Essai sur la connaissance approchée* he speaks of an 'essential mobility of knowledge' (ECA 261), arguing that

> Consciousness is [...] the function of mobility and consequently of a number of points of view. It is because objective knowledge multiplies itself that we manage to detach ourselves from sensations. [...] [T]o constitute an I, as for constituting an object, an epistemological pluralism is necessary. (ECA 259)

In *La Poétique de l'espace* Bachelard speaks of an image that flees the object and is straight away elsewhere, in the space of elsewhere, in a time that vibrates. And the following remark that he makes on Kafka's *Metamorphosis* is quite revealing. He is appalled by the slowness of movement of Gregor, The Insect:

> [Gregor] lives in a time with no future. [...] If it is true, as Georges Matisse says, that one of the greatest calamities that can befall a living being is the inability to exercise the motor functions at any but reduced speed, it would seem that Kafka's metamorphoses occur under a malevolent sign. (L 19, 8)

On Philosophical Aspirations

W. K. C. Guthrie, commenting on Pythagoras, remarks: 'The keynote of any philosophical system is struck when we understand its aims'; and he then adds in a footnote:

> In case this sounds a slightly cynical statement, implying that philosophy is no more than a rationalisation of beliefs held before the enquiry begins, let me add that although *this is in many cases a fair judgment*, clear thinking itself may be a philosopher's aim as much as anything else. If so, this does not make an understanding of the aim any less important. (Guthrie 1962: 182 italics added)

Guthrie's remark is very telling. There are certainly cases where the question of establishing ways of clear thinking is paramount (Wittgenstein comes to mind, although there is obviously more to his work than just establishing rules for clear thought). However, on reading most histories of philosophy one could get the impression that philosophy is a gentlemen's club, busying itself with sorting out clarity in philosophical thought; but it is not. Philosophical agendas are very often driven by motives that are themselves not of a philosophical nature. In such cases it is these that determine the ontological choices, not simply philosophical considerations. The aspirations and motives behind these choices should be called anthropological prejudices, that is, they are specific assumptions about human nature. Plato's hostility to Democritus was probably animated by such considerations as the two held entirely different views on this matter.

Plato's views on the nature of humans are apparent in his political convictions, in how he thought a state should be organised. His thinking on these questions evolved and what he says in his last text, the *Laws*, is quite chilling. His recipe was simple: purge the populace of the weak. The purgation must be effective ('The best method of all, like the most potent medicines, is painful' (*Laws* 735d)). Ensure that your citizens act and behave the same way, regulate the festivals, make them all sing the same songs. Punish all acts of dissent with firmness. Avoid change ('Change – except when it is change from what is bad – is always, we shall find, highly perilous' (797d).) Prevent the good citizens from becoming bewitched by evil teachings by banning foreign travel (950d–953e).

> [T]he principle is this – that no man, and no woman, be ever suffered to live without an officer set over them, and no soul of man to learn the trick of doing one single thing of its own sole motion, in play or in earnest, but, in peace as in war, ever to live with the commander in sight, to follow his leading, and take its motions from him to the least detail – [. . .] in a word, to teach one's soul the habit of never so much as thinking to do one single act [alone]. (942ab)

Following such a commander will instil proper respect for the gods and the laws of the city. Those who are found by the courts to have offended against this upbringing are to be given no less than five years of solitary confinement and will be subjected to a 'cure'; if the cure fails they will be put to death, or banished for life in an extremely inhospitable environment. All this is regulated by the watchful eye of the Transcendent. Where is this? It is embodied in the 'nocturnal council', which holds its meetings 'before daybreak' (961b) and whose task is to instil in the citizens a 'settled fear of god' (967d). Would a philosopher want to live in such a society? The trivia of society's woes and difficulties in handling disobedient citizens are of secondary concern to a real philosopher, as we are told in another dialogue that his gaze is turned elsewhere: 'true philosophers make dying their profession' (*Phaedo* 67e).

Democritus and Epicurus breathe a different air; they seek to eliminate terror. Epicurus understood the problem very well: 'A man who causes fear cannot be free from fear' (Fragment 84). The perspective is reversed. Rather than establishing a One, a Being, a Truth as philosophy's invisible centre, we have a horizontal ontology not burdened by any form of the transcendent, an ontology that knows no hierarchy and where we can allow ourselves the optimism of reason. Atomism allows us to invent concepts and consider new lives; it is, in the strict meaning of the word, a poetics. And last but not least, it was Democritus, the laughing philosopher, who left behind the beautiful Greek words, *athambia, euthymia, eudaimonia, euesto*.[13] Perhaps these were the sentiments that provoked Plato's ire.

In a larger scheme of things, one could say that Democritus was trying to create a philosophy that gives us a multitude of universes, a discontinuity in which new realities or worlds may appear while others disappear, a philosophy without transcendence, without *telos*. This is an ontology of welcome, very different from the closed and deterministic world of Newton and Laplace, and the opposite of the claustrophobia and violence of Plato's cave.

These aspirations are shared by Bachelard. Although we can only infer a general trend with regard to Democritus, Bachelard's aspirations are clearly stated. He seeks to develop an ontology in which the new, novelty, is central. In Bachelard's thought the new has ultimate value and ontological discontinuity is, in his view, the condition for the emergence of the new. Hence the necessity to break durations, to destroy them (by force, if necessary (*Lautréamont*)), otherwise we risk finding ourselves locked in a Bergsonian duration, where no event can be radically new as it is always anchored in the *élan vital*. The scientific (surrationalist) programme is animated by a thirst for the new, and Bachelard's so-called 'metaphysical' thought in his writings on time could be summed up as an attempt to promote a psychology of beginning. The *instant*, the *new*, the *beginning* are key terms in the Bachelardian universe; these rest in a vibrating repose out of which wise action emerges. In this he is certainly close to the spirit of Democritus. Bachelard rejected the concept of the atom as a bit of material substance and opted for the primacy of resonance, frequency and vibration, but it was atomism that gave him an ontology of discontinuity, of perfect mobility, in which he could articulate his project.

The one difference is that Democritus attempted to accommodate the Eleatic stipulation about the unchanging, immutable and imperishable One; Bachelard did not. He may have argued against naïve thought (a notion that we have, incidentally, found rather vague), but one could say that his entire work is deeply anti-Parmenidean. We will not find a systematic critique, nor is Parmenides specifically targeted, but throughout his *oeuvre* he is wary of the core ideas that have evolved out of the Parmenidean thought: the One, Being, Subject, Substance, Reason and Transcendence; he is hostile to totalising concepts; ideas of immutability and immobility are monstrosities.

Bachelard referred to philosophers that follow the speculative metaphysical path as 'being-ists' [*étristes*].

> Philosophers of Being, philosophers '*étristes*', are indeed too easily convinced of the permanence of being in all modes of being. They hang on to being into its very mist. Barely born, they exist. And the reality of the world is an immediate guarantee of their existence in the world. Therefore, every spoken expression has to be an echo of the natural sonority of to be, of their being. Philosophers of being speak the world and speak their being in one and the same language. (FPF 40)

Atomism is the antidote to this; atomism is the instant, discontinuity, mobility. It is an open world in which one can belong but from which it is possible to escape, if need be; 'atomism [. . .] is the symbol of opposition to the metaphysical spirit' (IA 158).

'More men become good by practice than by nature' (Democritus fr. 242). This is not by any means the most often quoted fragment of Democritus, perhaps because what he is saying may appear a little too obvious, a truism; but sometimes obvious things need to be repeated. And there is a further point to be made, this fragment exhorts us to *do* things rather than just trust some inborn, intrinsic disposition (not to mention divine guidance). We become good through practice. When we remember what Bachelard had to say in *L'Intuition de l'instant* about constructing creative habits, there is little doubt that he would nod his head in agreement. But, in fact, more than that, he goes further, as though echoing Democritus (although he makes no reference to the fragment). The question of 'nature' does not come into it, needless to say: for Bachelard, a positive moral life requires '*inventing* good and not just doing it' (DD 143, 148).

Notes

Introduction

1. 'It is well known that Homer appears to credit man with a *psyche* only after death, or when he is in the act of fainting or dying or is threatened with death: the only recorded function of the *psyche* in relation to the living man is to leave him' (Dodds 1951: 15–16). In fact, the notion of *psyche* is not rare in Greek thought and it would take a long exposition to present all the different meanings attributed to it, but it is not a psychological space as it is conceived today, that is, a closed off seat of thought, will, decision, etc. The one possible exception is Plato's concept of maieutics, which is a technique of drawing out of someone knowledge that the person could have not acquired, yet, when properly guided, can display. (Socrates demonstrates the principle by getting an uneducated slave to answer correctly some simple questions on geometry (*Meno* 81c–86b).) This hints at an interior space where unconscious knowledge dwells, but no more than hints at it, and it was not Plato's aim to discover an interior space but to demonstrate the immortality of the soul, as he toyed with the idea of transmigration of souls.
2. The *agrégation* prepares lycée teachers and gives a thorough grounding in the history of philosophy. One obtains the degree through a very competitive national examination.
3. 'Pagan' has also other connotations. Jean-François Lyotard, for example, wrote a text *Rudiments païens* (1982) which gives the 'pagan' a political, militant dimension.
4. In France to refer to someone as having a *tête bien faite* is a compliment and is often contrasted with a *tête pleine* (after Montaigne's '*Mieux vaut une tête bien faite qu'une tête bien pleine*'). The first are those who know how to use their head, the others have a head filled with facts but little else. Someone coming out of the

École Normale Supérieure would be expected to have a *tête bien faite*.
5. All italics in this and subsequent quotes are in the original unless indicated otherwise.
6. The school *Télégraphes* trained engineers for the Post Office. Entry into it was as tough as for *agrégation*.
7. 'Imaginary' used as a noun sounds a little strange to an Anglophone ear, but it is not incorrect. It has a somewhat different resonance than 'imagination' (although the nature of this difference seems difficult to tease out). It is also a literal version of the French 'l'imaginaire' as used for example by Sartre in *L'Imaginaire: Psychologie phénoménologique de l'imagination* or by Gilbert Durand in *Les Structures anthropologiques de l'imaginaire*; it is used frequently by Bachelard and it will be retained in the present work. (Sartre's work was translated into English as *The Imaginary: A Phenomenological Psychology of the Imagination*.) And here, in Bachelard's own words: 'The basic word in the lexicon of imagination is not *image*, but the *imaginary*. The value of an image is measured by the extent of its *imaginary* aura. Thanks to the *imaginary*, imagination is essentially *open* and *elusive*. It is the human psyche's experience of *openness* and *novelty*' (AS 7, 1).
8. Gaukroger 1976, Bhaskar 1975, Cutting 1987, Rheinberger 2005 are authors who wrote on Bachelard's epistemology. For writings dealing with his influence on literary criticism see Bibliography in Gaudin 1987. (A book *Gaston Bachelard* by Roch C. Smith (Boston: Twayne Publishers, 1982) appears in some bibliographies of earlier texts on Bachelard but I have not been able to trace it.)
9. Hacking's familiarity with Bachelard's work and some debt to it is quite obvious, and of the philosophers linked with the analytical tradition he has been the most open to French thought. In his later work the influence of Foucault is also clear. From 2000 to 2006, he held the Chair of Philosophy and History of Scientific Concepts at the Collège de France, a post that would seem to be a recognition of his links with the French tradition.
10. Three years later Caillois, Bataille, Monnerot and Leiris were involved in setting up the *Collège de Sociologie* which was aimed very much *against* the Surrealist movement which they perceived as too individualistic and lacking a social dimension. (The *Collège* folded at the outbreak of the war.)
11. It must be said, however, that despite the sense of discomfort the books provoked, Bontems gives a good account of them and makes

some pertinent observations, particularly about the role of the concept of 'rhythm' and 'rythmanalyse' in Bachelard's thought.
12. A recent collection of communications dealing with this question is *Bachelard Bergson: continuité et discontinuité* (Worms and Wunenburger 2008).

1 The New Scientific Mind

1. Quillet 1964, Serres 1970, for example.
2. In Roland Barthes' *La Chambre claire* we read 'As a living soul I am the very contrary of History, I am what belies it, destroys it for the sake of my own history'; in *The Human Province* Elias Canetti thought that 'people who cannot find their way out of history are lost'; and in James Joyce's *Ulysses* Stephen Dedalus says that history 'is a nightmare from which I am trying to awake'.
3. That it *sets an experimental programme* must be underlined. Mathematics alone does not secure the status of an epistemological act. Ptolemy's system, for example, was based on very strong mathematics, but it did not envisage any experiment, it was of a descriptive nature and, therefore, it was not an 'epistemological act'.
4. These reviews appeared in the no longer active journal *Recherches philosophiques* between 1935 and 1937.
5. However, Popper's drive for objectivity is animated by an ideological agenda. Stengers remarked that 'The invariant in his career was always the following: whatever the criterion, it should allow us to understand why Einstein is a scientist and why Marxists and psychoanalysts are not' (Stengers 1995: 38). The incongruous consequence of this is that if we were to pursue this line of argument to its extreme conclusion we would have to accord factual knowledge to animals but not to Marxists and psychoanalysts.
6. All citations and the numbering of Presocratic fragments are taken from Kathleen Freeman's *Ancilla to The Pre-Socratic Philosophers* (1962) which is a translation of the Fragments in Diels, *Fragmente der Vorsokratiker*.
7. Plato's scheme is, in fact, a little more complicated as he divides, for no apparent reason, the primary triangles into smaller ones, but this detail does not change the picture such as to effect the argument that Bachelard presents.
8. I base this non-expert remark on Morris Kline's *Mathematics and the Search for Knowledge* (1985).
9. The concept of *phénoménotechnique* has already attracted some

attention from Anglophone commentators, in the early study by Graukoger (1976) and more recently by Rheinberger (2005) and Chimisso (2008).
10. On a comprehensive analysis of the various borrowings from Husserl see Barsotti 2002. Whether Bachelard's engagement with Husserl went as far as Barsotti suggests is a point of debate, but it is a valuable study in that it traces all the affinities between Bachelard's thinking and phenomenology.
11. For an analysis of Cavaillès's work on Husserl see Webb 2004.
12. For example, Ervin Schrödinger: 'I believe it to be true that I actually do cut out my mind when I construct the real world around me' (Schrödinger 1996: 95). Alexandre Koyré expressed a similar thought: 'in what we call science [...] we are dealing with a particular attitude, with an opposition between the man in the world and the world in which he lives' (Koyré 1973: 87).
13. In *The Historian's Craft* Marc Bloch wrote:

> Our mental climate has changed. The kinetic theory of gases, Einstein's mechanics, and the quantum theory have profoundly altered the concept of science which, only yesterday, was unanimously accepted. They have not weakened it; they have only made it more flexible. For certainty, they have often substituted the infinitely probable; for the strictly measurable, the notion of the eternal relativity of measurement. Their influence has even affected the countless minds (and, alas, I must number mine among them) which, thanks to defects in intelligence or early training, have been able to follow the great metamorphosis only at a distance and as if by reflected light. Hence we are much better prepared to admit that a scholarly discipline may pretend to the dignity of a science without insisting upon Euclidian demonstrations or immutable laws of repetition. We find it far easier to regard certainty and universality as questions of degree. We no longer feel obliged to impose upon every subject of knowledge a uniform intellectual pattern, borrowed from natural science, since, even there, that pattern has ceased to be entirely applicable. (Bloch 2008: 14–15)

It seems probable that Bloch was influenced directly by Bachelard in formulating these thoughts. The kinetic theory of gases, Einstein's mechanics, and the quantum theory are examples that come in Bachelard's writings; they were both at the Sorbonne at the same time and may well have known each other.

One should also signal that Feyerabend gives a wonderful description of a change in mentality in ancient Greece between the seventh and fifth centuries BC in the almost fifty pages of Chapter 16 of *Against Method* (Feyerabend 1993: 164–208).

14. A very fine analysis of this comes in one of Bachelard's early short studies 'Substance et lumière' that can be found in *Études*, the same theme is treated in Chapter III of *La Philosophie du non*.
15. This subject is addressed by Bachelard in a number of books and articles, chiefly in *Les Intuitions atomistiques*, *Le Pluralisme cohérent de la chimie moderne* and *Le Matérialisme rationnel*.
16. I borrow this example from Paul Strathern's *Mendeleyev's Dream*. Strathern adds that the move from Lavoisier to Berzelius 'was the equivalent of mathematics changing from Roman to Arabic numerals (when the opacity of XL x V = CC gave way to the clarity of 40 x 5 = 200)' (Strathern 2001: 252).
17. Bachelard's most extensive commentaries on Mendeleyev's work come in *Les Intuitions atomistiques* and *Le Matérialisme rationnel*.
18. However, Mendeleyev did help himself by laying the elements out on a grid, like cards in the game of patience, to help him visualise the problem (Strathern 2001: 284).
19. Bachelard's *phénoménotechnique* was taken up by Silvia Di Marco in her *Towards an Epistemology of Medical Imaging* (2015). This is a study of the role of the image in medicine. Part of it deals with developments of techniques to obtain images of the inside of the living body, from stethoscopy to today's scanning techniques. At first, physicians tried to make sounds of the inside of the body audible and then, by squaring them with knowledge from anatomy, they would produce images of illnesses, lesions, etc. A marked shift takes place with the discovery (serendipitous) of X-rays by Wilhelm Röntgen in 1895; this was the beginning of technologically produced images, and with it mathematics begins to play a crucial role. (This is somewhat analogous to the entry of electronically produced sounds into music, only that image production in medicine is a longer and far more complex development.) Di Marco brings in Bachelard's *phénoménotechnique* to highlight a number of aspects of the new image-producing technology. One is the extent to which medicine transforms natural phenomena into scientific objects. She also shows how it affects ways in which illnesses and pathologies are conceptualised; how medical reasoning changes and evolves with the medical *phénoménotechnique*. We learn the extent of the mathematisation of medical technology. Admittedly, as Di Marco points out, one cannot

think of it as part of a surrealist project; those who are involved in constructing these new scanning machines want to produce images of the inside of the body rather than new effects that crown the rationalist effort. But the story is a little more complex. These new phenomeno-technical devices make visible what is, strictly speaking, invisible; they make visible images which under no conditions could the eye possibly spot, not even aided with the strongest conceivable microscope. What we see on a scan (of the inside of the brain, for example) is made visible by the mathematics of the machine. That the structure of the brain puts a limit on kinds of images that can be generated is obvious, but the same goes for microphysics' *phénoménotechnique*; the scientific effects may well be derived from mathematical formulas that have no grounding in the natural world yet this world imposes constraints on what kinds of effects can be produced. And when we read Di Marco's descriptions of how these scanning machines work it does feel quite surreal:

> PET allows visualizing the physiological activity of the inner tissues, by showing the variation of concentration of certain molecules in specific areas of the body over a given amount of time. It has several applications: it helps diagnosing cancer and monitoring possible metastases by detecting the elevation of glucose uptake by cells in rapid division; it allows tracking the levels of oxygenation of different areas of the heart or the brain; and it can be used to measure the activity of specific neural receptors. This kind of imaging is possible thanks to so called radiotracers or radiopharmaceuticals. These are molecules in which an atom of carbon, oxygen, nitrogen or fluorine has been replaced by a correspondent radioactive isotope. To produce a PET image, the radiotracer, selected according to the physiological process that one wants to monitor, has to be injected into the patient's blood. At this point it flows through the body as a normal molecule, but after a precise span of time (the isotope half life) it emits radioactivity in the form of a positron [that is a particle of *anti-matter*!] that, after colliding with an electron, produces two γ-rays that shoot off the body almost 180° apart. These two γ-rays are the signal detected by the imaging apparatus, and they are used to map the flow rate of the labelled molecule. As in the case of CT scans, the machinery delivers a set of images corresponding to the slices in which the original volume (the human body) has been divided. And as in the case of CT, the production of the images entails complex mathematical operations which require considerable computing power. (Di Marco 2015: 224)

Do we really know what we are seeing when we are looking at a brain scan?

2 The Imaginary

1. This does not appear in any of Bachelard's writings. Quillet quotes an anecdote recounted by L. Guillermit in *Les Annales de l'Université de Paris*, 1963, I (the reference that Quillet gives seems incomplete).
2. One should perhaps note that Françoise Bonardel, an eminent scholar of alchemical thought, is not very impressed with Bachelard's understanding of alchemy (Bonardel 1993). But it does not matter for our purposes; we may not be learning a great deal about alchemy from what Bachelard says but we get considerable insight into his way of laying out his own concerns, which is of primary interest here.
3. This problem has been noticed by psychoanalysts themselves. Jean Laplanche and Jean-Bertrand Pontalis, authors of *The Language of Psychoanalysis*, in reviewing the concept of narcissism, point out two risks in the concept:

   > First, there is a danger of running counter to experience by asserting that the newborn baby is without any perceptual outlet on the external world. Secondly, we may find ourselves re-opening the door, and in the naïvest way, to the version of the idealist fallacy made all the more flagrant by being expressed in 'biological' language: just how are we supposed to picture the transition from a monad shut in on itself to a progressive discovery of the object? (Laplanche and Pontalis 1973: 257)

4. For this brief sketch on the history of the place of imagination in philosophical thought I am much indebted to Jean Starobinski's 'Jalons pour une histoire du concept d'imagination' (Starobinski 1970).
5. Freud, incidentally, was perfectly aware that dreams are only recounted and not spoken, hence the idea of secondary revision during the recounting of the dream. It is for that reason that he concentrated on the associations to the dream, very much a phenomenon of language. It was Jung who spoke of dreams as constituting a narrative in their own right, complementary to the consciousness of the day. Curiously, Bachelard professed a liking for Jung exactly at the time when he no longer agreed with this particular view.

6. Blanchot's *The Space of Literature* offers a particularly instructive counterpoint to Bachelard as in a way there is something quite similar between *The Space of Literature* and Bachelard's two *Poétiques*. Both proceed in an unhurried way, free, it would seem, from the compulsion to rush into decisive and final statements. Both weave together their thought with an abundance of citations producing compelling and persuasive discourses. They also share some premises. Both reject psychological readings or biographical analyses; for both poetry is an overcoming of memory and a paean to solitude; finally, both speak of poetry in the context of philosophy (without, however, straitjacketing it in *a priori* metaphysical hypothesis). But this is where the similarities end. Blanchot is attuned to something very different than Bachelard – he is sensitive to the place of anguish and desolation in writing. His view, to put it as briefly as possible, is that poetry, literature, art, point towards an absence, an absence caused by the disappearance of the gods:

> Art was the language of the gods. The gods having disappeared it became the language in which this disappearance was expressed, then the language in which this disappearance itself ceased to appear. This forgetfulness now speaks all alone. The deeper the forgetfulness, the more the deep speaks in this language, and the more the abyss of this deepness can become the hearing of the word. (Blanchot 1982: 245–6)

Forgetfulness, absence, abyss, these are the words which for Blanchot are key terms in his meditation on the nature of the poetic work. It is a discourse on absence and poverty. The poet descends into the silence of the night where the word is no more and not yet. The writer takes on the ultimate risk; he works in the black, never being able to declare his work finished or unfinished, never able to take the place of the fallen gods. The poet is an outcast. Writing is a sacrifice; it places the poet in a radical impossibility where everything is effaced – the world, the other, the word. The poet's ordeal is that true writing cannot reveal anything, cannot give solace nor compensation, all it can do is to make apparent that which prompts writing – the abyss. The more the poet writes the more profound this experience. He starts from nothing and his words make things absent. 'For the work is possible only if absence is pure and perfect, only if, in the presence of Midnight, the dice can be thrown' (Blanchot 1982: 110).

In order to appreciate the difference between Bachelard and

Blanchot there follows a quick comparison of quotes, taken from Bachelard's La *Poétique de l'espace* and *La Poétique de la rêverie* and Blanchot's *The Space of Literature*, respectively:

'Gift of an hour which knows the plenitude of the soul' (PR 55, 64). 'Writing [...] the point where nothing reveals itself' (48). 'When the forces of matter must be awakened, praise is sovereign' (PR 62, 72). 'To see properly is essentially to die' (151). 'This new being is a happy man' (PE 6, xix). 'Art is primarily the consciousness of unhappiness' (75). 'The poem, through its exuberance, awakens new depths in us' (PE 6, xix). 'We have forgotten to die' (147). 'Passions simmer and re-simmer in solitude: the passionate being prepares his explosions and exploits in this solitude' (PE 28, 9). 'The poem is solitude's poverty' (247). 'There is a sort of innate optimism in all works of the imagination' (PE 144, 153). 'Art points into a sordid absence, a suffocating condensation where being ceaselessly perpetuates itself as nothingness' (243).

The differences are so marked that one has the impression that they speak about incompatible worlds. And incompatible they are, because Bachelard seeks out the principle of life and breath in poetry, while Blanchot, on the other hand, hears the whispering of death.

7. Jean François Lyotard makes a very similar distinction: '[T]he ruse of reason (masculine) differs from the snares of sensitivity (feminine): reason *makes use of death* [...] What is pertinent for distinguishing the sexes is the relation to death: a body that can die, whatever its sexual anatomy, is masculine; a body that does not know that it must disappear is feminine. Men teach women of death, the impossible, the presence of absence' (Lyotard 1989: 112).

3 The Poetics of Time

1. One should also mention in this context Emmanuel Levinas's *Existence and Existents* in which the question of the instant is also quite prominent (Levinas 1978). The book was published first in 1947, that is after Bachelard's texts, and although Bachelard is not mentioned one gets the distinct impression that Levinas was familiar with this work. However, he subjects the instant to an 'existential interpretation' (to use the expression from the Translator's Introduction by Alphonso Lingis). This entails situating it in a tissue woven between existence and existents. It is a complex and difficult text, in part an engagement with Heidegger, and it is impossible to

say anything meaningful about it in the confines of an endnote. What is clear, however, is that it has nothing to do with Plato's instant as a timeless moment of change, but it is not the Kierkegaardian instant either.

2. In fact, Bachelard does not give the title of Halbwachs's book, but the reference is unmistakable; and he clearly assumed that every reader would know it (and no doubt his French readers at the time did). It is depressing that this groundbreaking work is so roundly ignored today. For example, picked up at random, a collection of articles, *Les Histoires de la mémoire: pathologie, psychologie et biologie*, with eighteen contributors, does not have a single index reference to Halbwachs (Dupont 2005). This is probably due to the fact that the question of memory has been hijacked by neuroscientists (the cover of the book in question shows a brain in a jar), who try to convince us that memory can be located in the brain and reduced to the brain's activities (a wild goose chase, it is quite certain).

3. Quillet also made this point: 'Bachelard's Decision has nothing to do with the "Kierkegaardian" instant' (Quillet 1964: 54).

4. These terms are obscure, although they were not coined by Bachelard. They derive from *cata*, meaning 'down', and *ana*, meaning 'up', and *genic*, 'to be born'. So *catagenic* duration holds us back, while *anagenic* duration is the action that evolves out of a Decision.

5. It seems noteworthy that philosophers who reject the idea of death as a philosophically meaningful concept also reject time as an independent metaphysical entity, although without necessarily linking the two. Epicurus declared that 'Death is nothing to us: for that which is dissolved is without sensation; and that which lacks sensation is nothing to us' (*Principal Doctrines*, II in Epicurus *The Extant Remains*); as for time, this is the Epicurean position: 'Time also exists not of itself. [...] Nor may we admit that anyone has a sense of time by itself separated from the movement of things and their quiet calm' (Lucretius, *De Rerum*, 1.459–65). (I use a quote from Lucretius because of its clarity. It sums up faithfully the only extant utterance of Epicurus that deals with the notion of time (Letter to Herodotus, 72), which, although one can work out its meaning, is expressed in a rather obscure way.) Spinoza: 'a free man thinks of death least of all things; and his wisdom is a meditation not of death but life' (Spinoza 1933: prop. LXVII) and 'Time is not an affection of things but rather a mode of thought or, as we have said, a logical being; for it is a mode of thought serving to explain duration' (120). (One notes that Spinoza uses the term 'duration' but it is of

a different order than duration as discussed in this work; to demonstrate this would take a lengthy exposition which is not necessary for our purposes.) And Wittgenstein: 'Death is not an event of life. Death is not lived through. If by eternity is understood not endless temporal duration but timelessness, then he lives eternally who lives in the present. Our life is endless in the way that our visual field is without limit' (Wittgenstein 1981: 6.4311). The idea of the passage of time is rejected out of hand: 'We cannot compare any process with the "passage of time" – there is no such thing' (6.3611).
6. The Portuguese poet Fernando Pessoa, who had strong philosophical leanings, commented on a conversation between two poets (invented ones), Ricardo Reis and Alberto Caeiro, and finds a very neat and simple way of differentiating between the two different sentiments attached to the notion of nothingness: 'When Reis speaks of death, he seems to foresee being buried alive. [. . .] The sentiment [of nothingness] which in Caeiro is an empty field, for Reis is an empty tomb. He adopted Caeiro's nothingness but did not know how to keep it free of decay' (Pessoa 2007: 184).

Concluding Remarks

1. Vincent Bontems' chapter 'Le bachelardisme', that comes at the end of his monograph on Bachelard (2010), traces the lineage of specific influences that Bachelard exerted. Bontems identifies three regions in which this influence is tangible, two of them of a specifically philosophical nature. The first is the impact on epistemological thought. The influential position of Georges Canguilhem at the Sorbonne was of capital importance in implanting Bachelardian epistemology in the academic syllabus. Those who were introduced to Bachelard by Canguilhem include most notably Michel Foucault, François Dagognet and Gilbert Simondon. The second was the interest of Marxists in Bachelard's work, after Louis Althusser took from him the notion of the 'epistemological break' to try to establish the scientific credentials of Marxism. The third domain of influence can be seen in literary criticism. Here Roland Barthes is the most illustrious figure according to Bontems's account. In fact, Barthes refers to Bachelard rarely, but he did have this to say: 'Starting with the analysis of substances (and not works) following dynamic deformations of images in a great number of poets, G. Bachelard founded a veritable critical school so rich that one can say that French criticism is at its most flourishing under the Bachelardian inspiration' (in Bontems

2010: 194). Barthes is referring to what was known as the Geneva group, which included in its ranks Georges Poulet, Jean Starobinski, Jean-Pierre Richard and Jean Rousset.

2. The first, somewhat isolated, publications on the negative impact of science and industry on our environment only appeared in the 1960s. However, it was the think-tank The Club of Rome, set up in 1968, and the report that it commissioned, *The Limits to Growth*, published in 1972, that first alerted the wider public to the looming dangers implicit in scientific work.

3. We can find a very helpful survey of this philosophical terrain in David Webb's 'Background' to his commentary on Foucault's *The Archaeology of Knowledge*, where he discusses Cavaillès, Bachelard, Canguilhem and Serres (Webb 2013: 5–38).

4. It is interesting to note in this context the philosophical trajectory of Jean-François Lyotard. He began his project by positing a libidinal intensity that manifests itself in the figural which breaks the deadening logic of discursive reason. This route began with *Discours, figure* (1971) and ended with the howl of *Économie libidinale* (1974). However, Lyotard abandoned this route because he realised it was a philosophy of the will, which ultimately is a monism. But the necessity to account for intensities remained, and in *Le Différend* (1983), one of the truly great texts of that period, Lyotard presents a different picture. In this work he maps out a universe of language in which every utterance is linked with the one that preceded it and necessitates another one to follow. When there is a breakdown in the linkage of utterances – in other words, when for one reason or another a necessary utterance does not emerge – we witness a *différend*, a void, and it is there, in the gaps of discourse, that intensities emerge. Thus Lyotard located intensities in the intrinsic agonistics of language and in the inexpressible (which later he will refer to as the sublime). In other words, intensities are generated by the events of the 'in-betweens' of the utterances in language, but they do not have a substrate (libidinal, as in Lyotard's earlier work). (For a more detailed account of this aspect of Lyotard's thought see Kotowicz 2000.)

5. I borrow the notion of 'belonging' from the virologist Luis P. Villarreal, who introduces it in his *Origin of Group Identity*. The opening sentences of his work announce its scope:

> A sense of belonging is basic to the human experience. But in this, humans are not unique. Essentially all life, from bacteria to humans,

has ways by which it determines which members belong and which do not. This is a basic cooperative nature of life I call group membership which is examined in this book. (Villarreal 2009: v)

This is a rather daunting and intimidating work, the technical detail of which a non-biologist cannot hope to begin to understand. But it is possible to work out what is at stake in the book. The opening observation is that collective behaviour is observable at the very beginnings of life: in the behaviour of viruses. In everyday discourse we think of viruses as responsible for many diseases, yet there is a great deal more to them. They are strands of DNA or RNA contained within protein sheathes. They are very small and very numerous; we will find something to the tune of 100 million of them in a cubic millimetre of ocean water. Viruses are omnipresent; wherever there is life there are viruses; there is no known life process or event in which viruses are not implicated.

Viruses operate collectively and develop stable strategies which result in a development of a collective identity. One can trace an evolutionary pathway in which sensory systems necessary for maintaining collective identities (light, odour, pheromones) are developed, leading to the formation of the brain and the neocortex. Viruses are directly involved in all these developments. Our collective identities are hardwired into our bodies by how viruses (and the RNA they produce or induce) mould our DNA structure and social brain mechanisms. Recent research suggests that viruses provide a basic molecular and selective force that makes us social beings.

Villarreal's work is very thought provoking, and on a number of counts. Its premise is non-Darwinian: it argues that cooperation and group membership rather than competition and selection are the main guiding force in evolution; it demonstrates that belief systems that humans develop which are irrational (religions, for example) are biologically determined and, therefore, they effectively cannot be eradicated. However, although we learn that our social mind has a biological substrate, we are not reduced to it:

> [A] modern mind, can dissociate itself, to some degree, from the common belief needed for binding a social mind. In a sense, such a mind partially transcends the ancestral, normal biological state. A modern mind is mostly the product of intense education and training, and unlike the learning of language or other mental abilities it *does not have a specific or dedicated biological substrate in the brain for*

its development and maintenance. Thus it has an inherently dynamic (fragile) character to it. It is a bit unnatural in that it is developed in the individual, thus can be somewhat asocial. (Villarreal: 568–9, italics added)

The most important notion in the context of this study is that of 'belonging', a notion with strong resonances and deep meaning. But there are other intriguing avenues in Villarreal's work; it is also interesting to see a scientist with clear materialist thinking and not a hint of spiritual, mystical, or metaphysical leanings telling us that we have an escape route from our biologically determined state. (And it is almost uncanny how this chimes with Bachelard's insistence that we can escape our *catagenic* (biological) condition, and also that this escape is a solitary act.)

6. One could, in fact, extend the Buddhist dimension of Bachelard's thought. *Anatta* and *Anicca* are two of the three pillars of Buddhism, the third being *Dukkha*, suffering. Overcoming suffering can perhaps be read into a great deal of Bachelard's writings on the imaginary and on time. But again, it is not my intention to turn Bachelard into a Buddhist, although a careful study of this dimension of Bachelard's thought (philosophy and overcoming suffering) could yield some interesting insights, but this would necessitate a very different approach than is taken in this work.
7. It is noteworthy that Lyotard, while exploring questions around the sublime, developed an interest in Buddhist thinking, particularly the Japanese thirteenth-century Zen Buddhist thinker Dōgen Zenji, to whom he makes a specific reference (Lyotard 1988: 65–6). (This may be the only explicit reference in his writings but I know from a personal communication with someone who was a close friend of Lyotard that his interest in Buddhist thought was of a serious dimension).

Appendix: Bachelard and Atomism

1. Strictly speaking one should speak of Democritus and his predecessor Leucippus. But very little is known about the earlier man. He is credited with laying down the basics of the doctrine, but it was developed fully by the very prolific Democritus.
2. Because of somewhat conflicting doxographical evidence, commentators are not in agreement as to whether in Democritus' thinking weight was one of the characteristics of the atom.

3. This third century account of Democritus' views, given by Hippolitus, is particularly impressive and worth quoting: 'There are innumerable worlds, which differ in size. In some worlds there is no sun and moon, in others they are larger than in our world, and in others more numerous. The intervals between the worlds are unequal; in some parts there are more worlds, in others fewer; some are increasing, some at their height, some decreasing; in some parts they are arising, in others failing. They are destroyed by collision one with another. There are some worlds devoid of living creatures or plants or any moisture' (in Kirk, Raven and Schofield 1983: 418).
4. Guthrie draws our attention to the connection between heat and life in early Greek thought on several occasions (1962: 61, 101, 291 and 1965: 59, 207, 431ff).
5. Bohr's big house was covered with paintings of a traditional genre, portraits and landscapes, with one exception: he had a big Cubist painting by Jean Metzinger, *La Femme au Cheval*, which he had bought himself. He often showed this painting to visitors and had also read Metzinger's 1912 theoretical text *Du "Cubisme"* (penned with Albert Gleizes) which was the first major theoretical treatise on Cubism.
6. Interestingly, although by a completely different route, this, in a way, confirms Burnet's argument that 'all materialism depends on his [Parmenides'] view of reality' (Burnet 1945: 182), a view that seems to have been widely rejected.
7. On this see *The Great Chain of Being* by Arthur Lovejoy (1964); it was he who coined the term 'principle of plenitude'.
8. These two examples are borrowed from an article by David Sedley 'Two Conceptions of the Vacuum' (Sedley 1982), which is the most penetrating analysis of the problem of the Democritean (and Epicurean) void that I am aware of.
9. This means that in Democritus' thought discontinuity is constituted by the void and not by such concepts as limit or rupture. This would also mean, for example, that atoms could not push out the void into the periphery and huddle together to form a continuous material reality, as we find in the thought of the Stoics.
10. Paul Masson-Oursel recognises four different atomist systems in India (Jaina, Buddhism, Vaiśeiṣika and Nyāya (Masson-Oursel 1925)). And even this could be extended as the atomist thinking in Buddhist thought, at least, evolved; the somewhat materialistic atomism of early Buddhism is very different from the temporal atomism advanced later by the Dignāga school.

11. Serres also says the following: 'There we see, drawn on the plane of configuration, an infinite sheaf of parallels or lines, along which points spread out one ahead of the other. There we see atoms fall. Or move with an equal speed. From top to bottom, if you will, or in whatever direction you like, it's not important. Lucretian physics speaks in both ways, as far as I can see without any contradiction. Globally, no-one can imagine a top or a bottom to the universe. Locally, for a mechanical model, which has points of reference in relation to which a movement is described, direction is defined. It is, in general, unimportant. The explicit thesis of the plurality of worlds gives added coherence to this distinction between the global, the local, the whole, the part' (Serres 2000: 16).
12. Bachelard was not alone in holding this view, Schrödinger thought much the same: '[T]he [atomist] thought pattern is [...] based on the *a priori* structure, or at least the natural inclination, of the human intellect' (Schrödinger 1996: 83).
13. These can be found in the extant fragments of Democritus: *athambia* (215, 216), *euthymia* (3, 174, 189, 191, 286), *eudaimonia* (170, 171), *euesto* (257).

Bibliography

Works by Gaston Bachelard

(1928) *Essai sur la connaissance approchée* (Paris: Vrin).
(1928) *Étude sur l'évolution d'un problème de physique: la propagation thermique dans les solides* (Paris: Vrin).
(1932) *Le Pluralisme cohérent de la chimie moderne* (Paris: Vrin).
(1932) *L'Intuition de l'instant* (Paris: Denoël [Stock 1985]).
(1933) *Les Intuitions atomistiques (essai de classification)* (Paris: Boivin).
(1934) *Le Nouvel esprit scientifique* (Paris: Alcan [Paris: Presses Universitaires de France 1987]).
(1936) *La Dialectique de la durée* (Paris: Presses Universitaires de France [1972]).
(1936) *L'Expérience de l'espace dans la physique contemporaine* (Paris: Presses Universitaires de France).
(1938) *La Formation de l'esprit scientifique: Contribution à une psychanalyse de la connaissance objective* (Paris: Vrin).
(1938) *La Psychanalyse du feu* (Paris: Gallimard).
(1940) *Lautréamont* (Paris: José Corti).
(1940) *La Philosophie du non: Essai d'une philosophie du Nouvel esprit scientifique* (Paris: Presses Universitaires de France).
(1942) *L'Eau et les rêves: Essai sur l'imagination de la matière* (Paris: José Corti).
(1943) *L'Air et les songes: Essai sur l'imagination du mouvement* (Paris: José Corti).
(1948) *La Terre et les rêveries de la volonté: Essai sur l'imagination des forces* (Paris: José Corti).
(1948) *La Terre et les rêveries du repos: Essai sur les images de l'intimité* (Paris: José Corti).
(1949) *Le Rationalisme appliqué* (Paris: Presses Universitaires de France).

(1951) *L'Activité rationaliste de la physique contemporaine* (Paris: Presses Universitaires de France).
(1953) *Le Matérialisme rationnel* (Paris: Presses Universitaires de France).
(1957) *La Poétique de l'espace* (Paris: Presses Universitaires de France).
(1960) *La Poétique de la rêverie* (Paris: Presses Universitaires de France).
(1961) *La Flamme d'une chandelle* (Paris: Presses Universitaires de France).
(1970) *Études* (Paris: Presses Universitaires de France) (posthumous collection of articles).
(1972) *L'Engagement rationaliste* (Paris: Presses Universitaires de France) (posthumous collection of articles).
(1988) *Fragments d'une poétique du feu* (Paris: Presses Universitaires de France) (posthumous).

English Translations

(The chronology follows the order in which the publications appeared originally in French.)
(2013) *Intuition of the Instant*, trans. E. Rizo-Patron (Evanston: Northwestern University Press).
(1984) *The New Scientific Spirit*, trans. A. Goldhammer (Boston: Beacon Press).
(2000) *The Dialectic of Duration*, trans. M. McAllester Jones (Manchester: Clinamen Press). 2nd edition (London: Rowman & Littlefield International, 2016). (In this work references are made to the 1st edition.)
(2002) *The Formation of a Scientific Mind: A Contribution to a Psychoanalysis of Objective Knowledge*, trans. M. McAllester Jones (Manchester: Clinamen Press).
(1964) *The Psychoanalysis of Fire*, trans. A. C. M. Ross (Boston: Beacon Press).
(1986) *Lautréamont*, trans. R. S. Dupree (Dallas: The Dallas Institute Publications).
(1968) *The Philosophy of No*, trans. G. S. Waterston (New York: Orion).
(1942) *Water and Dreams: An Essay on the Imagination of Matter*, trans. E. R. Farrell (Dallas: The Dallas Institute Publications).
(1988) *Air and Dreams: An Essay on the Imagination of Movement*, trans. E. R. Farrell and C. F. Farrell (Dallas: The Dallas Institute Publications).

(2002) *Earth and Reveries of Will: An Essay on the Imagination of Matter*, trans. K. Haltman (Dallas: The Dallas Institute Publications).
(2011) *Earth and Reveries of Repose: An Essay on Images of Interiority*, trans. M. McAllester Jones (Dallas: The Dallas Institute Publications).
(1964) *The Poetics of Space*, trans. M. Jolas (Boston: Beacon Press).
(1969) *The Poetics of Reverie*, trans. D. Russell (Boston: Beacon Press).
(1988) *The Flame of a Candle*, trans. J. Caldwell (Dallas: The Dallas Institute Publications).
(1997) *Fragments of a Poetics of Fire*, trans. K. Haltman (Dallas: The Dallas Institute Publications).

Other Works

Aristotle (1941) *Metaphysics*, trans. W. D. Ross in *The Basic Works of Aristotle*, ed. R. McKeon (New York: Random House).
Aristotle, *Physics*, trans. R. P. Hardie and R. K. Gaye, in *The Basic Works*.
Aristotle, *Nicomachean Ethics*, trans. W. D. Ross in *The Basic Works*.
Aristotle, *Categories*, trans. E. M. Edghill in *The Basic Works*.
Aristotle, *On Generation and Corruption*, trans. H. H. Joachim in *The Basic Works*.
Augustine, St (1945) *Confessions*, trans. E. B. Pusey (London: J. M. Dent & Sons).
Barsotti, B. (2002) *Bachelard. Critique de Husserl: Aux racines de la fracture épistemologie/phénoménologie* (Paris: L'Harmattan).
Bergson, H. (1889) *Essai sur les données immédiates de la conscience* (Paris: Presses Universitaires de France [1991]).
Bergson, H. (1908) *L'Évolution créatrice* (Paris: Alcan).
Bhaskar, R. (1975) 'Feyerabend and Bachelard: Two philosophies of science', *New Left Review*, 94, 31–55.
Blanchot, M. (1959) 'Vaste comme la nuit', *Nouvelle Revue Française*, 7, 684–95.
Blanchot, M. (1982) *The Space of Literature*, trans. A. Spock (Lincoln: University of Nebraska Press).
Bloch, M. (2008) *The Historian's Craft*, trans. P. Putman (Manchester: Manchester University Press).
Bonardel, F. (1993) *Philosophie de l'alchimie: grand œuvre et modernité* (Paris: Presses Universitaires de France).
Bontems, V. (2010) *Bachelard* (Paris: Belles Lettres).
Breton, A. (1985) *Manifestes du surréalisme* (Paris: Gallimard).
Burnet, J. (1945) *Early Greek Philosophy* (London: A & C Black).

Canguilhem, G. (2002) *Études d'histoire et de philosophie de sciences concernant les vivants et la vie* (Paris: Vrin).
Caws, M.-A. (1966) *Surrealism and the Literary Imagination: A Study of Breton and Bachelard* (The Hague: Mouton).
Chimisso, C. (1996) *Gaston Bachelard: Critic of Science and the Imagination* (London: Routledge).
Chimisso, C. (2008) "From Phenomenology to Phenomenotechnique: the role of early twentieth-century physics in Gaston Bachelard's philosophy", *Studies in History and Philosophy of Science Part A*, 39 (3), 384–92.
Chinchore, M. R. (1995) *Anattā/Anātmatā: An Analysis of Buddhist Anti-Substantialist Crusade* (Delhi: Indian Books Centre).
Cicero (1979) *De Natura Deorum* and *Academica*, trans. H. Rackham (Cambridge, MA: Harvard University Press).
Cutting, G. (1987) 'Gaston Bachelard's Philosophy of Science', *International Studies in the Philosophy of Science*, 2 (1), 55–71.
Dagognet, F. (1965) *Gaston Bachelard, sa vie, son oeuvre, avec un exposé de sa philosophie* (Paris: Presses Universitaires de France).
Deleuze, G. (1990) *Pourparlers* (Paris: Les Éditions de Minuit).
Descartes (1968) 'Meditations on First Philosophy' in *The Philosophical Works of Descartes*, trans. E. S. Haldane and G. R. T. Ross (Cambridge: Cambridge University Press).
Di Marco, M. S. (2015) *Towards an Epistemology of Medical Imaging*, Doctoral dissertation (University of Lisbon/University of Milan).
Diogenes Laertius (1980) *Lives of Eminent Philosophers*, trans. R. D. Hicks (Cambridge, MA: Harvard University Press).
Dodds, E. R. (1951) *The Greeks and the Irrational* (Berkeley: University of California Press).
Duhem, P. (1962) *The Aim and Structure of Physical Theory*, trans. P. P. Weiner (New York: Atheneum).
Dupont, J.-C. ed. (2005) *Les Histoires de la mémoire: pathologie, psychologie et biologie* (Paris: Vuibert).
Epicurus (1926) *The Extant Remains*, trans. and notes C. Bailey (Oxford: Clarendon Press).
Feyerabend, P. (1993) *Against Method*, 3rd edn (London: Verso).
Foucault, M. (1994) *Dits et écrits*, vol. IV (Paris: Gallimard).
Freeman, K. (1962) *Ancilla to the Pre-Socratic Philosophers* (Oxford: Basil Blackwell).
Gaudin, P. trans. and intr. (1987) *On Poetic Imagination and Reverie: Selections from Gaston Bachelard* (Dallas: Spring Publications).
Gaukroger, S. W. (1976) 'Bachelard and the Problem of Epistemological

Analysis', *Studies in History and Philosophy of Science*, 7, 189–244.

Guthrie, W. K. C. (1962 and 1965) *A History of Greek Philosophy*, vols I and II (Cambridge: Cambridge University Press).

Halbwachs, M. (1925) *Les Cadres sociaux de la mémoire* (Paris: Félix Alcan).

Heidegger, M. (1973) *Being and Time*, trans. J. Macquarrie and E. Robinson (Oxford: Basil Blackwell).

Heisenberg, W. (1971) *Physics and Beyond: Encounters and Conversations*, trans. A. J. Pomerans (New York: Harper and Row).

Heisenberg, W. (1990) *Physics and Philosophy* (Harmondsworth: Penguin).

Hume, D. (1978) *A Treatise of Human Nature*, 2nd edn (Oxford: Oxford University Press).

Husserl, E. (1982) *Cartesian Meditations*, trans. D. Cairns (The Hague: Martinus Nijhoff).

Hyppolite, J. (1957) 'Gaston Bachelard ou le romantisme de l'intelligence', *Revue philosophique de la France et de l'étranger*, 1–3, 13–27.

Kant, I. (1950) *Critique of Pure Reason*, trans. N. Kemp Smith (London: Macmillan).

Kierkegaard, S. (1973) *Kierkegaard's the Concept of Dread*, trans. W. Lowrie (Princeton: Princeton University Press).

Kirk, G. S., Raven, J. E. and Schofield, M. (1983) *The Presocratic Philosophers* (Cambridge: Cambridge University Press).

Kline, M. (1985) *Mathematics and the Search for Knowledge* (Oxford: Oxford University Press).

Kojève, A. (1947) *Introduction à la lecture de Hegel* (Paris: Gallimard).

Kotowicz, Z. (2000) 'Notes on Lyotard's Route to Atomism', *Parallax* ('To Jean-François Lyotard'), 6 (4), 114–26.

Koyré, A. (1973) *Études d'histoire de la pensée scientifique* (Paris: Gallimard).

Kuhn, T. (1962) *The Structure of Scientific Revolutions* (London: University of Chicago Press).

Lacan, J. (1977) 'The Mirror Stage as Formative of the Function of the I', in *Écrits: A Selection*, trans. A. Sheridan (London: Tavistock Publications).

Lalande, A. (2002) *Vocabulaire technique et critique de la philosophie* (Paris: Presses Universitaires de France).

Laplanche, J. and Pontalis, J.-B. (1973) *The Language of Pycho-Analysis*, trans. D. Nicholson-Smith (London: Hogarth Press).

Latour, B. (1987) *Science in Action* (Cambridge, MA: Harvard University Press).
Latour, B. (1997) *Nous n'avons jamais été modernes* (Paris: La Découverte).
Lautréamont, Comte de (1970) *Lautréamont's Maldoror*, trans. A. Lykiard (London: Allison & Busby).
Lecourt, D. (1969) *L'Épistémologie historique de Gaston Bachelard* (Paris: Vrin [11th edition 2002]).
Lecourt, D. ed. (1971) *Bachelard: Épistémologie* (Paris: Presses Universitaires de France).
Lescure, J. (1983) *Un été avec Bachelard* (Paris: Luneau Ascot Éditeurs).
Levinas, E. (1978) *Existence and Existents*, trans. A. Lingis (The Hague: Martinus Nijhoff).
Lovejoy, A. (1964) *The Great Chain of Being* (Cambridge, MA: Harvard University Press).
Lucretius (1982) *De Rerum Natura*, trans. W. H. D. Rouse and M. F. Smith (Cambridge, MA: Harvard University Press).
Lyotard, J.-F. (1970) '«L'eau prend le ciel»', *L'Arc*, 42, 38–54.
Lyotard, J.-F. (1971) *Discours, figure* (Paris: Klincksieck).
Lyotard, J.-F. (1974) *Économie libidinale* (Paris: Éditions de Minuit).
Lyotard, J.-F. (1982) *Rudiments païens* (Paris: Christian Bourgois).
Lyotard, J.-F. (1983) *Le Différend* (Paris: Seuil).
Lyotard, J.-F. (1988) *L'Inhumain* (Paris: Galilée).
Lyotard, J.-F. (1989) 'One of the Things in Women's Struggles' in *The Lyotard Reader*, ed. A. Benjamin (Oxford: Blackwell).
Marx, K. (1975) *Notebooks on Epicurean Philosophy*, trans. R. Dixon in Karl Marx and Frederick Engels, *Collected Works*, vol. 1 (London: Lawrence and Wishart).
Masson-Oursel, P. (1925) 'L'Atomisme indien', *Revue Philosophique de la France et de l'Etranger*, 99, 342–68.
Minkowski, E. (1963) 'Vers quels horizons nous emmène Gaston Bachelard?' *Revue Internationale de Philosophie*, 66, 419–40.
Mookerjee, S. (2006) *The Buddhist Philosophy of Universal Flux: An Exposition of the Philosophy of Critical Realism as Expounded by the School of Dignāga* (New Delhi: Motilalal Banarsidass).
Nef, F. (2011) *La Force du vide: Essai de métaphysique* (Paris: Éditions du Seuil).
Nietzsche, F. (1968) *Beyond Good and Evil* in *Basic Writings of Nietzsche*, ed. and trans. W Kaufmann (New York: Random House).
Nietzsche, F. (1974) *The Gay Science: With a Prelude in Rhymes and an Appendix of Songs*, trans. W. Kaufmann (New York: Vintage Books).

Onians, R. B. (1988) *The Origins of European Thought about the Body, the Mind, the Soul, the World, Time, and Fate* (Cambridge: Cambridge University Press).
Ovid (1984) *Metamorphoses*, trans. F. J. Miller, revised by G. P. Goold (Cambridge, MA: Harvard University Press).
Pagels, H. R. (1986) *The Cosmic Code* (Harmondsworth: Penguin).
Pascal, B. (1958) *Pensées*, trans. W. F. Trotter (New York: Dutton & Co.).
Penrose, R. (1990) *The Emperor's New Mind: Concerning Computers, Minds and the Laws of Physics* (Oxford: Oxford University Press).
Pessoa, F. (2007) 'Notas Para a Recordação de Meu Mestre Caeiro' in *Prosa de Álvaro de Campos*, ed. J. Pizarro and A. Cardiello (Lisboa: Ática).
Plato (1985) *Phaedo*, trans. H. Tredennick in *The Collected Dialogues of Plato* (Princeton: Princeton University Press).
Plato, *Meno*, trans. W. K. C. Guthrie in *The Collected Dialogues*.
Plato, *Parmenides*, trans. F. M. Cornford in *The Collected Dialogues*.
Plato, *Laws*, trans. A. E. Taylor in *The Collected Dialogues*.
Plato, *Timaeus*, trans. B. Jowett in *The Collected Dialogues*.
Poirier R. (1974) 'Autour de Bachelard épistémologue' in *Bachelard: Colloque de Cerisy* (Paris: Union Générale d'Éditions).
Popper, K. R. (1972) *Conjectures and Refutations* (London: Routledge and Kegan Paul).
Prigogine, I. and Stengers, I. (1978) *La Nouvelle alliance: Métamorphoses de la science* (Paris: Gallimard).
Pullman, B. (1998) *The Atom in the History of Human Thought*, trans. A. Reisinger (Oxford: Oxford University Press).
Quillet, P. (1964) *Bachelard* (Paris: Seghers).
Rheinberger, H.-J. (2005) 'Gaston Bachelard and the Notion of "Phenomenotechnique"', *Perspectives on Science*, 13 (3), 313–28.
Roupnel, G. (1927) *Siloë* (Paris: Stock).
Sambursky, S. (1956) *The Physical World of the Greeks* (Princeton: Princeton University Press).
Sartre, J.-P. (1956) *Being and Nothingness: An Essay on Phenomenological Ontology*, trans. H. E. Barnes (New York: Philosophical Library).
Schrödinger, E. (1996) *Nature and the Greeks* and *Science and Humanism* (Cambridge: Cambridge University Press).
Sedley, D. (1982) 'Two Conceptions of the Vacuum', *Phronesis*, 27, 175–93.
Serres, M. (1970) 'La réforme et les sept péchés', *L'Arc*, 42, 14–28.

Serres, M. (1978) *Hermès II. L'interférence* (Paris: Les Éditions de Minuit).
Serres, M. (1992) *Éclaircissements: Entretiens avec Bruno Latour* (Paris: Éditions François Bourin).
Serres, M. (2000) *The Birth of Physics*, trans. J. Hawkes (Manchester: Clinamen Press).
Silburn, L. (1989) *Instant et cause: Le discontinue dans la pensée philosophique de l'Inde* (Paris: De Broccard).
Spinoza, B. (1933) *The Ethics* in *Philosophy of Spinoza*, trans. R. H. M. Elwes (New York: Tudor Publishing).
Starobinski, J. (1970) 'Jalons pour une histoire du concept d'imagination' in *La Relation critique* (Paris: Gallimard).
Starobinski, J. (1984) 'La double légitimité', *Revue Internationale de Philosophie*, 38 (150), 231–44.
Stcherbatsky, T. (1970) *Buddhist Logic*, 2 vols (New Delhi: Motilalal Banarsidass [First edition 1930–32])
Stengers, I. (1995) *L'Invention des sciences modernes* (Paris: Flammarion).
Strathern, P. (2001) *Mendeleyev's Dream: The Quest for the Elements* (Harmondsworth: Penguin).
Tiles, M. (1984) *Bachelard: Science and Objectivity* (Cambridge: Cambridge University Press).
Villarreal, L. P. (2009) *Origin of Group Identity: Viruses, Addiction and Cooperation* (New York: Springer).
Webb, D. (2004) 'Cavaillès, Husserl and the Historicity of Science', *Angelaki*, 8 (3), 59–72.
Webb, D. (2013) *Foucault's Archaeology: Science and Transformation* (Edinburgh: Edinburgh University Press).
Wittgenstein, L. (1981) *Tractatus Logico-Philosophicus*, trans. C. K. Ogden (London: Routledge and Kegan Paul).
Worms, F. and Wunenberger, J.-J. eds (2008) *Bachelard et Bergson: Continuité et Discontinuité* (Paris: Presses Universitaires de France).

Index

a priori, 46, 52, 60, 78, 80, 81, 147, 189n, 197n
alchemy, 44, 46, 47, 62, 72, 84–5, 88, 103, 107, 188n
Althusser Louis, 9, 192n
ambivalence (poetic), 97, 102–5
anagenic, 125, 137, 191n; *see also* catagenic
Anderson, Carl D., 166
anima/animus, 10, 115–16
anti-(electron, matter), 166, 168, 171, 187n
Aristotle, 30, 36, 49, 60, 67, 100, 103, 119, 122, 132, 135, 158, 159, 160, 163–4, 168, 169, 170
Arnold, Matthew, 117–18
aspirations (philosophical), 11–12, 21, 74, 134–5, 148, 179–80
ataraxia, 127
atom, 35–6, 40, 63–4, 100, 123, 126, 137, 149, 157, 160, 161, 165–8, 169–71, 172–4, 176, 177, 180, 197n
  atomic number/weight, 63–5
  Bachelard's view on classical concept of, 172–4, 176, 180
  temporal, 126, 137, 177; *see also* time: instant
  see also electron; isotopes; particles
atomism, 20–2, 35–6, 40, 99, 149, 156, 157–9, 161–2, 164–5, 167–8, 171, 172, 173–5, 181, 196n
  ancient, 21, 109, 159–60, 160–1, 171–2; *see also* Democritus; Epicurus
  contemporary, 21, 167–8, 171, 174, 177

as 'natural philosophy', 21, 174; *see also* Gassendi; Laplace; Newton
Augustine, St, of Hippo, 1, 44, 132, 161, 172

Bachelard, Gaston
  L'Activité rationaliste de la physique contemporaine, 8, 15, 46–7, 157, 172, 174
  L'Air et les songes, 8, 92, 106
  La Dialectique de la durée, 7, 18, 84, 121, 126–7, 130–1, 139, 142, 153, 176
  Essai sur la connaissance approchée, 6, 15, 55, 75, 121, 146, 177
  L'Expérience de l'espace dans la physique contemporaine, 7, 113
  La Flamme d'une chandelle, 116–17
  La Formation de l'esprit scientifique, 3, 32, 39, 41–3, 44, 47, 75, 82, 86, 98–9, 126, 154
  Fragments d'une poétique du feu, 8, 18, 93, 102, 117–18, 154, 155
  L'Intuition de l'instant, 7, 18, 84, 119, 121, 125–7, 130, 131, 153, 166–7
  Les Intuitions atomistiques, 75, 99, 157, 173
  Lautréamont, 18, 88–92, 96, 98, 100, 105, 108, 154, 180
  Le Matérialisme rationnel, 8, 15–16, 41, 72, 75, 100
  Le Nouvel esprit scientifique, 7, 10, 37, 43
  La Philosophie du non, 29, 52, 113
  La Poétique de l'espace, 1–3, 5, 8, 18, 56, 107–9, 113, 144, 149, 154, 178, 190

206

La Poétique de la rêverie, 8, 97, 109, 115, 190
La Psychanalyse du feu, 8, 82–3, 85, 88, 93, 100
Le Rationalisme appliqué, 8, 15, 151
La Terre et les rêveries du repos, 8, 92–3, 102, 107
La Terre et les rêveries de la volonté, 8, 92, 102, 107, 117
Bacon, Francis, 17, 30–1, 32, 49, 99
Barsotti, Bernard, 185n
Barthes, Roland, 46, 184n, 192–3n
Bataille, George, 13, 183n
Beckett, Samuel, 119, 142–3
Being, 2, 11–12, 103, 114, 115, 141, 147, 180, 181
belonging (belongingness), 150–2, 193–4n; see also inter-subjectivity
Bergson, Henri, 19–20, 96, 131–5, 136, 140, 177, 180; see also substance: *élan vital*; time: *élan vital*
Berzelius, Jöns, 12, 186n
Blanchot, Maurice, 9, 118, 146
  The Space of Literature, 189–90n
Bloch, Marc, 59, 185n
body (flesh), 95–7, 98, 100, 131
  muscle, 91, 96, 97–8
Boehme, Jacob, 88, 104
Bohr, Niels, 40, 165–6, 173, 196n
Bolyai, János, 25
Bonardel, Françoise, 188n
Bontems, Vincent, 9, 19, 183n, 192n
Boscovich, Ruder, 149
brain, 32, 126, 187–8n, 191n, 194n
  Bachelard's view, 32, 126
Brand, Henning, 61–2
breath (breathing), 96–7, 111, 126, 155, 190n
Breton, André, 12, 15, 145
Bruno, Giordano, 104
Brunschvicg, Léon, 6, 23, 146
Buddhism, 20, 22, 136–40, 142, 155, 195n, 196n
  Dignāga (School of), 20, 136, 155, 196n
Burnet, John, 196n

Caillois, Roger, 13, 183n
Canetti, Elias, 48, 184n
Canguilhem, George, 9, 23, 146, 192n

catagenic, 90, 125–6, 128, 137, 191n; see also anagenic
Cavaillès, Jean, 56, 146
Caws, Mary-Ann, 9
Chimisso, Cristina, 9, 185
Cité scientifique, 145
clinamen, 161, 172
Club of Rome, 193n
cogito, 37, 110–11; see also ego; psyche
complex (Charon, Hoffman, Jonas, Novalis, Oedipus, Ophelia), 101
concept vs image, 10–11, 27, 29, 39–40, 100, 115
Cros, Charles, 42
cubism, 165, 196n
  Metzinger, Jean, 196n

Dagognet, François, 9, 146, 192n
de Broglie, Louis-Victor-Pierre-Raymond, 7e duc, 74, 176
death, 8, 14–20, 95–6, 134–5, 139–40, 142, 190n, 191–2n
  fear of, 10, 140–2
  feminine/masculine, 115–18, 192n
  overcoming, 105–7, 142
Decision, 123, 125, 127, 155, 191n
Deleuze, Giles, 38–9
Democritus, 20, 35, 99–100, 157–71, 177, 179–81
Descartes, René, 5, 13, 17, 36, 37, 46, 110, 148, 150, 155, 169, 174
Destouches, Jean-Louis, 25
Di Marco, Margherita Silvia, 186–7n
dialectic, 13–14, 29, 51–2, 73, 75, 77, 78–9, 81, 83, 103, 104–5, 111, 114, 116, 118, 127, 128, 130, 139, 169, 171, 176
Diogenes Laertius, *Lives of Eminent Philosophers*, 67, 158–9, 168, 171
Dirac, Paul, 17, 166–8, 172
discontinuity
  atomist, 170–5, 180–1
  in history of science, 16, 23, 26, 41, 45, 59, 68, 73, 76, 147
  temporal, 19, 20, 73, 128, 131, 135–6, 138, 140, 142, 176–7
Döberheimer, Johann Wolfgang, 63
Dodds, E. R., 182n
dream (nocturnal), 109–10, 111–12, 188n

dream (of reverie), 87, 96–8, 100, 103, 107, 110–11, 114–17
Duhem, Pierre, 23, 43, 53, 73, 146
Durand, Gilbert, 183n

Eckhart, Meister, 120
École Normale Supérieure, 5, 183n
Eddington, Arthur, 40, 68
effect (Compton Raman, Stark, Zeeman), 56
ego, 37–8, 66, 95, 148, 150, 151, 155; see also cogito; psyche
Einstein, Albert, 15, 27, 36, 68, 99, 175, 184n, 185n
Elea (Eleatic), 159–60, 169, 181
electron, 27, 39–40, 42, 66, 72, 165–7, 187n; see also particles
elements (chemistry), 24–5, 45, 54, 57–8, 61–5; see also particles
elements (four), 8, 18, 24, 30, 33, 39, 52–3, 85–6, 88, 92, 93–5, 96–8, 100–8, 113, 116, 156
  air, 8, 18, 24, 53, 86, 93, 96–7, 102, 106–7
  earth, 8, 18, 24, 53, 86, 92, 93, 101–2, 107
  fire, 8, 18, 24, 53, 59, 82–5, 93, 97, 100, 101–3, 116–18
  water, 8, 18, 24, 53, 59, 86, 93–5, 101–2, 106, 107
Éluard, Paul, 12
Empedocles, 67, 97, 103, 117–18
Epicurus, 20, 38, 127–8, 141, 157, 160–1, 164, 172, 177, 179–80, 191n
episteme, 23, 26, 73, 175
epistemology, 7, 10, 11, 14, 16–19, 21, 26, 27, 29, 31, 39, 41, 43, 47, 54, 72–6, 82, 84–5, 98, 100, 107, 113, 116, 129, 136, 144, 146–8, 149, 153–4, 172, 176, 178, 183, 184n, 192n
  break/rupture (epistemological), 7, 10, 16, 23, 43, 47, 82
  obstacle (epistemological), 16–17, 29–30, 32–3, 35, 43, 44, 47, 82
epoché, 41, 55
experiment (experimental, experimentally), 7, 13, 25, 28, 30–1, 41, 47, 56, 58, 60, 65, 69, 71, 72, 73, 78, 79–81, 99, 184n

Faraday, Michael, 45
Feyerabend, Paul, 7, 30–1, 186n
  Against Method, 145, 186n
Foucault, Michel, 38, 146–7, 183n, 192n
Frege, Gottlob, 49–50
frequency, 7, 42, 61, 69, 70, 101, 129, 130, 180; see also radiation; resonance; rhythm; vibration
Freud, Sigmund, 1, 4, 8, 12, 93–5, 101, 110, 134, 146, 188n

Galileo, Galilei, 62, 68
Gassendi, Pierre, 20, 157, 161, 162
Gaudin, Colette, 3, 183n
Gilson, Étienne, 5, 6, 144
Gorgias, 135
Guthrie, W. K. C., 66, 68, 178, 196n

habit, 19, 98, 125–6, 128–9, 138, 181
Hacking, Ian, 7, 10, 183n
Halbwachs, Maurice, *Cadres sociaux de la mémoire*, 122–3, 150, 191n
Hamelin, Octave, 121
Hannequin, Arthur, 175
Hegel, Georg Wilhelm Friedrich, 1, 8, 36, 44, 52, 78, 104, 118
Heidegger, Martin, 9, 12, 141, 190n
Heisenberg, Werner, 43, 165–7, 168–9
Hertz, Heinrich, 54
history, 23, 31, 43–8, 73–6, 80, 110, 113, 123, 147, 156, 184n
  historicity, 44–5, 48, 73, 76, 156 see also tradition
Hölderlin, Johann Christian Friedrich, 117–18
Hooke, Robert, 46
Hume, David, 60, 155
Husserl, Edmund, 4, 8, 38, 55–6, 185n
hylozoism, 18, 95, 97, 151, 156, 162–3
Hyppolite, Jean, 9, 147

image, 2, 10–12, 17–19, 30, 32, 35–6, 39–40, 56, 70, 85–91, 95–117, 141, 149, 153–4
imaginary/imagination, 8, 10–12, 17–19, 39, 83–92, 95–114, 135, 153–4, 183n
impermanence, 114, 155
  vs permanence, 37, 131, 138, 175, 181
incommensurability, 16, 59, 67, 73

intermittence, 7, 68, 142, 172, 177
inter-subjectivity, 151–2; *see also* belonging
Iona, 18, 59, 97, 156, 159–60, 163
isotopes, 48, 57, 58, 68, 164, 187n

Jaloux, Edmond, 105
Janet, Pierre, 19, 176
Joyce, James, 46, 184n
Jung, Carl Gustav, 188n

Kafka, Franz, 178
Kant, Immanuel, 17, 28, 29, 36, 60, 174
Kepler, Johannes, 67
Kierkegaard, Sören, 120, 141, 191n
  The Concept of Dread, 141
Kline, Morris, 184n
Kojève, Alexandre, 8
Koyré, Alexandre, 146, 185n
Kuhn, Thomas, 7, 10, 16

Lacan, Jacques, 9, 93
Laplace, Pierre-Simon, 68, 162, 172, 180
Latour, Bruno, 7, 11, 16, 32, 33–4, 39
Lautréamont, Comte de, 12, 88–92
  Le Chants de Maldoror, 12, 88–92, 98
Lavoisier, Antoine, 24, 45, 46–8, 61, 62, 63, 186n
laziness (lazy), 11–12, 19, 76, 133, 173
Lecoq de Boisbaudran, Paul Émile, 63
Lecourt, Dominique, 9, 39, 74
  L'Épistémologie historique de Gaston Bachelard, 74
Leibniz, Gottfried Wilhelm, 122, 174
Leiris, Michel, 13, 183n
Leucippus, 35–6, 100, 167, 168, 170–1, 195n
Levinas, Emmanuel, 141, 190n
Lippmann, Gabriel, 42, 50
Lobachevsky, Nicolai, 14, 25, 78–9
Locke, John, 46
logic, 15, 43, 49–50, 73, 77, 79, 87–8, 91, 109, 116, 136, 160
Lovejoy, Arthur, 196n
Lucretius, 160–1, 191n
Lupasco, Stéphane, 52
Lyotard, Jean-François, 9, 146, 182n, 190n, 193n, 195n
  Le Différend, 193n

Mach, Ernst, 162
Marx, Karl (Marxists), 1, 8, 38, 44, 146, 184n, 192n
Masson-Oursel, Paul, 196n
mathematics, 9, 15, 17, 25, 27, 29, 47, 49–50, 52–4, 57, 58, 64–5, 66–71, 91–2, 168, 175, 184n, 186–7n
  chemistry, 60–2, 64–5
  Euclidian/non-Euclidian geometries, 13–14, 17, 25–6, 40, 43, 57, 113, 167, 172, 185n
  music, 68–70
  poetics, 91–2, 108
  tensor calculus, 17, 43, 57–8
Maxwell, James Clerk, 47, 54
memory, 13, 77, 88, 90–1, 95, 106, 110, 122–3, 124–5, 132, 139, 150, 154, 189, 191n; *see also* Halbwachs, Maurice
Mendeleyev, Dmitri, 45, 47, 48, 54, 62–5, 186n
  periodic table, 45, 47, 62–5
Merleau-Ponty, Maurice, 9, 146
Meyerson, Émile, 23, 49, 50, 146
mind (rationality, soul) (at work), 11–12, 51, 71, 87, 148
Minkowski, Eugène, 9, 147
Monnerot, Jules, 13, 183n
Montaigne, Michel Eyquem de, 141, 182n
Moseley, Henry, 65
movement (mobility), 29, 31, 67, 78–9, 81, 95, 96, 105, 109, 130, 160, 163, 171–2, 173–5, 177–8, 180–1, 191n, 192n
multiplicity, 38, 68, 96, 167, 171–2
mystical (instant), 120, 124

naïve (naïvety), 16, 18, 22, 29–30, 32–8, 64, 82, 84, 86, 98–100, 107, 154, 156
narcissism, 83, 93–5, 188n
nature, 17, 25, 33–4, 51, 53, 57–8, 145, 160, 161, 162, 169
Nef, Frédéric, 169
new (the) (novelty), 45, 76, 125, 133, 142, 147–8, 177, 180
Newlands, John Alexander Reina, 63
Newton, Isaac, 56, 62, 162–4, 169
  Newtonian (mechanics, world, space), 25–6, 29, 113, 147, 169, 170, 173, 174, 180

Nietzsche, Friedrich, 38, 60, 81, 117–18, 125, 148–9, 155
nirvana, 142, 177
Nothingness, 116, 122, 130–1, 134, 140–2, 190n, 192n; *see also* void
noumenon (noumenal, noumenology), 4, 28–9, 40, 54–5, 58, 69, 111, 149
nougonal, 29, 111, 149

ontology, 21, 52, 54, 72, 85, 104, 108, 110–11, 129, 134, 149, 151, 159, 162, 167, 172, 175, 177, 178, 180
  mathematics, 54, 175
  negative (Jean Wahl), 52
Ostwald, Wilhelm, 162

pagan, 2, 4, 18, 151, 182n
Paracelsus, 62, 85, 88, 104
Parmenides, 36, 59, 76, 156, 159–60, 164, 167–8, 181, 196n
particles, 27, 52, 54, 72, 129, 160, 165–7, 168, 174, 187n; *see also* electron
Penrose, Roger, *The Emperor's New Mind*, 176
Perrin, Jean, 162
Pessoa, Fernando, 192n
phénoménographie, 55
phenomenology, 4, 7, 9, 10, 11, 18, 33, 38, 41, 51, 55–6, 108–9, 112–13, 114, 130, 185n
  intentionality, 51, 55–6, 152
  of the soul, 18, 56, 112
phénoménotechnique, 17, 52, 55, 57–8, 66, 69, 71, 148, 175, 184n, 186–7n
phlogiston, 24, 46, 48, 62
Pinheiro dos Santos, Lucio Alberto, 130, 135, 176
  La Rythmanalyse, 126, 130, 135, 176, 184n
Planck, Max, 166
Plato, 28, 52–3, 67–8, 76, 105, 120–1, 127, 156, 158–9, 179, 180, 182n, 184n, 191n
  Laws, 179
  Parmenides, 120–1
  Timaeus, 62–3
Poe, Edgar Allan, 106
Poincaré, Henri, 23, 26
Poirier, René, 6

Pontalis, Jean-Bertrand, 188n
Popper, Karl, 48–9, 184n
Presocratic, 18, 29, 156, 184n
psyche, 1, 30, 81, 83, 86, 97, 98, 108, 113, 117, 128, 131, 182n, 183n; *see also cogito*; ego
psychoanalysis, 3, 4, 16–17, 18, 30, 39, 43, 44, 46, 93–5, 98–100, 101, 109, 113, 154, 184n, 188n
  of a philosophical mind, 98–100
  of a scientific mind, 16–17, 30, 39, 43–4, 46
Ptolemy, 184n
Pythagoras, 52–3, 66–71, 72, 156, 169, 178

quantum physics, 10, 17, 19, 25, 27–8, 36, 49, 84, 99, 166, 170, 176, 185n
Quillet, Pierre, 4, 9, 12, 31, 72, 84, 146, 153, 188n, 191n

radiation, 60–1, 130–1, 175; *see also* frequency; resonance; rhythm; vibration
rationalism, 7, 8, 10, 13–15, 17, 29–31, 33, 35–7, 42, 43, 45–6, 48–54, 58–9, 64, 68, 69–70, 71, 73–4, 76, 77–81, 83, 95, 98–100, 145, 147, 151, 153, 168, 172, 175–6; *see also* surrationalism
relativity, 10, 15, 17, 25, 27, 36, 99, 185n; *see also* Einstein, Albert
Remarque, Erich Maria, 156
resonance, 17, 61, 66, 101, 129, 176, 180; *see also* frequency; radiation; rhythm; vibration
reverie, 83, 92, 97–8, 101–2, 105, 109–13, 115, 117; *see also* dream (of reverie)
Rey, Abel, 6, 146
rhythm, 61, 65, 66, 81, 98, 101, 128, 129–31, 138, 153, 163–4, 176–7, 184n; *see also* frequency; radiation; resonance; vibration
Riemann, Bernhard, 25
Rouault, George Henri, 112, 149
Roupnel, Gaston, 16, 122, 124, 130, 135, 177
  Siloë, 19, 121, 124, 130, 135
Russell, Bertrand, 49
Rutherford, Ernest, 40

Sartre, Jean-Paul, 9, 19, 104–5, 116, 141, 146, 183n
  Being and Nothingness, 105, 141
Sassoon, Siegfried, 156
Schrödinger, Erwin, 15, 153–4, 170, 185n, 197n
Sedley, David, 169, 196n
Serres, Michel, 7, 9, 16, 32–3, 34, 39, 145, 161, 172, 197n
  'La réforme et les sept péchés', 33
Silburn, Lilian, *Instant et cause: Le discontinu dans la pensée philosophique de l'Inde*, 20, 136–42
Socrates, 159, 182n
solitude, 11, 111, 117, 126, 189–90n
  historical, 46
Sorbonne, 4, 5, 6, 7, 8, 23, 185n, 192n
soul, 18, 37, 56, 97, 102, 110, 111–13, 115, 123, 132, 134, 138, 142, 149, 152, 153–4, 163, 182n, 184n, 190n; *see also* phenomenology: of the soul
Soupault, Philippe, 15
space
  physical (Euclidian), 14, 25–6, 40, 162, 169–72
  poetic, 108–15, 178
  psychological (interior), 1, 182n; *see also cogito*; ego; psyche
Spinoza, Baruch, 191n
Starobinski, Jean, 9, 146, 188n, 193n
Stengers, Isabelle, 7, 16, 32, 34, 39, 144, 145, 184n
Strathern, Paul, 186n
substance
  chemistry, 25, 66, 68, 72, 150
  élan vital as, 132–3
  ex-tance, 60, 66, 150
  philosophy, 35, 36–7, 59–61, 138, 148, 155
  poetic, 83, 84–6, 87, 90, 101–3, 113, 118
  radiation, resonance, rhythm, vibration, 17, 130–1, 180
  self as, 95
  thinking (Descartes), 37; *see also cogito*; ego; psyche
  time as, 74, 135

unitary, 35–6, 72, 77, 84–5
vs void, 168–70
surrationalism, 10, 13–15, 17, 21, 48, 71, 74, 77–80, 84, 153, 180
surreal (surrealist), 9, 10, 12–15, 18, 21, 22, 70, 77, 78–9, 89, 92, 109, 145, 147, 154, 155, 174, 175, 187n
Surrealism, 9, 10, 12, 13, 15, 18, 88, 92, 104, 145, 154, 183n

telos, 2, 18, 44, 76, 147, 171, 180
Thompson, Joseph John, 165
Tiles, Mary, 9, 10, 54
time, 2, 7, 18–20, 48, 61, 73, 75–6, 115, 119–42 *passim*, 148, 149, 155, 156–7, 176, 178, 180, 191–2n
  chronos, 135
  duration, 19–20, 120–9, 132–40, 142, 152, 176, 177, 180, 191–2n
  élan vital, 19, 132–4, 136, 180
  horizontal/transitive, 124, 126, 128, 138
  instant, 7, 19, 92, 100, 119–31, 133–5, 136, 138, 140, 142, 152, 155, 176–7, 180, 181
  interval, 121, 127, 128, 140
  kairos, 135–6
topophilia, 113
tradition, 1, 2, 36, 44, 48, 76, 77, 80–1, 124, 136, 140, 146, 148, 155, 159–60, 183n; *see also* history
transcendence (transcendental), 2, 8, 17, 56, 147, 167, 179, 180–1
Tzara, Tristan, 13, 78, 109

universe, 11, 68, 97, 116

vertigo, 91, 117–18, 134
vibration, 17, 69–70, 128, 129–31, 177, 180; *see also* frequency; radiation; resonance; rhythm
Vienna Circle, 10, 12, 15, 48–9
Villarreal, Luis P., *Origin of Group Identity*, 193–5n
violence
  Platonic, 105, 180
  poetic, 88–92, 96, 100, 154

void
    in atomism, 160–3, 169–72
    in contemporary science, 169–72
    temporal, 107, 117, 119, 126, 139, 140, 142, 159, 174, 177, 193n, 196n
    see also Nothingness

Webb, David, 185n, 193n
well-being, 2, 15, 22, 84, 86, 115, 153, 156
Winkler, Clemence, 63
Wittgenstein, Ludwig, 178, 192n

Zeno, 120–1

EU Authorised Representative:
Easy Access System Europe Mustamäe tee 50, 10621 Tallinn, Estonia
gpsr.requests@easproject.com

Printed and bound by CPI Group (UK) Ltd, Croydon, CR0 4YY
17/11/2025
01998987-0005